THE BRIDGE AT NO GUN RI

THE BRIDGE
AT
NO GUN RI

A HIDDEN NIGHTMARE FROM THE KOREAN WAR

CHARLES J. HANLEY, SANG-HUN CHOE
AND MARTHA MENDOZA

WITH RESEARCH ASSISTANCE BY RANDY HERSCHAFT

HENRY HOLT AND COMPANY

NEW YORK

Henry Holt and Company, LLC
Publishers since 1866
115 West 18th Street
New York, New York 10011

Henry Holt® is a registered trademark of
Henry Holt and Company, LLC.

Library of Congress Cataloging-in-Publication Data

Hanley, Charles J.
The bridge at No Gun Ri : a hidden nightmare from the Korean War / Charles J. Hanley,
Sang-Hun Choe and Martha Mendoza.—1st ed.
p. cm.
ISBN 0-8050-6658-6 (hc.)
1. Korean War, 1950–1953—Atrocities. 2. Massacres—Korea (South)—Nogæn-ni.
3. Nogæn-ni (Korea)—History. 4. Korean War, 1950–1953—Campaigns—Korea
(South)—Nogæn-ni. 5. Korean War, 1950–1953—United States. 6. United States.
Army. Cavalry, 7th. I. Choe, Sang-Hun. II. Mendoza, Martha. III. Title.

DS920.8.H36 2001
951.904'27—dc21   2001032690

Henry Holt books are available for special promotions and
premiums. For details contact: Director, Special Markets.

First Edition 2001

Designed by Kelly S. Too
Maps by Bob Bianchini

Printed in the United States of America

1   3   5   7   9   10   8   6   4   2

CONTENTS

On August 11, 1945, as World War II drew toward a close, two U.S. Army planning officers in Washington chose an invisible line across Korea, the 38th Parallel, for dividing the Japanese colony into Soviet and American zones, north and south. Five years later, on June 25, 1950, Korean troops from the north invaded the south to try to reunify the nation. They were led by communists. The resulting war, which ended in 1953 in stalemate, was the first great clash of arms of the Cold War.

Within days of the invasion, the United States rushed American troops from police duty in Japan to fight alongside its South Korean ally. The Americans who were shipped across the Sea of Japan were mostly green, teenaged recruits, with insufficient combat training, led in many cases by inexperienced officers in units that were under-strength and poorly equipped. They reeled before the North Korean attack, in weeks of desperate retreat, until finally holding a last-ditch defense line. Hundreds of thousands of South Korean civilians fled south with them. It was a bleak, humiliating chapter in U.S. military history, soon forgotten by the American people.

Almost a half century later, on September 29, 1999, the forgotten chapter burst into newspaper headlines worldwide, with a story of buried history, of unforgiven acts from that long-ago war, at a place called No Gun Ri. The Associated Press reported that a dozen graying ex-soldiers, young GIs of 1950, had confirmed what South Korean villagers claimed: U.S. forces in July 1950 killed large numbers of civilian refugees—up to 400, the Koreans said, mostly women, children and old men—under and around a railroad trestle at the hamlet of No Gun Ri. The AP also published declassified military documents showing that U.S. commanders had issued standing orders to shoot civilians rather than risk infiltration by disguised enemy soldiers.

The highest levels of the U.S. and South Korean governments immediately ordered investigations, military inquiries that then dragged on for many months, ending in weeks of conflict between American and Korean investigators. In its final report in January 2001, the U.S. Army, after years of dismissing the villagers' story, affirmed the AP's finding that American troops killed the refugees. But it assigned no blame. Instead, it said, "What befell civilians in the vicinity of No Gun Ri in late July 1950 was a tragic and deeply regrettable accompaniment to a war."

Here is the story of No Gun Ri and that war, of what accompanied it, preceded it, and followed it, as seen through the eyes of the only people who could really know—Korean villagers and American soldiers who were there.

The No Gun Ri Area

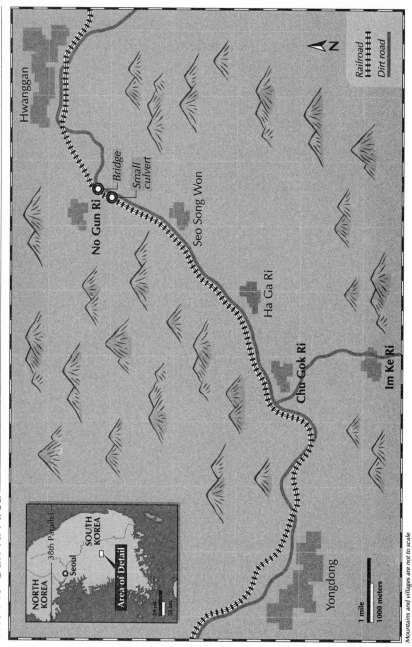

Mountains and villages are not to scale

THE U.S. ARMY IN KOREA, JULY 1950

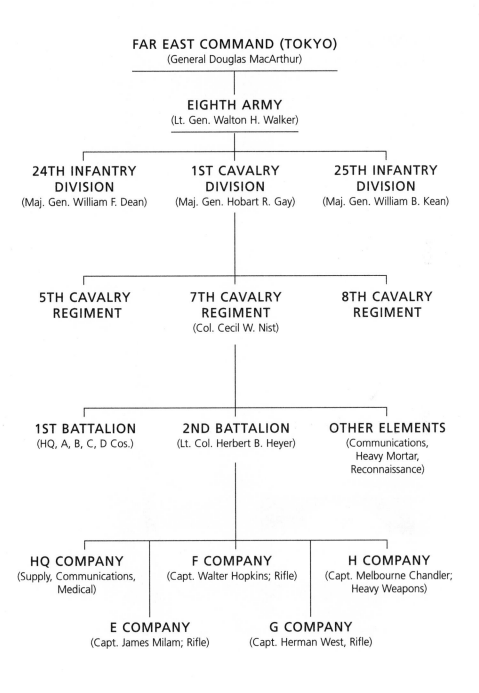

FAR EAST COMMAND (TOKYO)
(General Douglas MacArthur)

EIGHTH ARMY
(Lt. Gen. Walton H. Walker)

24TH INFANTRY DIVISION
(Maj. Gen. William F. Dean)

1ST CAVALRY DIVISION
(Maj. Gen. Hobart R. Gay)

25TH INFANTRY DIVISION
(Maj. Gen. William B. Kean)

5TH CAVALRY REGIMENT

7TH CAVALRY REGIMENT
(Col. Cecil W. Nist)

8TH CAVALRY REGIMENT

1ST BATTALION
(HQ, A, B, C, D Cos.)

2ND BATTALION
(Lt. Col. Herbert B. Heyer)

OTHER ELEMENTS
(Communications, Heavy Mortar, Reconnaissance)

HQ COMPANY
(Supply, Communications, Medical)

F COMPANY
(Capt. Walter Hopkins; Rifle)

H COMPANY
(Capt. Melbourne Chandler; Heavy Weapons)

E COMPANY
(Capt. James Milam; Rifle)

G COMPANY
(Capt. Herman West, Rifle)

THE KOREAN FAMILIES

A NOTE ON NAMES: Koreans place family names first; in Chung Eun-yong, for example, Chung is the family name. Women don't take their husbands' family names. The given names of siblings, and sometimes of cousins, usually carry a common root. "Koo" in the names of Chung children is an example. Literally, it means "to seek," as in Koo-hun, "to seek the law"; Koo-hak, "to seek learning"; and Koo-ok, "to seek the jade." Because some Korean surnames, such as Chung and Park, are so common, *The Bridge at No Gun Ri* generally uses only given names of villagers on repeated references to avoid confusion.

(Key: D=Killed at No Gun Ri; W=Wounded;
S=Survived without wounds. Main figures in the book are in ALL CAPITALS.)

CHUNG EUN-YONG'S FAMILY

Chung Tae-nyon (father) (S)
Park Hee-moon (mother) (W)
   CHUNG EUNG-YONG (the ex-policeman; not present at No Gun Ri)
   PARK SUN-YONG (wife) (W)
      Chung Koo-pil (four-year-old son) (D)
      Chung Koo-hee (two-year-old daughter) (D)
   Chung Kwan-yong (Eun-yong's brother; the prison guard; not present)
   Min Young-ok (wife) (D)
      Chung Jong-ja (daughter) (W)
      Chung Soon-ja (daughter) (S)
      Chung Soon-rye (daughter) (D)
      Chung Koo-sung (baby son) (D)
   Chung Soon-yong (Eun-yong's sister; not present)
   Chung Kun-yong (Eun-yong's brother) (S)
   Chung Kum-yong (Eung-yong's brother) (S)
   Kim Hong-ki (servant boy) (W)

CHUNG KOO-IL'S FAMILY

Chung Hee-yong (father; the "1919 patriot") (S)
Lee Soon-kum (mother) (D)
   Chung Tae-gu (daughter; not present)
   Chung Koo-yon (daughter) (D)
      Kim Sung-ja (daughter) (W)
      Kim Kook-hun (baby son) (D)
   CHUNG KOO-IL (son; the college student; later disappeared) (S)
   CHUNG KOO-OK (daughter; the schoolteacher) (D)
   Chung Koo-hong (son) (S)

CHUNG KOO-HUN'S FAMILY

Chung Ssang-yong (father; the fishmonger) (S)
Hwang Eun-yon (mother) (D)
    Chung Koo-soon (daughter; not present)
    CHUNG KOO-HUN (son; the tall seventeen-year-old) (S)
    Chung Myong-ja (daughter) (W)
    CHUNG KOO-HAK (son; the sickly eight-year-old) (S)
    Chung Young-sook (baby daughter) (D)

YANG HAE-SOOK'S FAMILY

Lee Ja-sun (grandmother; the reluctant refugee) (D)
    Yang Ho-yong (father; the "loyal son") (S)
    Lee Soon-yi (mother) (W)
        Yang Hae-young (son) (D)
        YANG HAE-SOOK (daughter; "Golden Girl") (W)
        YANG HAE-CHAN (ten-year-old son) (W)
        Yang Hae-yong (son) (D)
    Yang Ke-soon (father's sister) (D)
        Min Eun-soon (Ke-soon's daughter in-law) (D)
            Chung Hyun-mok (Eun-soon's baby son) (D)
    Yang Mal-soon (father's pregnant sister) (D)
    Park Ne-eung (Mal-soon's husband) (D)
        Park Chung-ha (son; not present)
        Park Sang-ja (daughter) (D)
        Park Hwa-ja (daughter) (S)
        Park Hwa-soon (daughter) (D)

CHUN CHOON-JA'S FAMILY

Chun Kyong-moon (grandfather who protected Choon-ja) (D)
Kim Suk-jin (grandmother) (S)
    Chun Soon-pyo (father; the "possessed" widower) (S)
    Kim Ae-shim (mother) (D)
        CHUN CHOON-JA (ten-year-old daughter) (S)
        Chun Tae-sung (baby son, "Great Success") (D)
    Chun Joon-pyo (father's newlywed brother) (D)
    Lee Young-ja (Joon-pyo's wife) (D)
    Chun Ok-boon (father's sister) (W)

PARK HEE-SOOK'S FAMILY

Park June-ha (father) (D)
Sohn Soon-nam (mother) (D)
    Park Hee-soo (son; not present; long missing overseas)
    Park Hee-un (daughter; not present)
    Park Hee-soon (daughter; the nervous new mother) (D)
        Lee Young-ja (Hee-soon's daughter, the crying baby) (D)
    PARK HEE-SOOK (daughter; the pigtailed sixteen-year-old) (S)

THE BRIDGE AT NO GUN RI

THE END OF THE ROAD

Summer 2000
Fauquier County, Virginia

In the coves and hollows of the Blue Ridge foothills, the peace deepens with the summer night. The roar from the interstate has faded. Crickets fall silent one by one. Televisions and computer screens have flickered off. A breeze stirs the stillness and mosquitoes drift lightly through the heavy air.

Inside a cottage a mile up the dirt roads of Apple Mountain, an old soldier tosses in his sleep. His early morning visitors have arrived again, as they always have, night after night, year after year. They stand over him, an old man and an old woman, indistinct faces, Asian faces, blurred by time but close at hand, accusing faces, faces of the dead.

Restless spirits abide, it is said, in a landscape not found on any map. In old Buddhist lore, it's a place called "Nine Springs," Ku-chun in Korean. The souls of those who died unjust deaths wander there in search of peace, crying for the injustice, the *han*, to be set aright.

On this quiet Virginia night, the visitors once more take the old machine gunner back to a place and time of mud and stinking rice paddies, of flares in the blackness, of bugles and screams from the wounded, of lost babies' cries in a landscape without life. He cannot escape. He rises from his bed and shuffles across the room. He lifts his rifle surehandedly and slowly makes his way to the porch. And there he sits in the shadows once more, weapon at the ready, and peers into the night, down the hillside, and watches. And waits. And again it is the summer of 1950.

PART I

THE ROAD TO
NO GUN RI

1

Waves raced over the sea in long, broken ranks to batter the port bow of the *David C. Shanks.* The steel hull shuddered with each blow as the troopship rolled, lifted up, pitched forward and plowed on into the gloom. It held at a steady and stubborn 8 knots.

The four ships of the little westbound convoy, carrying 2,000 men of the 7th U.S. Cavalry Regiment, struggled to stay in sight of one another in thick sheets of rain and foam, their U.S. Navy colors whipping wildly in force 8 winds. On the bridge of the *Shanks,* the crewmen tugged at the wheel over and over, nosing the bow back on course toward the wide mouth, still distant, of the Osumi Strait.

If all went well, the three lumbering transports—the *Patrick,* the *Ainsworth* and the *Shanks*—and their escort, a Navy corvette, would make the strait tomorrow, then skirt around the lighthouse point of rocky Cape Sata, at Japan's southern tip, to emerge among the islands of a stormy East China Sea. The next day, they would turn the corner and bear north toward Korea's southern coast, toward an unexpected war in an unknown land.

MAYBE A COUPLE OF WEEKS IN KOREA, BUDDY WENZEL THOUGHT. Maybe a couple of months. That's what they say. Private Leonard B. Wenzel, like the rest of the green troops buttoned up inside the *Shanks,* wanted to believe that his regiment, the famed "Garryowens," could handle anything thrown at them—once they got through this typhoon.

The U.S. Navy had seen the giant storm coming for days, as it spun toward the sea lanes where the legendary "kamikaze" typhoon, the "divine wind," sank a Chinese-Korean fleet another July day seven centuries earlier, saving Japan from invasion. But heavy weather would not deter the American planners of 1950, at General Headquarters in Tokyo. The need was urgent for the human cargo that had crowded in the hundreds aboard the troopships last Monday at the Yokohama piers. "The situation in Korea is critical," the supreme commander, Gen. Douglas MacArthur, had told Washington. Now the *Shanks*'s crewmen could do little but watch 30-foot seas crash over their bow, hoping to hear the wind's howl drop an octave, glancing nervously at the barometer. It had to bottom out soon.

The difficult passage—a three-day crossing turned into five days—was especially hard on one group of passengers. When they boarded days before, forty-five Japanese stevedores had been herded down the main deck to the stern and ordered to settle down on the open fantail. Now these quiet men in rough clothes were fending for themselves, finding shelter where they could on the jam-packed ship. Like other Japanese since the war, the stevedores had grown used to American bosses, and they were uncomplaining. At least they had a few days' work, loading and unloading hardware and food for the soldiers, and knew they'd be returning home when the Americans would not.

Below deck, in stifling quarters beneath the waterline, the young Americans, their fresh fatigue uniforms now crumpled and soiled, sat pale-faced amid the reek, stumbled into the head holding stricken stomachs, or curled up weary on fold-down cots, stacked five high, trying to reread letters, mutter conversation or sleep while bracing themselves against bulkheads or gripping bunk frames, praying for shore or at least an even sea.

For the proud 7th Cavalry, George Armstrong Custer's regiment, it was an inauspicious journey into war.

NINETEEN-YEAR-OLD BUDDY WENZEL HAD BEEN COUNTING THE days until his discharge, until he could go home to New Jersey and to Dot, his girl. He had been counting the days, that is, until the Army had thrown him a curve ball—the "Truman year," they were calling it. All enlistments were being extended for twelve months because of the Korea "emergency." Now, as he lay in his narrow sleeping space, Private Wenzel suddenly faced two years left to serve, instead of 388 days.

Up and down the rows of racks, the story was the same for the others, almost all of them 4745s—riflemen in Army personnel parlance—and most still in their teens. Their return home would now be delayed for many months. They would miss a lot: the family's new television, the latest car models, the high school girls growing up and getting married.

Since VJ Day in 1945, the country had been racing ahead in every way. It came out of the war an economic giant. Older brothers, home from Europe and the Pacific, had stepped out of uniform and into new jobs, started families, bought houses. America was building new suburbias and roads; producing automobiles, washing machines and babies by the millions; sending veterans to college; introducing gadgets and new ideas daily.

But just when things were so good, the headlines were turning bad. Almost overnight, it seemed, a confident America had found a challenge in the Communist governments of the Soviet Union and China, and now North Korea had invaded South Korea. The Korean peninsula had been split into southern and northern halves by American and Soviet occupation forces after World War II, and the two Korean governments—with armies built up by Washington and

Moscow—had been skirmishing across their dividing line, each bent on reuniting the Korean nation under its rule. The two great powers, one a northern neighbor of Korea, the other far across the Pacific, had failed to develop a plan for peacefully restoring an independent, whole Korea. Now that the north was trying to end the division by force, the price of that failure would be paid in blood.

As inevitable as it became, it was an unforeseen war for the crew-cut, fresh-faced infantrymen aboard the *Shanks*. Now these younger brothers, peacetime pickets on occupation duty in Japan, were suddenly in the front line.

For some of them, those without much to go home to, President Harry Truman's "year" may have been a godsend. Many came from broken families and had dropped out of school long ago. Some were brawlers and misfits. Some wound up in the regiment because judges back home gave them a choice between the Army or jail. Some couldn't even write.

One who could was Buddy Wenzel. He loved to write. The curly-haired, pug-nosed Wenzel's strong right hand, below the bulging biceps and red-and-blue DOT tattoo, produced two or three letters a day in Tokyo, not just his daily note to Dot, but others to two-dozen pen pals, all female, all in different states. He'd picked up the addresses from friends. One favorite was Dorothy Hodges, blond sister of his George Company buddy James Lamarr Hodges, an easygoing, harmonica-playing farm boy from Florida.

Wenzel was a letter writer even as a kid in South River, New Jersey, when he wrote them for his father, a Polish immigrant and cannery worker. During World War II, Albert Sr. would sit with the boy and tell him what to write to big brother Albert, an Army medic on the Belgian front. The boy's scrawled pages were fraught with a father's anxiety. But the hardest letter Buddy had to write was the one his father sent to his mother. "Why did you leave us?" the heartbroken husband asked through the confused son. "I tried to give you what I could. If you come home, I'll even buy new furniture."

Lydia had walked out of their tall, narrow country house at three o'clock one morning when Buddy was thirteen and moved in with another man. She was fed up with raising five children, Buddy came to believe. It fell to the boy to care for two small sisters. He washed clothes and dishes, ironed, cleaned the house, and he dropped out of school. Then in June 1947, four years after his wife left him, Albert Wenzel Sr.'s broken heart quit beating. Buddy's mother moved back into the house with her boyfriend, and Buddy rebelled. Learning his friends were enlisting in the Army, he joined them. It was an "out." Since he was only seventeen, the minimum age, he needed a parent's signature, and his mother gladly supplied it.

Some of the other recruits sweating it out in the *Shanks*'s lower decks had found their "out" even before turning seventeen.

Pfc. James Hodges had arrived in Japan on the same ship as Wenzel and ended up as a George Company bunkmate in Tokyo. The quiet, sandy-haired Hodges was another rebel, a runaway from a sharecropping family's hard life among Florida's baking hot citrus groves and strawberry fields. His father, Cauley Hodges, taciturn and strict, worked James, Dorothy and his nine other children at all hours in the fields, keeping them from school whenever he could, keeping them picking berries or cotton, planting peas, harvesting beans. They moved from town to town, school to school, had little time to do homework, and dropped out one by one.

Eldest son James, a boy who would sing country songs alone on the porch in the evening, finally packed some things and left. He borrowed a few dollars from Juanita, his married older sister, and found someone to pose as a parent and sign him up with the Army, attesting the runaway was older than his sixteen years. He would never return home.

Fox Company's Ralph Bernotas had already turned seventeen when he set his sights on the service, having been baptized at the Lithuanian Catholic church in Girardville, Pennsylvania, in 1931. But his Pop was a reluctant cosigner. The youngest son among twelve children in a coal-mining family, Ralph was a good boy, an altar boy—"That's when I learned to drink wine." He was a poor boy, too. "I was the only one who didn't have a suitcoat for the class picture." But he had a happy childhood in a town where it was natural for a fifteen-year-old to descend 300 feet into a hole on a weekend to load coal into wagons and earn a couple of bucks.

By the time Ralph turned seventeen, however, his father's black lung disease was fast worsening and the boy felt a need for more than a couple of bucks. He decided the Army was one place to make and save some money. He and eight high school pals rode the 15 miles to Pottsville together to meet the recruiter. But only Ralph, back home, finally got his father's signature and a uniform. "Pop took me to the train in Pottsville. All he said was, 'Don't worry about us. We'll be all right. Just take care of yourself.' "

Now, aboard the *Shanks,* the affable, chatty Bernotas was suddenly worried about taking care of himself. His sergeant, Lonnie Burrow, had been reassigned out of the regiment at the last minute, and Ralph and the rest of F Company's 3rd Platoon were without the one leader they trusted.

Ralph was a model soldier, a reader of field manuals who had quickly made corporal and dreamed of an officer's commission someday. Down in a *Shanks* latrine, meanwhile, another kind of soldier was swabbing up the mess of seasick shipmates.

For Art Hunter, who had drawn the unpleasant cleanup duty after crossing his sergeant, the Army was a fresh chance in a frustrating young life. Back home in Lynchburg, Virginia, at age fifteen and still in fifth grade, he was finally expelled from school as disruptive and impossible to teach. He painted Coca-Cola signs for a while, until laid off, and then simply quit a second job, working for his second cousin, a plumber. "You ain't going to lay around here on me," his father, a fire marshal, told him. "You're going into the Army."

On his seventeenth birthday in 1948, Art headed off to Fort Jackson, South Carolina, for basic training. It was his first time away from Lynchburg, and the homesick teenager, a big but insecure boy, cried through the night in a strange bunk far from home. Now Art Hunter, having failed at Army supply clerks' school, was steaming into war, this time very far from home, as an assistant machine gunner for G Company.

Somewhere in the H Company racks, nineteen-year-old Norm

Tinkler had crammed his 200-plus pounds into a tight bunk space as the *Shanks* heaved and slid in what seemed to him "100-foot waves." Norm grew up among an ocean of wheat in Cloud County, Kansas, and became an intimidating young man, a local boxer and "rassler" who tangled with his own father before finally deciding to try the Army. He had only an eighth-grade education. "I had nowhere to go."

But even the brawling Norm Tinkler, now toting half of a 100-pound machine gun for How Company, a heavy weapons unit, had not expected to find a war in his future. The one that had ended just a few short years before in the atomic incineration of two Japanese cities had seemed finally to be the war to end all wars. The biggest battles these teenagers had contemplated were the drunken free-for-alls that erupted late at night in the dance halls of the Ginza, after guard duty or parade drills or patrolling in Tokyo.

It can't last long, they told each other aboard the *Shanks*. They had us take along only two sets of fatigues, underwear and socks, poncho, steel helmet, weapon. Whatever it is, wherever we're going in this Korea place, "we'll just clean it up and get back," they said— back to Tokyo, to their *koibitos,* their Japanese girlfriends, to the cheap beer, to the $10 and $20 black-market deals that made them rich Americans. Buddy Wenzel, the quiet one, would get back to writing his twenty-five "girls."

THEIR OFFICERS, TRYING TO ORGANIZE BRIEFINGS, RUN THEIR troops in shifts to the mess for meals, and then get them to clean up after seasick bunkmates, were not so cocky. The higher the rank, in fact, the greater was the unease.

Lt. Col. Gilmon Augustus Huff knew firsthand that these parade-ground soldiers were being rushed unready into war. In Japan, Huff had been the chief infantry instructor for the 1st Cavalry Division, the regiment's parent unit, before being named regimental executive officer, the 7th Cavalry's second-in-command, just six days before they shipped out.

A Bible reader from South Carolina's "Possum Kingdom" country, he had learned to hate war, but he'd also become extremely good at it. The curly-red-haired Gil Huff was only twenty-eight, one of the Army's youngest lieutenant colonels, when he fought through Normandy in 1944 in command of an infantry battalion. He won a Silver Star for his "coolness under fire" in overwhelming a German fortress in France.

In Japan, Huff had plans for whipping the 1st Cavalry Division's three infantry units—the 5th, 7th and 8th Cavalry Regiments—into shape for their primary mission, combat. But he ran out of time. Now his regiment was headed for an amphibious assault on a Korean beach, a landing that would begin with troops clambering dangerously down cargo nets spread across the side of the ship, nets that Huff's men had barely seen before. Some boys had not even received full basic training.

Not only was the division's training incomplete, but the division itself was also incomplete, missing components every infantry officer considered essential. After World War II, Washington planners felt the new atom bombs would make giant land armies obsolete. Budget slashing shrank the mighty, victorious, 100-division Army of 1945 to ten combat divisions. In Japan, those three-regiment divisions in turn were hollowed out by the deactivation of one of each regiment's three battalions. Each regiment was also short one of three artillery batteries, and the company of medium tanks allotted to it could be found only on paper.

Already understrength, the 1st Cavalry Division got a call from Eighth Army headquarters at 2:30 A.M. on June 27, two days after North Korea's invasion, to round up more than seven hundred sergeants and other enlisted men and send them off to help fill the ranks of the 24th Infantry Division, the first unit to head for Korea.

The 7th Cavalry Regiment lost 168 key noncommissioned officers, among them Ralph Bernotas's platoon sergeant, a decorated combat veteran. Melbourne C. Chandler, a 7th Cavalry company commander, later described the stripping away of the platoon sergeants as "a blow to the heart and soul of the regiment."

As for the troops that remained, the U.S. command had noted

confidentially that replacements arriving in Tokyo in 1949 had a high percentage of low intelligence ratings and more men of "questionable character" than it would have liked. The current emergency only worsened that situation: The Eighth Army had opened the gates of its stockade and sent one hundred prisoners to the 1st Cavalry Division for deployment to Korea. If they could not repair the soul of the 7th Cavalry Regiment, they would at least replace some bodies.

As the *Shanks* pitched and rolled through the wild seas, Lieutenant Colonel Huff looked around and knew that the seasick privates and corporals were not the only unready ranks.

At one point, Huff had called on his boss, regimental commander Col. Cecil W. Nist, the man leading the 7th Cavalry toward the unknown in Korea, and found him hurriedly poring through a primer in his cabin—*Army Field Manual 7-40: Infantry Regiment.* Its words were not reassuring. "The means which a regimental commander has to capture his objectives are his three battalions and his tank company," read the chapter on attack, envisioning a regiment much different from the thinned-out one Nist commanded.

Nist had spent twelve months in Korea in 1945–1946 as an intelligence staff officer, but the bespectacled, pipe-smoking colonel, in twenty-seven years as a soldier, had never led troops in combat. He spent most of World War II at Fort Jackson and the past three and a half years at the Pentagon, largely in the comptroller's office. He had arrived in Japan a mere six weeks earlier, in early June, to take command of the storied 7th Cav.

Many senior officers in the Eighth Army, the garrison force in Japan, had been given prestigious infantry commands because of connections, not because of demonstrated abilities. Some were nearing retirement, like Nist, who would soon turn fifty.

In the officers' cabins of the crowded *Shanks,* the lack of familiarity with war's front lines reached right down the chain of command. Lt. Col. Herbert B. Heyer, leading Nist's 2nd Battalion, had spent the last war as an Army post commander among the peaceful Eskimos of Greenland. Before World War II, back home in Iowa, the lanky Heyer had been a postmaster, doing two weeks' Army

Reserves training each summer. In Japan, the battalion commander had been afflicted by ulcers. Now he faced a hard sea journey, and greater challenges beyond.

A few of the 7th Cavalry's junior officers had seen action in World War II. The troops spotted them in the full-dress parades in Tokyo, when they could size up the medals spread across the chests of men like G Company's Capt. Herman L. West. But other company commanders, each in charge of 150 young Americans packed into the heaving holds of the *Shanks*, bound for uncertain war, had never heard the whine of incoming enemy artillery.

Mel Chandler was one of them. A son of small-town Kansas, Chandler had dropped out of Oklahoma University's premed program in 1940 to join the Army. A skinny nineteen-year-old, he stuffed himself with bananas to make sure he made the minimum weight at the physical exam. Through the war years and after, the young officer oversaw civilian staff at the Kansas City medical depot and at other Army medical facilities. Then, in 1949, Captain Chandler attended infantry school and was assigned to Japan, to take command of H Company in the 7th Cavalry, the Army's most famous regiment.

The square-jawed captain, now filled out and solid, soon won the respect of his men. Fellow officers considered him "Army"—thoroughly professional. A less tolerant type or two frowned on his determined partying and drinking, but others joined him in what had become a natural part of occupation duty in Tokyo, where officers could buy a fifth of Canadian Club for little more than a dollar, and GIs could pick up a Japanese party girl for even less.

Melbourne Caldwell Chandler was still rated as a Medical Service Corps officer, though in charge of an infantry company now pounding through the waves toward war. Fellow officers, all infantry, wrote it off to the political machinations of Army life—that is, connections.

On the bottom rung, almost to a man, the lieutenants who led platoons lacked combat experience. One of Chandler's enthusiastic platoon leaders, Second Lt. Bill Kaluf, had set his heart on the 7th Cavalry ever since seeing, as a boy, his first Budweiser beer poster of Custer's Last Stand. He wanted to hit the beach in top shape for his first war, and so he was walking the tilting decks of the *Shanks* in search of a doctor. He needed to have his chronically waxed-up ears cleaned out.

Over in F Company, the men worried that Second Lt. Edwin M. Byles Jr. was losing his bearings. At the Tokyo barracks, Byles had been all over his platoon, an unpopular stickler on inspections. But on the *Shanks,* Byles could be seen sitting off alone, withdrawn, oddly fixated on a tommy gun, a Thompson submachine gun he was anxiously stroking.

THE GALE AND HEAVIEST SEAS BEGAN TO EASE ON THE FOURTH DAY as the tiny American flotilla carrying the fourteen companies of the 7th Cavalry moved into the stream of the warm Tsushima current, which brushes up the Korean coast. Between bouts of rain, the teen-aged infantrymen could roam again behind the chest-high gunwales of the open main deck, in the fresh salt air. Officers pulled out maps, briefed the troops on where they were going in Korea, gave them tips on map reading, instructed them in radio operation, distributed antimalaria tablets. The men were told they were unlikely to go up against a regular enemy army in Korea. Guerrillas in civilian clothes were more likely, and they would certainly not see any enemy tanks.

Regaining their sea legs, young soldiers tried to get their minds off the unknown with poker games and craps played against the *Shanks*'s damp gray bulkheads. Some masked apprehension with bravado. A corporal and a couple of privates had assembled their machine gun on a hatch cover. "Hey, Wenzel! We're getting up a suicide squad. Wanna join?" It was like some kind of war movie, Wenzel thought, and walked by.

The bravado showed in other ways, too. A few "warriors" had shaved their heads. When Heyer spotted a Mohawk haircut on F Company's Bill Collins, the mild-mannered battalion commander chewed the young soldier out: "We're not animals."

On the evening of July 21, as they bore in on the battle zone, the Navy crew blacked out the *Shanks*. The darkness that enveloped the sea spread through the ship as well. Those who knew Gil Huff imagined the young colonel pulling out a bottle of vodka from somewhere in the dimness, to sip himself into a mood, perhaps recalling the grief of the Norman hedgerows in '44, the men lost before the Rhine. Down below, hundreds of men and boys—farmers' sons, miners' sons, delinquents on probation—were left with their own thoughts about tomorrow and what they might face, about the unknowables of an amphibious landing: How deep will the water be? Will I get down the net OK? Will we be fired on? As the ship plowed on through the East China Sea, they could listen to the waves thud against the hull, recheck their gear in their minds, let their thoughts drift back to Tokyo, to the bars, to the cheap hooches where they could disappear with their girlfriends, to the parades, to the scenes played out to snatches of "Garryowen," the tune embedded in every 7th Cavalryman's unconscious.

WHEN THEY WERE EIGHTEEN ABREAST, PARADING BY BATTALION, these seasick soldiers could be an inspiring sight, among thousands of men from various divisions striding in synchronized shining boots over the bleached gravel of the Imperial Palace Plaza. On that same vast plaza, just a few momentous years ago, Japan's Emperor Hirohito, on a white horse, in glittering regalia, had reviewed the loyal troops of his Imperial Army. Now it was General of the Army Douglas MacArthur, in battered cap and open khaki shirt, taking the salute of the U.S. occupation forces marching through the heart of Tokyo. Hirohito sat unseen nearby in his secluded palace, figurehead of a defeated nation.

Parades were a fixture of the late 1940s in Tokyo, when congressional delegations, cabinet secretaries and military chiefs flew in regularly from Washington on inspection tours. The troops, in even ranks of gleaming helmets and bloused pant legs, with M-1 rifles angled smartly over their shoulders, thundered past the reviewing stand behind company guidons and regimental flags. The highlight, always, came when the band struck the first insistent, prancing chords of "Garryowen" and the 7th Cavalry, MacArthur's favorite regiment, stepped into view.

That quick march, an old Irish drinking song whose Gaelic title means "Owen's Garden," was adopted by the 7th Cavalry's celebrated early commander, Lt. Col. George A. Custer. He first had it played in 1868 to launch the regiment's attack on a Cheyenne Indian encampment on the Washita River in Oklahoma. President Theodore Roosevelt later called it "the finest military march in the world." But to the natives of the American Plains it was "devil's music."

Buddy Wenzel, Ralph Bernotas and other fresh recruits heard the uplifting tune soon after docking at Yokohama at the end of their two-week journeys from the States. They were sent to the movies as part of their orientation, to watch Errol Flynn play the doomed Custer in *They Died with Their Boots On,* the story of the Battle of the Little Bighorn, where Sioux Indians massacred Custer and two hundred men of the 7th Cavalry. Like much of what Hollywood produced in the early 1940s, the film and its heroic music, keyed to "Garryowen," set a tone of uncomplicated patriotism at a time when Americans faced the challenges of a global war. The bluecoated horsemen of Warner Bros.' 7th Cavalry had helped make America what it was by sweeping the Plains clean of "hostiles."

"We'd get them to love the regiment," a young sergeant from the Japan days, Robert C. "Snuffy" Gray, said of the initiation. What were said to be Custer's saber, boots and uniform were on display, under glass, at the Tokyo barracks.

The green recruits learned still more by reading a brief history handed out in the barracks, a pamphlet that said the 7th Cavalry troopers "firmly established their reputation as Indian fighters in the Battle of the Washita," and recounted regimental exploits elsewhere. But behind the cover sheet emblazoned with a horseshoe-and-saber shield, the booklet had gaps. It did not explain that the 7th Cavalry, in the snowstorm at the Washita, had slaughtered more than one hundred Native Americans—mostly unarmed old men, women and children—who had been ordered into the area by the U.S. Army itself, and that the soldiers carried off other women, killed 875 ponies and destroyed whatever Indian property they did not loot.

The history also did not include some later 7th Cavalry operations, including one of the nineteenth century's most infamous massacres, the killing of up to 370 Sioux, many of them women and children, at Wounded Knee Creek in South Dakota in December 1890. Troopers later said a Sioux had fired on them first, and they could not distinguish the Indian women from men.

Nor did the newest recruits read that many young men who rode to their deaths with Custer had been poorly trained, some of them immigrants who had never ridden a horse until they put on the blues and set out toward the Little Bighorn.

When the West was won, the 7th Cavalry found new frontiers. The seven-page history noted the regiment was sent to the Philippines in 1905 to help with the "organization of the islands" a few years after the United States seized the East Asian archipelago in the Spanish-American War. In reality, the U.S. Army had been engaged in an anti-guerrilla struggle against a Filipino independence movement, resisters whom President Theodore Roosevelt vilified as "Apaches." The Army, led in many cases by old Indian fighters, mounted a frontier-style campaign, burning villages to the ground and killing thousands of Filipino peasants. In a letter home a soldier told of the slaughter of one thousand men, women and children in one town and wrote, "I am probably growing hard-hearted for I am in my glory when I can sight my gun on some darkskin and pull the trigger."

From somewhere, American soldiers picked up a harsh little epithet for these unfamiliar Asians: "gooks."

Unease over the atrocities in the Philippines led to congressional hearings. A U.S. military governor from Manila, old Indian Wars cavalryman Arthur MacArthur, assured the congressmen that America was carrying out the civilizing mission of its "Aryan ancestors" in its Philippine campaign.

IT WAS GEN. ARTHUR MACARTHUR'S SON, FOUR DECADES LATER, who rode triumphantly into a defeated Tokyo on September 8, 1945, with a handpicked escort—the 2nd Battalion of the Garryowens.

That day, war-weary veterans of the 7th Cavalry raised the Stars and Stripes once more at the old U.S. Embassy to fly over a Japanese capital blanketed with ash, choked with debris, a city that had lost one-third of its buildings to American firebombing and lost half its prewar population of seven million to the bombings, to the warfront as soldiers, or to the poor but bomb-free countryside as refugees.

The 7th Cavalry Regiment, now a modern infantry unit, fought under Douglas MacArthur through his campaigns from 1943 to 1945, hopscotching with the rest of the 1st Cavalry Division up the island chains of the southwest Pacific. Its men had fallen by the hundreds in a war without mercy.

The war's ferocity was marked early on by the "Rape of Nanking" and other bloodbaths perpetrated by the Japanese army in China, and by the Bataan Death March, on which thousands of American and Filipino soldiers perished after being captured by the Japanese. Eventually, American GIs and Marines began routinely killing Japanese soldiers who tried to surrender. A major psychological study found almost half of American soldiers said they would "really like to kill a Japanese soldier," but only 6 percent said the same about the German enemy. Then the war ended in the deathly flash of U.S. atomic weapons over Hiroshima and Nagasaki, where well over 100,000 Japanese civilians were killed.

As the mass killings drew toward a close, one of MacArthur's own top aides took note of the cruel conflict's special nature. "The war in the Pacific was racial," Brig. Gen. Bonner F. Fellers, the general's military secretary and psychological warfare chief, wrote in an internal memo. Even before Hiroshima, this American general concluded that his country's bombings of Japanese cities were "one of the most ruthless and barbaric killings of noncombatants in all history."

Gil Huff, the junior colonel, got his own good look at the nature of that Asian war when he took up his infantry assignment in Japan in 1945, fresh from Europe and a war in which Americans and Germans frequently did take each other prisoner. The daring Huff, in fact, had himself been captured by the Germans that January. When his family back home in Greenville was told he was missing, they filed into the Second Baptist Church every day to pray for a miracle. Then, 92 days later, he returned to American lines leading a group of escapees. On turnips, water and dandelion greens, the onetime 190-pound bulldog lost one-third of his weight.

In Japan, Huff joined a military team that traveled to Nagasaki not long after the atomic bombing. He had seen a lot of war, but never anything like that plain of devastation, the bizarrely twisted steel—"like a corkscrew"—the stench of death, of burned, decaying flesh, that gripped the site of the vanished city center.

Possessing the atomic bomb put a swagger in the step of Americans. They stood unchallenged on the world stage. It was a swagger that could be seen at the top in Japan, where the erect, stern-jawed MacArthur assumed the role of Asian proconsul for a kind of American global empire. "Our frontier lies here where half the world's population lives," MacArthur took to telling American visitors in Tokyo. "We haven't begun to realize its potentialities."

As Supreme Commander Allied Powers—SCAP in Army shorthand—MacArthur set about transforming occupied Japan, his actions enforced by a "strong right arm," the 1st Cavalry Division. The division, including the 7th Cavalry, was entrusted with overseeing all of Tokyo and eventually all of central Honshu, the main Japanese island.

Throughout the war, Americans had developed vile images of the Japanese—as "savages," President Truman's term, and as the "monkey men" shown in propaganda art spilling decent people's blood and raping white women. The U.S. troops pouring into Japan in 1945 were apprehensive. Die-hard militarists might mount terror attacks. When the 7th Cavalry first moved into permanent barracks, taking over the yellow brick buildings of the Japanese Merchant Marine Academy, the troopers stashed their M-1 rifles beneath their cots, with ammunition clips, in case of trouble. But the Jeep patrols and off-duty GIs, dispensing chocolate and chewing gum to kids and cautious smiles to adults, soon broke through the chill.

Eventually, MacArthur and his SCAP brain trust would rewrite the defeated nation's constitution, redistribute agricultural lands in a vast reform and put their stamp on a host of other institutions of postwar Japan. But first the occupation forces had to disarm a heavily militarized country, and Sgt. Snuffy Gray and the rest of the 7th Cavalry took part.

A brawny, canny New Yorker, Gray and his men traveled to Chiba prefecture outside Tokyo in 1946 to collect guns and arms-making equipment and dump them at sea. They even seized antique samurai armor and cut it up. The enterprising sergeant did manage to save about two hundred classic samurai swords and take them to Tokyo for the "regimental museum." But the museum did not exist, many valuable swords were given away to departing veterans, the rest were eventually stolen, and it all typified the casual plundering the conquering army grew accustomed to. They owned Japan.

In the post–World War II years, most of the cavalrymen's working hours were spent on guard duty, punctuated by occasional full-dress parades. For both they needed to look sharp. Pfc. Don MacFarland was surprised when he first reported to F Company and was sent to the "tailor shop" to get his fitted uniforms, with military creases sewn into the pants. MacArthur wanted the new recruit from Massachusetts and the rest of his 7th Cavalry to impress the Japanese. Not only did the men spit-shine their tanker boots, but they also car-waxed their helmet liners to wear as dress headgear, and soaked their web belts in salt water to bleach them to a showy white. "We weren't infantry," MacFarland said of those days before Korea. They were a praetorian guard fit for a proconsul.

They had little time and Japan had little space for full infantry training. They fired their M-1 rifles and .30-caliber machine guns once or twice a year on ranges, and in the summer of 1949 the regiment spent a few weeks at Camp McNair, a training ground near Mount Fuji. Gray, the reconnaissance platoon sergeant, called the training at McNair "haphazard and sketchy."

"All we did was ride around," he said. When John Ramirez, a nineteen-year-old sergeant in G Company, tried to give his platoon some bayonet training outside the Tokyo barracks, a passing regimental staff officer told him to forget it. "We're never going to be in another war where there'll be bayonet charges," he said.

The troops did no large-unit maneuvers, and little or no live-fire training. Lieutenant Colonel Huff eventually could report that only one company in the 8th Cavalry Regiment, among the dozens in the division, had received complete combat training by the time of the Korea emergency in the summer of 1950. One segment completely missed by the 7th Cavalrymen instructed troops in how to handle civilian refugees in a war zone.

An Army historian later concluded that the occupation army in Japan had simply become "flabby and soft." Too much beer can do that. Once when the men were scheduled for a long march at McNair, they planted caches of beer along the route beforehand.

THE TEENAGED AMERICANS WERE NOT TRUE INFANTRY, BUT GUARDS, and they manned critical posts across Tokyo—the ordnance depot, a major pier, railroad stations. The showiest was at the moats of the Imperial Palace, where Hirohito and his family remained largely hidden behind the glossy, nine-foot-high stone outer walls, and where meticulously turned-out 7th Cavalry troopers, pairing up with Australian, British Gurkha, or other Allied soldiers, would stand at parade rest at the gatehouse for four hours at a time.

They stood across the broad avenue as well, guarding the austere office building of the Dai-Ichi insurance company, where "acting emperor" MacArthur was chauffeured up to the columned entrance each morning in a black Cadillac to rule Japan from a sixth-floor office. His SCAP bureaucracy of U.S. military officers and civilian specialists eventually filled up a 278-page telephone directory, taking over the office blocks of the Marunouchi financial district and turning it into a "Little America."

Wherever they could, the SCAP bureaucrats put an American stamp on Tokyo, superimposing a U.S.-style grid of street names, for example, over the unfamiliar Japanese address system. New wooden street signs went up across town. The 7th Cavalry's home, renamed McKnight Barracks, was instantly relocated from Fukagawa-Etchujima to the intersection of 22nd Street and Avenue W. A giant post exchange opened in the heart of the Ginza, purveying everything from Buicks to lunch-counter beef hash. Before long *The Aldrich Family,* Jack Benny and *Amos 'n' Andy* were crowding the Tokyo broadcast band, thanks to the U.S. Armed Forces Radio Service.

Across a canal from the SCAP buildings, well-armed Garryowens settled in for days at a time at the Bank of Japan, an imposing Romanesque stone pile. Behind its heavy front doors, troopers descended by elevator through four underground levels, where guards guarding guards stood outside vaults holding uncounted riches in Japanese government gold and silver and imperial trinkets.

The security was not always airtight. One veteran 7th Cavalry sergeant made off with a kilogram bar of gold from the bowels of the bank, pounded it exceedingly thin, sewed it into the lining of foldover luggage, and successfully spirited it back to the States.

Ralph Bernotas would not have dreamed of attempting such a caper. The eighteen-year-old corporal, pleased with a paycheck approaching $100 a month, regularly did his "four hours on" in the subterranean corridors and simply wondered what lay inside the giant vaults.

Lois Findley could have told him. In the war's dying days, Japanese officials had dumped tons of gold ingots into Tokyo harbor, hoping to secretly recover them someday. But the Americans happened on the treasure, in waters just off the 7th Cavalry's motor pool area. Now the efficient Miss Findley, twenty-four, a civilian Army employee, was working every day down in the Bank of Japan vaults, two regiment guards beside her, trying to match recovered ingots with bank registration numbers. During her time in Tokyo, she never completed the task, but the pretty, lively Nebraskan did manage to meet a 7th Cavalryman who took her fancy.

Up at ground level, above this storehouse of wealth, Tokyo was a metropolis of the newly poor. It could, in pockets amid the ruins, still be a charming place of meandering alleys and long rows of tiny houses, their occupants' shoes arrayed outside, their light flowing warmly through paper windows onto the passing scene. The cherry trees still blossomed a sublime pink each spring. But in the central city, where the healthy Americans with the yellow-and-black "Cav" patches on their uniforms towered over the Japanese throngs, the hard times could be seen everywhere.

Tokyoites jammed dangerously onto rickety old streetcars or into the too few trains. Even some of the most important Japanese offices went unheated in winter. The aftermath of war—unemployment, inflation of 10 percent a month, chronic food shortages—crushed the urban workingman and his family. Hundreds of thousands resorted to a barter economy: taking the train to the countryside, or meeting farmers in the city, to trade clothing, household goods, even heirlooms for a bag of rice.

On guard duty behind an Army mess hall, the 7th Cavalry's Joe McAnany spotted a Japanese man breaking in and stealing food one night. "I could have shot him, but he was hungry and I let him go."

In such desperate times, millions of ordinary Japanese stepped over the line into the black market, which, with the help of almost every American soldier, quickly became the real economy of Japan. Rationing of rice and other staples at times permitted only half the daily requirement of calories. The Japanese had little choice but to pay the ever-inflating prices of the black market. Some hoped to make money themselves there.

The Garryowens became enthusiastic black marketers, and their barracks' location, beside the oily dark waters of Tokyo harbor, made movement of goods easy. Even quiet Buddy Wenzel joined in. The arithmetic, from Army post exchange to black market, was too persuasive. "A carton of cigarettes cost us a dollar. You could take a carton down there and make $10 on it."

Men reported their bed linen or clothing lost at the laundry and got new supplies that quickly turned up in the open-air markets around town. On guard duty at the quartermaster depot, men would help themselves to Army footwear—choosing smaller sizes for the Japanese. Some even stole .45-caliber pistols to sell to the black market. The troops grew to expect the extra income. MacArthur's fiscal officers reported that servicemen in Japan each month were sending home $8 million more than their total pay.

Black-market cigarettes became a currency in a land whose citizens could smoke only two "legal" cigarettes a day. In fact, American soldiers would remember for the rest of their lives the days in Tokyo when a single Lucky Strike could buy them sex with a "gook girl."

The hard times had driven tens of thousands of young Japanese women to prostitution—part-time, full-time or in an *onrii wan* relationship, with only one GI. Some hungry families encouraged their daughters to become bar girls, taxi dancers, bathhouse attendants.

Prostitution had long been accepted, even licensed, in Japan. Under pressure from the U.S. military, the Tokyo government tried to outlaw it after the war. American commanders even sent troops, including Snuffy Gray's platoon, on raids through Yoshiwara, a centuries-old red-light district. "Guys would be jumping out windows in their underwear," Gray recalled. One was big Norm Tinkler, who dodged military police once by diving for a ditch behind a bathhouse, only to find he had landed in an open sewer. Once the commotion died, the "panpan girls" washed him down. The night was still young.

Off-limits signs went up all over Tokyo, but 7th Cavalrymen ignored them. The U.S. command, in a way, encouraged the red-light expeditions by setting up "pro stations" in convenient spots, where partying soldiers stopped to pick up condoms or dose themselves with after-sex medication. For inexperienced country boys, half a world away from parents and American puritanism, it was an idyll of parades, easy money and cheap sex. "I didn't have a care in the world then," Norm Tinkler said.

But not everyone went out every night. Buddy Wenzel, for one, wanted time alone. Buddy had not taken to Army life, bucking some of the petty discipline. At one point, because of a childhood musical talent, he was shunted over to the regimental bugle corps, but the tricky notes of "Retreat" defied him and he was passed around some more, spending time as an MP.

When he was off duty, Buddy would sit atop his bunk for hours, pencil in hand, writing to a long list of girls in California, Idaho, Ohio and beyond. "It was interesting to hear what the different states were like." Every day he wrote to "Green Eyes," his girlfriend Dot back home in New Jersey, and once a month he sent her $10 or $20 from his $80 pay. He knew they'd be getting married.

Other 7th Cavalrymen were scared off the circuit of bars and guesthouses by venereal disease. They latched onto a single girl, and usually put her up in a little rented house, a hooch. Don McFarland paid secretarial school tuition for his girlfriend, Kiyo. Girl, house, school, laundry—the cost for all was about $30 a month, "a couple of cartons of cigarettes."

A teenager in bangs named Yoshiko found the blue-eyed ex–altar boy Ralph Bernotas. She was "Cookie" to him. Ralph had her checked by a doctor, paid her rent in a cramped, hibachi-heated house. She made him happy. "If we didn't have the war," he said, "I might have brought her home."

Art Hunter, no longer homesick, plunked down $200 to buy a hooch for his pretty girlfriend. The shy, blond James Hodges had a *koibito,* too, a lovely young woman whose photograph puzzled his sisters back at the Florida farm. Whose child was in the photo with her, they wondered, and why did James urgently ask that the savings he'd sent home now be sent back to him in Japan?

In occupied Tokyo, before Korea, no Garryowen was a hermit. The unlimited Class-A passes, the sake rice brew and inexpensive beer, the live music, the lipsticked girls, all drew the young soldiers to the Ginza. Even Buddy Wenzel learned to samba there.

At the Oasis, the biggest, hottest Ginza nightspot, the taxi dancers all wore long evening dresses, copied from old American magazines, and loose-limbed GIs tried out the jitterbug they'd picked up in high school. The big Japanese band, its sound a dead ringer for what they left back in the States, would play "Tokyo Boogie Woogie" and, always, "China Nights," a wistful Japanese tune that became the late-night anthem for these boys far from home. It was a few cents a dance, and girls were available for more than dancing later.

Beneath the spinning, mirrored chandelier, in a haze of cigarette smoke, the vast sunken dance floor of the Oasis was a sea of libido, liquor and five hundred girls, and was also a notorious cauldron for trouble. Brawls broke out repeatedly, and in late 1948 one erupted that Sgt. John Ramirez, a tough barrio kid from Los Angeles, called the biggest free-for-all he ever saw. Paratroopers passing through Tokyo took exception to the Garryowens they found around the Oasis dance floor, and forty-five minutes of fistfights ensued, among hundreds of GIs. "The 720th MP Battalion would not go down into the club. They were afraid," said Ramirez, who was in the thick of the action. The MPs finally did venture inside. "They arrested the ones still on the floor."

While drunken squads of enlisted men roamed the Ginza, the regiment's commissioned ranks found their Glenn Miller and Artie Shaw music at the officers' clubs, especially the former University Club of Tokyo, a grand expropriated building where General MacArthur's officer corps dined on continental cuisine, played the slot machines, took in the floor shows and danced, with wives or girlfriends, to the nightly music of a fourteen-piece band. The amusing Mel Chandler, crew-cut and dark, was one of the regular ladies' men around the dance floor.

For these "honorable conquerors" in occupied Japan, on the eve of an unexpected war, life was almost aristocratic. At a time when millions of Japanese remained homeless, the U.S. occupation requisitioned more than six hundred houses for Army officers and others, naturally choosing the finest. A twenty-nine-year-old major, Harold D. Steward, and his wife had a 14-room house, fronting a private lake, with five servants. "It was a very pleasant life, with maids, cooks, manservants, gardener," said Steward. Even sergeants often had two maids.

The conquerors could travel free on the trains to visit the city of Kyoto and other Japanese treasures that had escaped the U.S. bombing. Back in Tokyo, the division's ex–horse cavalrymen took over a city stadium for regular polo matches, riding quarter horses from the Japanese imperial stables. On weekends, regimental and division football teams clashed before stands full of cheering Americans.

Even junior officers like Captain Chandler, whose wife and small son stayed behind in the States when he shipped out to Asia, drew comfortable Japanese-style homes for quarters. At his place, near the 7th Cavalry's McKnight Barracks, Chandler had H Company men build him an un-Japanese wet bar, and the twenty-eight-year-old company commander threw frequent parties, popular with young officers, nurses and other civilian American women, and pretty Japanese.

Army officers were more discreet than the privates who "lost" their laundry, but they, too, routinely ventured into the black market—at times too deeply. When the Tokyo provost marshal's wife, spouse of the Army's top policeman, began flaunting her fur coats, an underling turned the major in for enriching himself on seized contraband recycled back into the illicit market. The ex–police chief ended up serving stockade time in the States.

NO MATTER WHAT THEY DID, BOTH TEENAGED RECRUITS AND HIGH-living officers enjoyed immunity in one sense: The Japanese couldn't touch them. In fact, public criticism of the U.S. military was forbidden under all-encompassing censorship. After posters appeared in 1949 accusing American troops of widespread rapes of local women, six Japanese held responsible for the "rumors" were sentenced to five years in prison by a U.S. military court.

The censorship obscured a violent, criminal side of the American presence. One Japanese calculation found an average of 330 rapes and assaults daily on Japanese women at one point during the occupation. Reckless Army Jeep drivers ran down Japanese civilians and simply drove on. Half-drunk soldiers, unprovoked, would kick or beat Japanese on the street, sometimes shouting, "Remember Pearl Harbor!" At times those responsible would be traced and prosecuted by the U.S. military, sometimes not.

On a petty level, crude abuse was common. Clownish GIs took to pushing tram drivers aside and taking trolleys, with terrified passengers, on headlong joy rides. Soldiers "playfully" nudged Tokyo's pedicabs with their Jeeps, sending their runner-drivers sprawling. Photos of those rickshaw cabs show the unequal relationship: Teenaged white soldiers, buck privates, sit grandly above grim and sweaty Japanese, often war veterans, hauling them through Tokyo.

Officially, the U.S. Army was a racist institution at the time. Black soldiers were still segregated in their own units; the 7th Cavalry Regiment was all white. President Truman had ordered the armed forces desegregated in 1948, but the Army was slow to comply, especially in MacArthur's Far East Command. When his father signed Art Hunter into the Army back in Virginia, the young man chose the 1st Cavalry Division because recruiters assured him it had not been integrated.

Anti-Asian racism, inflamed by the recent war, underlay many American attitudes on the far side of the Pacific. MacArthur's own intelligence chief, Maj. Gen. Charles A. Willoughby, had proclaimed at the outset of World War II his belief in the "military supremacy of the white race." In Japan, a visiting U.S. journalist found ranking Army officers who told him, "Dumbness has almost been bred into these people," and, "They are sneaky right down to their pagan souls. They are like animals." MacArthur himself viewed his mission to include "Christianizing" the Japanese. His aides kept him informed on missionaries' successes.

One observant visitor to MacArthur's Tokyo, the Navy veteran and writer James Michener, captured this khaki-clad mentality at the time in his short novel *Sayonara,* in which an American officer, son of a general, is pressured into abandoning the Japanese actress he loves. "We don't want officers with yellow wives," declares his father.

That kind of poignant clash of worlds played out in real life uncounted times. Gil Huff, unmarried and in his thirties, reborn survivor of the European front, met a beautiful young woman at a dinner in Tokyo, a member of a prominent Japanese family. The millworker's son was entranced. He pursued her, called on her. She seemed interested in him, too, he thought. But the gap was too great, the liaison was doomed. It would have hurt the young colonel's career.

" 'Squaw man,' the Army would have called me in the old days," says Michener's hero, who in his *sayonara* to Japan regrets that he lives in an age "when the only acceptable attitude toward strange lands and people of another color must be not love but fear."

THE 7TH CAVALRY REGIMENT IN JAPAN WAS SURROUNDED BY strange lands it could fear. One lay just across the Korea Strait, an ancient place of mountains, paddies, almost medieval poverty, a mystery to all but a few who served in an Army contingent there after World War II. Those U.S. troops withdrew from Korea in 1949, four years after Soviet and U.S. forces first occupied the Japanese colony and divided it north and south.

As he flew home in August 1948, the man in charge of that Korean occupation, Lt. Gen. John R. Hodge, looked ahead for reporters. The 7th Cavalrymen, in their bunks at McKnight Barracks, could have read about it in the newspaper: KOREA CIVIL WAR POSSIBLE, HODGE SAYS. But the headline did not concern them. The U.S. Army's mission was to defend Japan.

Although they didn't know Korea, the Garryowens did, to some extent, know Koreans—a one-million-strong minority in Japan, many imported and impressed into hard labor during World War II. The Japanese looked down on the Korean "garlic eaters," and MacArthur allowed Japan's reconstituted parliament to pass discriminatory laws against them. The Americans considered them a troublemaking minority from the outset of the occupation, when hungry Korean coal miners in Japan agitated for a better deal. In 1948, U.S. troops of the 25th Infantry Division killed five Koreans in rioting over demands for minority rights in the Japanese city of Kobe.

Year by year, the SCAP regime's political attitudes had been shifting. MacArthur began with attacks on the pillars of Japan's "fascism" by dismantling its military institutions and by working to break up the wealth of the *zaibatsu,* family business monopolies. He had authority from Washington to promote labor unions and wider income distribution in Japan. He even legalized Japan's long-suppressed Communist Party. But by 1947 the SCAP planners were themselves under attack from right-wing critics back home who called their plans a war against capitalism. Anti-leftist fervor was building daily in America because of the news from Europe, where communists had gained control of the governments in Poland and

Czechoslovakia, and from China, where the communists were advancing in the civil war.

Japanese conservatives lobbied MacArthur's aides to view their country as a bulwark against a leftist tide. Willoughby's counterintelligence corps began reporting any political or labor protest as "communist agitation." MacArthur pushed through legislation restricting the rights of Japan's labor unions. The efforts to "deconcentrate" giant conglomerates were largely abandoned. Japan began to look like its prewar self again.

Political surveillance became a major mission for the 1st Cavalry Division. In one monthly report, it said its men had monitored thirty-one meetings of communists in the Tokyo area and—the other troublesome group—"ten meetings of Koreans."

The troops still carried out other occupation duties as well, among them escorting accused war criminals to their trials. On December 22, 1948, two 7th Cavalry companies were trucked out to Sugamo Prison, where they stood around the dark, glowering fortress, almost shoulder to shoulder, while U.S. Army hangmen inside, just after midnight, dropped the gallows trap door under Hideki Tojo.

The wartime Japanese prime minister was declared dead within minutes. But his voice lived on in a final testament in which he declared the Americans had committed major blunders in the postwar period, one of the most serious being the division of Korea. That had sown the seeds of future disaster, Tojo wrote.

If so, American generals believed, it would not be their disaster. South and North Korea, armed by the United States and the Soviet Union, were trading threats and artillery fire across their dividing line. But the U.S. Joint Chiefs of Staff decided in 1949 that the peninsula was of little strategic value, and "any commitment to United States' use of military force in Korea would be ill-advised."

Other voices were also being heard, however. Presidential advisers told Truman that Korea was a symbolic battleground of ideologies, and in February 1950 a U.S. senator, Joseph M. McCarthy, stoked the fears of ordinary Americans by telling them that leftist traitors had infiltrated their very own government. The proof,

McCarthy said, could be seen in America's "loss" of China to the communists in October 1949. Out of nowhere, it seemed, a "Red" tide was threatening America.

NOW IT WAS JULY 1950, AND BUDDY WENZEL AND RALPH BERNOTAS, Captain Chandler, Gil Huff and the nervous Colonel Nist were all on the high seas in a lonely convoy strung out along the back side of a typhoon. They would soon land in Korea, but the Garryowens hoped to return before long to the girls and football, the scams and sukiyaki, to their own little "Bali Ha'i," the paradise in that new Rodgers and Hammerstein musical about the last war.

One Garryowen, Bill McKown, knew a Bali Ha'i off through the stormy murk past Cape Sata. He and Lois Findley, the "girl from the vaults," had spent their honeymoon there, at a hotel among the Unzen hot springs of Japan's south coast.

Lois hadn't liked Cav men until her blind date with the tall, sensible mess sergeant from West Virginia. Six months later, they got married—after first obtaining his commanding officer's permission and then waiting through a 60-day cooling-off period, designed to discourage soldiers from impulsive marriages to Japanese, but applicable to everyone.

When the wedding day finally came, it was an unforgettable, all-American blowout. Friends took care of that. An MP Jeep with siren blaring escorted Bill and Lois to the ceremony at the U.S. Consulate. A colonel's driver later chauffeured the newlyweds to the front door of Tokyo's Civilian Club, where two hundred guests—sharply uniformed Garryowens, young American women in stylish bright dresses—packed the ballroom for their reception. Lois, the star, wore a headband of white satin and a flared suit of brown gabardine.

A 20-piece Japanese band, an affordable luxury picked up by a generous sergeant friend, played jitterbugs, fox-trots, two-steps. They sang along to "She Ain't Got No Yo-Yo," the Americans' nonsense mimic of the Japanese lyrics of "China Nights." They all drank and joked, flirted and danced the night away, in a party that, in its way, captured a carefree moment in time for a generation and an army that had grown too used to peace too quickly.

Around midnight, the driver whisked the McKowns to a Japanese-style home, an officer's quarters vacant at the time, to spend the night. Just as they settled in behind rice-paper doors, the street outside exploded with gunfire. Snuffy Gray and a few of the boys had descended on them to perform a "shivaree," a traditional raucous serenade, Sergeant Gray squeezing off a magazine of rounds from his .45 pistol, the others banging on pots and pans.

Then, as the smell of gunpowder floated off into the night, the noisy interlopers sat down with Bill and Lois and drank champagne and beer and laughed until dawn, toasting the happiness of the newlyweds and basking in their own good fortune, at being young and American and on top of an American world.

2

December 20, 1944
Yongdong County, Korea

The newlyweds threaded their way slowly through the bare and twisting winter valleys, their little cortege heading home beneath jumbled ridges and peaks a traveler once likened to the sight of the sea in a gale.

The crew-cut young man, Chung Eun-yong, small and intense, his slight build buttoned up in a stern high-necked jacket, sat hunched inside a closed sedan chair at the head of the humble procession. Slung between two poles, he was an easy morning's work for the two bearers loping along front and rear.

The bride, Park Sun-yong, some paces behind, sat atop a bouncing rickshaw whose runner swung left and right in hopes of dodging the road's ripples and rocks. She was a gentle, big-eyed young woman, and she was on a short, seven-mile journey of a lifetime, the trip to her new village. She was petrified.

New husband Eun-yong, twenty-one years old, had much on his mind: How would his parents take to his bride? Would she soon bear him a son? Would she make a good wife for a policeman? For that matter, would he make a success of himself?

His eighteen-year-old wife wondered the same things. But now, with the cold December air pricking her plump pink cheeks, Sun-yong also had the warm memory of yesterday's wedding to draw upon. The weather, it was true, had forced them to wear a layer of everyday clothes beneath the brilliant colors of their wedding costumes. A winter wedding is unusual in Korea. But they had their reasons for not waiting, and things went perfectly in the minutely choreographed ceremony on the *matang,* the foreyard of her parents' house in the village of Shimchon. Now they were traveling, in the traditional homecoming, from Shimchon to the young Mr. Chung's ancestral village, Chu Gok.

Behind the couple and their hired conveyances, porters leaned into the road carrying her luggage on their *ji-gae,* the wooden back frames, shaped like the letter *A,* that Korean men used to transport everything from rice sheaves to frail grandmothers. Along with Sun-yong's clothes and household items, they bore gifts of clothing and food for Eun-yong's family.

Yongdong County's gray-brown slopes, much of their tree cover stripped for firewood, seemed lifeless, except for the black-and-white magpies and the rare pheasant or hare that might startle from the scrub. The roads themselves always teemed with Korean life in winter, especially on this highway of packed earth and gravel that for centuries had served as the peninsula's main north-south route, meandering diagonally through the jigsaw of valleys and up and down passes, from the old royal capital at Seoul, 100 miles northwest of Yongdong town, to the ancient seaport of Pusan, the same distance to the southeast.

On the road to Yongdong, oxen snorted frozen clouds of breath as they hauled their carts of bagged rice. Sturdy men in flimsy sandals, with weathered faces and calloused hands, strode along under loads of firewood. Women passed with bulging cotton bags atop their heads. All were dressed in the usual winter garb of quilted and padded white cotton. Even in ancient times the Koreans were known to the Chinese and others as the "people in white."

Like China, Korea in the mid–twentieth century remained a land of villages in a maze of terraced valleys. They stretched in chains along the roads or reached into tight, steep side hollows, each village, or *ri*, a cluster of thatched roofs of graying yellow, ringed by fields wet and green with rice in the summer, and where barley was now taking root for the winter.

The smell of wood smoke met travelers along the road. Beneath the chimneys, inside the mud-walled homes, villagers worked at sorting rice straw for weaving or other wintertime chores, or readied some red bean porridge for the winter solstice meal, the holiday dish that, tradition said, warded off ghosts on the year's longest night.

Steam whistles, at regular intervals, pierced the mountain stillness. The peninsula's main rail line paralleled the road, and the Japanese, Korea's colonial masters since annexing the country in 1910, were running trainloads of war matériel northward from ships at Pusan, to their hundreds of thousands of troops in Manchuria and at the fighting fronts of China. After crossing a tiny trestle at nearby No Gun Ri, the trains rumbled on another five minutes and past Eun-yong's home village. The punctual sound of hissing locomotives told Chu Gok Ri residents the time of day.

By late 1944, the global war had reached into Chu Gok and each of Korea's 29,043 other villages. Local Japanese administrators were demanding more and more rice to feed the troops and the Japanese home front. The colonial government and other landlords who once took half the rice crop now were seizing up to 70 percent. And the Japanese took more than food. They dug up Seoul's water mains for their iron and even seized gongs from little village bands for their brass, and they impressed many thousands of young Koreans into hard labor at mines and factories in Japan, and some into Imperial Army service at the warfront. Young men from Chu Gok Ri were among them, and some never returned.

It was a difficult, hungry time for Koreans, but the latest bad news for Japan—despite censorship, people heard of American victories in the Philippines—secretly cheered some in Chu Gok Ri.

For now, the war meant shortage and hardship, even for a wedding. The bridegroom was supposed to ride a horse royally from the wedding back to his home, but the horses had gone to war and Eun-yong had to settle for a rented sedan chair. The bride's neighbors would normally receive an invitation to a feast of wine and song, but Sun-yong's family had to limit the celebration to a handful of relatives.

The two had been brought together in the usual way, by family arrangement. Village grapevines had told the parents that each was eligible. A female go-between checked each family's wealth and standing. The prospective bride's father was relatively well-to-do, a low-ranking township official with money and land. Eun-yong, as a policeman, was a good catch. Eun-yong knew the arranged marriage had to be, but he got one modern concession: He could see the girl before agreeing to marry her.

That day, accompanied by a male cousin for a second opinion, the young man first met Sun-yong's father, honoring him with a formal bow, kneeling, nose almost to the floor. Then he was led to a small room where the girl waited in a pink *hanbok,* the high-waisted Korean gown.

"She was beautiful," Eun-yong said. "We didn't talk at all, and someone brought in jujube fruit and dried persimmon. I may have eaten one or two. Then they said it was time to go." The minutes flew for Sun-yong, too. "Not bad," she thought of this stranger with the small, serious face.

On the appointed wedding day, a date chosen by a fortune-teller, it dawned snowy, not a deep snow but enough for the cows to leave hoofprints. Sun-yong's family spread a rice straw mat in the center of the *matang,* and placed a table on it laden with the Korean symbols of matrimony: a live hen and cock bound in cloth, rice cakes, fruits, candles, alternating red and blue colors representing the bride and groom.

Now she stood before him across the wedding table, hair pulled up into a tight bun, face thickly powdered, a bright red dot placed on each cheek. Her coat and skirt were a rainbow of primary colors. He wore the costume of a court official—red, black and blue. They performed the solemn rituals—delicately timed bows, precise postures for sitting and facing each other, she always with head bowed, never talking or smiling, because a smile, it was said, would doom her to bear only girls, a dreadful prospect in a society that tells a wife her sacred duty is to carry on the male family line.

They sealed their marriage with a *hapkunlye,* a ceremonial sharing of cups of wine. She then retired to her room. He then ate a meal alone, and after sunset joined her. By age-old custom, women of the family gathered outside, to learn what would happen. Inside, according to script, he would blow out the candle, and the eavesdroppers outside were obliged to retreat, with giggles or grumbles.

As a policeman, Chung Eun-yong was exempt from Japan's draft. Having a family would insulate him still further. But the union was even more important to the Parks. Japanese police had been taking away young unmarried Koreans to become "comfort women"—a euphemism for sex slaves, working in front-line military brothels. The roundups that began in southernmost Korea were now rumored to be moving toward the Yongdong area. To Sun-yong, then, this sober young man was not just a husband. He was a savior.

The war was far from their homes, but still it cut deep into Korean souls, just as wars on their doorsteps—wars always brought to them by others—had done in centuries past. One scar from a long-ago war lay just over the hills the newlyweds skirted as they made their way, the day after the wedding, toward Chu Gok Ri. The women of Yul village had fled into those hills three and a half centuries earlier as a huge Japanese army poured up the main road, slaughtering and pillaging along the way. Two village women, pursued by invaders, threw themselves to their deaths from a cliff rather than be raped and killed by the foreign soldiers. The people of Yongdong County have since memorialized the place as the "Hill of the Japanese Barbarians."

KOREANS HAD LONG SOUGHT TO BE LEFT ALONE IN THEIR "HERMIT kingdom." In the end, when their walls crumbled in the nineteenth century and they could no longer keep out the world, they were the last East Asian nation to open up to Western trade and ideas.

Their rugged, sharp-peaked peninsula, the size of Great Britain, juts out 500 miles into natural trade routes of northeast Asia, putting Korea at a crossroads among larger nations. Yongdong, meanwhile, was a crossroads of southern Korea. Through its valleys, hemmed in by highlands reaching to 3,000 feet, Korean tribes and kingdoms contacted and fought each other. Twentieth-century boys playing "knights" and scaling the heights near Yongdong could still find the ruins of stone bastions, remains of forgotten wars. One giant battlement circled the summit of White Horse Mountain, looming across the main road from Chu Gok Ri.

Around A.D. 935 the kingdoms were united under the Koryo dynasty. Since then, although outside powers had brought war to the land, Koreans themselves had lived at peace with one another.

The 200,000-man Japanese army that terrorized Korea in the late 1500s, driving the women of Yul off the cliffs, was dispatched by the shogun Hideyoshi, who wanted Korea as a stepping-stone to the conquest of China. In thousands of boats, the invaders plowed through the waves of the Korea Strait to Pusan and marched north toward Seoul, the capital. Unprepared, with outdated weapons, a "Righteous Army" of Korean peasants held off the invaders for three days east of Yongdong, at Autumn Wind Pass, until the Japanese broke through and flooded the area, plundering and burning, raping and killing thousands before moving on to Seoul. Surviving peasants pulled back into the forested mountain valleys to carry on a guerrilla resistance. It is believed that Chu Gok Ri's more isolated sister village, Im Ke Ri, arose during this period.

Harassed by guerrillas, strangled at sea by the Koreans' revolutionary ironclad "turtle" boats, facing a Chinese army marching down from the north, the overextended Japanese pulled back after seven years to a perimeter in the southeast. Hideyoshi's generals ordered a scorched-earth campaign and burned down Kyongju, an ancient Korean capital, and then finally left the peninsula. The Koreans soon disentangled themselves from the Chinese and withdrew into centuries of isolation.

The Korean people absorbed and refined the cultures of others. Confucianism, the Chinese creed of devotion to ancestors and family, arrived around the fourth century, most scholars believe, and was still the village religion of Koreans sixteen centuries later. It had a heavy overlay of Buddhism, the religion of contentment through self-denial, which came to the peninsula about the same time and was eventually passed on to Japan as a Korean product.

The Koreans' own prehistoric shamanism also survived in the hearts of villagers, like those of Chu Gok Ri. This was a set of unorganized beliefs in a host of spirits that must be respected and appeased—spirits of the household, in old trees and great rocks, of the dead. A shaman, a village woman known as a *mutang,* could be called on to deal with the spirits and cure ailments.

At the same time, Koreans could be modernizers. They developed movable type long before Gutenberg. They devised their own simple alphabet, freeing Korea from the shackles of Chinese character-writing. They taught techniques of ceramic making to the Japanese. They instituted civil service exams and organized the nation into political subdivisions centuries before Western societies did.

Down the centuries, however, the people were kept in serflike poverty. An elite called the *yangban* owned the land, and masses of simple farmers labored endlessly to pay them rent with their rice crop. The Yongdong area, picturesque and peaceful, became the home of *yangban* with positions in the royal government in Seoul. This semifeudal society, which also included a small population of Korean slaves, largely survived until the late nineteenth century, when an outside world intrigued by tales of gold, of "pagans" needing God, or simply of new commercial frontiers, grew ever bolder—and sometimes violent—with the Koreans.

In 1866, the *General Sherman,* an armed, U.S.-owned ship carrying a Chinese crew and a few Americans seeking to open Korea, defied warnings and steamed up the Taedong River to the city of Pyongyang. Korean accounts say the crew went ashore and looted, and the ship exchanged fire with Koreans on shore. An armed stand-off ended when the *General Sherman* grounded in shallows, and the Koreans killed all nineteen on board. In response, a U.S. Navy squadron later appeared off Korea's west coast. It, too, was fired upon, but it managed to land Marines on Kanghwa Island, where they killed hundreds of Korean defenders before withdrawing. It was the Koreans' first encounter with the American military.

Korea's five-century-old Yi dynasty came under growing pressure from many sides, and by the 1880s had signed treaties allowing trade with Western powers and Japan, even opening the land to Christian missionaries. From that time, Korea simply became a piece in the chess game of great powers, none of whom wanted a rival to dominate the strategically situated peninsula. Soon Japan was check-mating the others, defeating China and then Russia in wars in 1895 and 1905. The United States then negotiated a secret agreement with Tokyo recognizing Japan's "suzerainty" over Korea in return for a Japanese pledge not to interfere with U.S. interests in the Philippines. In 1910, Japan finally forced Korea's weak Yi regime to cede power to direct Japanese colonial rule. America and Britain, whose bankers helped finance Japan's expansion, ignored the appeals of Korean patriots for support—something Koreans never forgot.

THE JAPANESE WANTED MORE THAN A COLONY; THEY WANTED TO make Koreans an integral part of a greater Japan, to the point of replacing their language with Japanese and forcing them to adopt Japanese names. In Chu Gok Ri, young Chung Eun-yong had to take the name Ingyo Matsukawa. The emperor's hand would endow Korea with the "the gift of good administration and peace," the first colonial governor-general wrote.

The Koreans showed they didn't want the emperor's gifts, or to give up their language or their right to speak their minds and work out their own affairs. From 1905 to 1915, armed with antiquated weapons and fighting from the hills, Koreans resisted Japanese power. They called themselves the Righteous Army. The Japanese called them bandits and rooted them out. When nationalist dem-onstrations filled the streets of Seoul and other cities in 1919, the Japanese brutally crushed them. It was the era when President Wood-row Wilson was championing "self-determination" for nationalities, but Korean nationalists, like those in Vietnam and elsewhere in

Asia and Africa, found little help in America for their anticolonial cause.

Seven men from Chu Gok Ri were leaders of the "March 1 Protests" in 1919 in Yongdong County, distinguishing their little village as a home of patriots. One, Chung Hee-yong, was taken away by the Japanese police, interrogated and beaten nearly to death. He was found semiconscious on a street in Yongdong town by Chung Tae-nyon, the bridegroom Eun-yong's father, who carried him home on his back. Chung Hee-yong lived as a fugitive for years afterward, and anti-Japanese sentiment among Chu Gok villagers intensified.

The new colonialists saw Korea as a rice bowl for the homeland. A Japanese monopoly land corporation expropriated public lands and pressured private owners into selling. Tens of thousands of Japanese emigrated to the new farming frontier. In some fertile areas, more than two-thirds of the land came under Japanese ownership. Remaining Korean landlords worked with the "New Order."

The Japanese industrialized the underdeveloped economy to some extent, particularly in the north, building hydroelectric plants, harvesting the vast forests. They laid the rail line that cut through Autumn Wind Pass and ran by No Gun Ri and Chu Gok Ri and on to Seoul. The foreigners went prospecting, too, even around Chu Gok Ri, digging small gold mines in the mountainside behind Im Ke Ri and forcing some of the valley's poor to work there.

The new masters had some good ideas. In a country where only twenty thousand children were being educated in 1910, almost a million were in school a generation later. But Korean children were taught only in Japanese, and Korean newborns had to be registered with Japanese names.

The Japanese brought modern farming techniques to the rice paddies, boosting yields, but demands for rents and taxes—rice or money—grew onerous, to the point of extortion and near-starvation. Per-capita consumption of rice, the Korean staple, dropped almost 50 percent between 1915 and 1938, as harvests were sent to Japan by the shipload. Overall calorie intake fell with it, in a farming nation whose peasants, if impoverished, at least had eaten adequately in the past. The demands of World War II, when livestock was being seized and the rice tax grew, pushed villagers even closer to starvation. With the harvest, police descended on Chu Gok Ri and Im Ke Ri and searched the nooks and crannies of households for hidden rice. When any was found, responsible villagers would be flogged or jailed.

Ambitious young men like the newlywed Eun-yong found the Japanese hand oppressive in other ways, too. Eun-yong was a bright child in a proud line of Chungs that included noted Yi dynasty scholars, but his village-poor family could never afford a real education for him. From middle school, he won admission to the prestigious, costly Kyongsung technical school in Seoul. He had dreams of becoming an architect. Instead he went off to the one-year railroad school in the capital, a free government institution. Home on a vacation, he received a letter from the Kyongsung principal telling him they would extend their enrollment deadline especially for him. The teenager crumpled the letter, threw it into the kitchen fireplace and wept.

Once out of school, Eun-yong worked on the telegraph at Seoul's Yongsan railroad station, relaying messages of military shipments and imminent U.S. air attacks on Japanese targets. Outnumbered by Japanese coworkers, ground down by anti-Korean discrimination, he got into a fistfight with a Japanese coworker and eventually quit.

In 1944, the war was going badly for Japan, and Eun-yong knew he would be seized and thrown into the Imperial Army. But he managed to join the police force and now had married Sun-yong. A few days after the wedding, they left for his assignment in Taejon, a bustling city 25 miles north of Chu Gok Ri.

Like all Chu Gok Ri travelers, the young couple passed the Sonangdang at the village's entrance, a gnarled old tree and imposing six-foot-tall rock where the village "guardian spirit" dwelled. Some still placed a small stone there, a prayer to the Sonang for a safe journey home, as they ventured out into the uncertain world.

CHU GOK RI, FRONTING THE MAIN ROAD AND THE RAILROAD beyond, lay at the mouth of a side valley that reached back to where sister village Im Ke Ri sat in a cul-de-sac below the 2,500-foot-high backdrop of Three Peaks Mountain. From above, as graceful white herons flew in each spring, the little valley was a patchwork of rice paddies and vegetable gardens edging right up to the farmers' rice-thatch roofs.

The villages were a collection of extended families, totaling about 570 people in Chu Gok Ri and 390 in Im Ke Ri in the late 1940s. The Chung, Yang and Suh clans were dominant, networks of brothers and cousins—up to eight degrees of separation were carefully tracked—that supplied the social underpinning, the support system, that allowed a village to stand almost independently. Whatever the upheavals nationally, whatever local officials might be appointed from outside, the village stayed essentially democratic, led by a consensus of elders and clan chiefs. This gave villagers a sense of unity and security in a world of tax collectors and police.

The elders were the men in black hats—the distinctively Korean horsetail-hair *got,* a six-inch-high crown ringed by a wide flat brim, worn by married men with recognized social standing. If of *yangban* descent, the Chu Gok Ri elder might also be distinguished in his speech, his words few but important, delivered in a leisurely regional drawl.

The "people in white" wore natural-colored clothing, in the warm months usually made of coarse hemp, sometimes cotton—pajama-style with baggy pants for men, and high-waisted, ankle-length skirts and a light jacket top for women. Some middle-aged women bared their midriffs to the bottom of their breasts, and some removed their tops on the hottest days working the fields. On the rainiest days, villagers donned wide bamboo hats and rice-straw capes. Almost all wore homemade, high-slung sandals of rice straw, which hard use could wear out in a day. The children went shoeless in summer and usually tramped through winter's mud and snow on wooden clogs. Many children could be seen running down village lanes in oversized clothes, hand-me-downs from older brothers and sisters.

Confucianism put a patriarchal stamp on the Korean family. The elder in his mud-and-straw house was "king in his castle," sometimes aloof to an extreme. Because of women's presumed inferiority, some husbands conversed with wives only when necessary. Past the age of seven, except for close family, the sexes did not mix.

The elder got the best food and was served first, sitting cross-legged on the floor at his individual dining tray. Younger males followed, and then the women and children. A better-off village family might eat potatoes or sweet potatoes mixed with rice, and some kimchi, the Korean trademark dish of pickled cabbage or radish. The food came from an earth-floor kitchen at the left end of the rectangular Chu Gok Ri house. The oven's smoke drifted out a chimney at the house's opposite end, having first warmed the flues under the one or two tiny bedrooms on the right, where the family rolled out quilts to retire each night atop a clay floor layered with rice-straw mats. Before each home, inside an outer fence of mud and stone, was its dusty *matang,* where mats were laid so an elder could lounge or rice could dry. Inside the fence, a hog, chickens, perhaps a beehive were kept. If a family was rich it had an ox and wooden-wheeled cart.

Putting down their chopsticks at dinner's end, the villagers returned to their endless chores, often making rope or bags or sandals from rice straw. Rice was everything, and the government exacted a quota of straw products from villagers as a tax. The light went out early to save kerosene, and the sounds of the night took over in Chu Gok Ri—bamboo rattling in the breeze, a sick cow lowing, a hungry baby crying, a widow's muted sobs. The children dropped off to the rhythmic *tock, tock, tock* of mother and daughter-in-law, before a rounded stone, pounding wrinkles out of the freshly laundered family clothes with wooden ironing bats.

Children were everywhere. Most of the village's population was under twenty. Many died young of tuberculosis, measles, typhoid, smallpox—almost half didn't make it to age six. More were conceived to ensure the family's future. Midcentury Korea had one of the world's highest population growth rates, and new generations would find little available farmland around Yongdong. In Chu Gok Ri, only a half-dozen families owned any land; the rest rented, mostly from absentee landlords. To many parents, education was the children's way out of the narrow valleys.

The Japanese opened a school less than a mile from Chu Gok Ri in 1942, a marvel of wood, with wooden floors that the children would sweep and wipe in the morning before sitting down to learn.

Before that, those going to school had to trek almost two hours to Yongdong, or get only classical Confucian training from a village sage at the Seodang, the "House of Letters."

Not every child attended the new school. To Yang Ho-yong and his wife, their Hae-sook was "Kum Yi," Golden Girl. Born in 1937, she was an energetic, talkative child, the only daughter in a family from a *yangban* line that had descended into poverty as small rice farmers. She stood out among her friends, a head taller, as they jumped rope to singsong or played *kongki,* a marbles-like game with pebbles. But when they set off with their books each morning for school, Hae-sook didn't join them. Her parents were old-fashioned: they didn't believe girls should be educated.

In a cramped, century-old house in Im Ke Ri, with a little bent pear tree out front, seven of them lived: grandmother, parents, eldest son Hae-young, middle boy Hae-chan, a baby brother and the "golden" daughter.

Hae-chan ranged the mountain slopes around Im Ke Ri with other boys, climbing trees for wild chestnuts, setting snares for rabbits. They caught crayfish in the stream, and in the winter, when it froze, they would find a piece of wood and push themselves on this "sled" all the way down to Chu Gok Ri. Small for his age, Hae-chan was beaten up once by the village bully. Instead of running off, he stood outside the boy's house, yelling for him to come out again, until the father finally did and apologized. "My brother was a small kid and weak, but he had a lot of guts," Hae-sook said. It was an inner strength that would be tested sooner, and more cruelly, than any ten-year-old deserved.

Yongdong, three miles to the west, was the outer limit of most village children's lives. They might accompany adults to the open-air market, held every five days, and see an itinerant clown or musicians clad in traditional yellow, blue and red. The routine distractions were nonstop: the noise of townspeople and travelers; gossips from other villages; men driving cattle, women with barrels on their heads and babies on their backs; *mutangs* interpreting dreams; rich landlords' sons pedaling their own bicycles; haughty Japanese surveying the natives from rickshaws.

Back in the village, however, life for these midcentury Koreans remained a daily struggle, one that led each year to a climb up "the hill of barley," the grim season of late winter and early spring when the autumn harvest's reserves of rice and other food ran out, and families survived day to day, hand to mouth, until they could bring in the winter barley.

During those gray days, they climbed the hills around them, collecting firewood to sell in Yongdong. Year by year, they ascended higher, deeper into the mountains as the slopes lost more cover to their little iron axes. It was exhausting work. The villagers felled pine or scrub oak, laboriously chopped it up into firewood, and then descended the rugged mountainsides with their back A-frames piled high with heavy loads. They would stop at the village for lunch, then push on to Yongdong, returning as the sun dipped behind the mountains, with a little barley, the food of poverty, to last them another day.

Although the Japanese distributed rations of rotting "bean cake," barely edible pulp left after oil was squeezed from soybeans, the villagers had to resort to eating roots and grass in the hardest times. The children grew famished; their ribs stuck out; white spots spread on their faces. They dug into hillsides for starchy arrowroot, which turned their mouths chocolate-brown. When pink azaleas covered the mountain meadows, the children would eat the flowers. They hunted down snakes and frogs to roast. Their mothers made noodles or buns from roots, sprouts and grain husks to fill their stomachs, giving them digestive problems, bloated bellies and little nutrition.

During these worst of times for the people of Chu Gok Ri, a tall schoolboy from the Chung clan, Chung Koo-hun, was approaching his teens and seeing the injustice of the world around him. Toting his baby brother, Koo-hak, around the village, Koo-hun found that neighbors agreed. "I can tell you that many people back then dreamed of some miracle, some revolution to happen," Koo-hun said. "After years of living under extortion, they wanted a change in the world."

But for now, the people of Chu Gok Ri had only each other to lean on, and their ancestors. Those departed generations remained close by in spirit, guardians whose eternal happiness would, in turn, bestow good fortune on the families left behind. The devotion took its most ceremonial form at New Year's, when ancestral tablets, small plaques of polished chestnut, were displayed in the house and meals were symbolically shared with deceased parents and grand-parents. On the most important holiday, autumn's Chusok harvest moon, villagers climbed to family burial mounds on the hillsides overlooking the valley, trimmed the grass and made offerings of new rice to those who gave them life.

In recent decades, some around Yongdong had found another place of solace as well—in Christianity. The Salvation Army had established a small mission in Chu Gok Ri in 1915. In its 1934 yearbook, the organization boasted of Korea, "There have been many striking instances of conversion from devil worship." Ameri-can missionaries may have shown little respect for the Koreans' reli-gious traditions, but some villagers nonetheless found the church novel and exciting—the singing, the camaraderie at services, the reassuring promise of a better life in the hereafter. Americans in uniform, church "captains" and "majors" waging religious "war-fare," traveled the countryside. The Salvation Army even built a small modern hospital in the town of Yongdong.

But these American "soldiers" were expelled by the Japanese in 1941 and the congregation languished. Then, on August 15, 1945, word reached the villages that Japan had surrendered to end World War II, and three weeks later a genuine American army, the war's victors, landed on the peninsula to take the surrender of Japanese troops in southern Korea, while the Soviet army did the same in the north.

ON THE *MATANGS* OF 29,000 VILLAGES UP AND DOWN THE KOREAN peninsula, millions sensed a gate was opening to a bright future. Liberated from Japanese rule, they danced in the streets of Seoul.

"I thought, I can have a real Korean education," Koo-hun said of the time when Japanese teachers had to pack up and leave for their homeland. "And I could have pride. I could learn that Korean people could actually be better than Japanese people." Ordinary Korean families were filled with expectation and hope in those early days. But within months the future of their reborn country suddenly looked less promising, and less their own to decide, than it did on Liberation Day.

Korea's fate, they learned, had been determined by men half a world away in a sterile Washington office. Officers on the Army General Staff in Washington, pressed by deadlines, meeting past midnight on the morning of August 11, 1945, had arbitrarily chosen the latitude of 38 degrees north, a parallel running north of Seoul, to separate U.S. and Soviet zones for the purpose of demobilizing the Japanese. The line, accepted by the Soviets, had no intrinsic sense. It sundered the dependent halves of the Korean economy, the more industrial north, with its 10 million people, from the more agricultural south, population 20 million. The line's only advantage was that it was easy to find on the crude map the major and colonel had available in that distant Washington office.

The 38th Parallel, meant as a line of convenience for two armies' temporary operations, immediately took on characteristics of a political boundary, infuriating the divided people. Just two weeks after his troops landed in Korea on September 8, the U.S. commander, Lt. Gen. John R. Hodge, sent a message to General MacArthur in Tokyo: "Dissatisfaction with the division of the country grows."

Hodge had received no detailed guidelines from Washington for the operation, and his relations with his hosts got off to a bad start. Even before reaching Korea, he had instructed his officers to view the Koreans as an enemy. When his 78,000 troops began landing, he ordered Japanese police to keep local welcoming crowds away. The police shot and killed two Koreans in the process.

Hodge, a combat commander with no preparation for this job, alienated Koreans further by taking his time removing the Japanese colonial governor-general. A temporary assembly of prominent Koreans, mostly moderates to leftists, had declared a republic two days before the Americans arrived, but Hodge would not recognize it. He soon banned such activity, and in November 1945 shut down a Seoul newspaper sympathetic to the republic.

Officers of a new U.S. Army Military Government in Korea took over the administrative functions in Seoul. The Koreans quickly saw they were not being liberated, but occupied, just like defeated Japan. In December 1945, the victorious Allies agreed in Moscow they would exercise a five-year "trusteeship" leading to a united, sovereign Korea. Word of this further delay in independence set off work stoppages and street demonstrations in Seoul.

The American officers had limited scope. Not very international-minded to begin with, knowing little about Korea, they relied on a relatively few Koreans who spoke English, often politically conservative men who had ties to Christian missions and who reinforced the Americans' inclination to the right. Koreans sneered at it as the "interpreters' government." In the streets, a song spread among children: "Don't believe Americans! Don't be cheated by Soviets! The Japanese will rise again!"

In February 1946, Hodge established a Representative Democratic Council of Koreans as an advisory group, and named as chairman a seventy-year-old right-wing Christian, Syngman Rhee, who had spent years as an exile in the United States campaigning for Korean independence. More liberal groups, all but excluded, refused to cooperate with the council, and it withered.

In the fall of 1946, the U.S. military authorized elections to an interim legislature for southern Korea, but the results were clearly fraudulent. Even General Hodge privately wrote that right-wing "strong-arm methods" had been used to control the vote. The winners were almost all rightists, including Rhee supporters, even though a survey by the American military government that summer had found that 70 percent of 8,453 southern Koreans polled said they supported socialism, 7 percent communism and only 14 percent capitalism. Generations of subservience to a Korean or Japanese elite had whetted the appetite for egalitarianism.

"They were not 'communist sympathizers.' They were simply against the pro-Japanese forces," Chung Koo-hun, the observant young student of the late 1940s, said of the villagers' attitude. "The Americans simply re-employed the pro-Japanese Koreans whom the people hated."

In the national police and other sensitive areas, the U.S. military often relied on Koreans who had collaborated with the colonial regime. Continuity seemed to come first for the Americans as they asserted control over a strange land 9,000 miles from home. Seventy of 115 top Korean officials in the Seoul administration in 1947 had held office during the Japanese occupation.

Hodge's soldiers began to feel a Yankee-go-home hostility. In some areas, they carried carbine rifles on the briefest errands, and they vented their dislike and incomprehension of the impoverished millions around them with the harsh "gook," the slur picked up a half-century earlier in the Philippines. Its use may have grown because of the similarity in sound to *han guk sa ram,* the Korean word for "Korean." Even high staff officers used the epithet freely, and in an official document Hodge referred to Koreans as "muddle-headed."

The Soviets, who shared a short border with Korea, had it easier in the north. Behind the Red Army came thousands of Koreans who had lived in exile or as economic migrants in the Soviet Far East, or had fought with China's revolutionaries. Many were communists. These returnees, along with political prisoners freed in Korea as Japanese rule collapsed, took over local "people's committees," originally established as "committees of law and order" by the temporary government Hodge had outlawed in the south. Peasants and industrial workers filled out committee ranks.

The Soviets never established a full-fledged military government in the north, moving quickly to local control. Political parties sprang up, but the Korean communists, well organized and highly motivated, maneuvered all into a united New People's Party in early 1946. Suppression of the opposition press then followed, and Kim Il Sung, a leader of anti-Japanese guerrillas in neighboring Manchuria, took charge of a central Provisional People's Committee in the north's largest city, Pyongyang, the old Koryo dynasty capital.

The transition in the north was tumultuous. The new regime not only seized Japanese-held farmland for redistribution, but also evicted Korean landlords from any but small plots they cultivated themselves. Many wealthier northerners, especially those with Japanese connections, had fled south at the first approach of the Soviet army. Now still more landlords joined the exodus, along with thousands of other northerners driven south by food shortages.

Such political thresholds were crossed in 1946—both north and south—because the Americans and Soviets failed to work out a formula for establishing a united, independent Korea. Their own concerns, back in Washington and Moscow, outweighed the commitment made to the Korean people under the Moscow accord. The Russians, as they had since the nineteenth century, sought a Korea on their border that was friendly, or at least neutral, and not a launchpad for anti-Soviet activities. The Americans, whose global confidence had been bolstered by the atomic bomb, began to view Korea, a land that had meant almost nothing to them, in a new light, as an "ideological battle ground upon which our entire success in Asia may depend," as adviser Edwin Pauley put it to President Harry S. Truman in mid-1946.

At joint meetings in early 1946, the two powers were to set up negotiations for a unified Korean state. But the Americans tried to freeze southern leftists out of the process, and the Soviets wanted to exclude Rhee's far right, because it opposed trusteeship and Moscow's role. The talks collapsed and Korea's division solidified. Pauley, a California oilman and Democratic fund-raiser who had toured the peninsula, told Truman that in Korea communism "could get off to a better start than practically anywhere."

By whatever name, something was starting in the southern Korean countryside. The leftist National Farmers' Committee, favoring land redistribution, worked hard to reach into even the smallest villages. When the southern Korean police began arresting young village men indiscriminately for real or imagined interest in the farmers' group, its membership rose sharply, as peasants reacted against the heavy-handed, Japanese-style tactics.

The U.S. military government had pleased the farmers by decreeing a limit on the "rice rent" of 30 percent of the crop. That was on paper. In reality, enforcement was lax, landlords still gouged tenant farmers and the military government did actual harm with a related ordinance lifting price controls and imposing a "free market" on rice. That set off a binge of speculation, corruption and smuggling of Korean rice abroad, which left subsistence rice farmers and other poor southerners with little to eat. They exploded with resentment.

In the southern city of Taegu, people verged on starvation. When 10,000 demonstrators rallied on October 1, 1946, police opened fire, killing many. Vengeful crowds then seized and killed policemen, and the U.S. military declared martial law. The violence spread across the provinces, peasants murdering government officials, landlords, and especially police, detested as holdovers from Japanese days. American troops joined the police in suppressing the uprisings. Together they killed uncounted hundreds of Koreans.

The division at the 38th Parallel sharpened along with resentments in the countryside. In August 1948, with U.S. approval, South Korea declared itself a separate republic. The north followed suit. Each claimed jurisdiction over the whole peninsula. Soviet troops withdrew from the peninsula by late 1948, and American units a few months later. The military leaderships of both great powers feared becoming ensnared in the Korean web.

American anthropologist Cornelius Osgood, spending much of 1947 in a village west of Seoul, watched as police carried young men off to jail by the truckload. A "mantle of fear" had fallen over once-peaceful valleys, he wrote. The word "communist," he said, "seemed to mean just 'any young man of a village.' " On August 7, 1947, the U.S. military government outlawed the southern communists, the Korean Workers' Party. Denied a peaceful political route, more and more leftist militants chose an armed struggle for power.

Police officers lived in fear, too. Chung Eun-yong, now a police lieutenant, was ordered from the relative quiet of Taejon in the fall of 1948 to the southern island of Cheju, where serious trouble had broken out. He worried about himself and about his family: Sun-yong had borne him two children, the first a boy, whom they named Koo-pil, and just recently a baby girl, Koo-hee. The young mother worried, too, lonely in their roomy Taejon home, a "tatami house" left by the Japanese. Persuaded by a local Presbyterian deacon, she tried religion, every Sunday carrying two-year-old Koo-pil and the newborn to church to pray for Eun-yong's safety.

Her husband landed on lush Cheju on October 1, 1948, at the head of a police squadron. Within a week, two of his men lay dead, killed by leftist guerrillas who attacked his station at night. Rhee, now president of South Korea, had ordered his embryonic army to crush the island revolt. Villagers were driven from their homes with a few pitiful belongings, and soldiers then set the thatched roofs ablaze. Thousands of islanders were killed in the campaign.

One South Korean army regiment mutinied in protest of the tactics, briefly seizing the southern city of Yeosoo, and another rebelled in Taegu. The rebels were suppressed by forces loyal to Rhee, advised by U.S. officers, but some managed to flee into the mountains to become guerrillas.

All across the south, insurgent bands were recruiting young men, often transient farm workers and others of the lowest social classes. As in thousands of other villages, the great majority of people in Chu Gok Ri were not political. Villagers later recalled, however, that one well-to-do family had been closely allied with the Japanese colonial regime and then with Rhee's police, and that on the other side three young villagers left to take up arms with the guerrillas. One of the three was eventually shot to death by police, another was arrested and a third disappeared. Two other Chu Gok Ri youths— Sohn Seok-tae and Chung Chan-young—were called in to the Yongdong police station and accused of collaboration: They had given food to a friend who was a guerrilla. They were freed, but were forced to join a political "rehabilitation" group, and for them, as for countless unsuspecting Koreans in those fearful days, the repercussions would never end.

Word in Seoul was that wealthy citizens had put a high price on the heads of leading left-wingers in South Korea, and one by one they were, indeed, assassinated. In Yongdong, meanwhile, police entered the Salvation Army hospital, interrogated patients suspected of being insurgents, and then took them outside and shot them, the hospital's director later reported.

WHEN THE INSURGENCY WAS MOST INTENSE, IN 1949, GUERRILLAS came down from the Yongdong County hills to sabotage the main rail line and attack and set fire to police stations. The terror also reached beyond the guardian rock of Sonang and far into the narrow valley of Chu Gok Ri and Im Ke Ri.

The farmers worked hard in the summer, from before sunrise to past sunset, weeding their rice paddies and cutting wild grasses from the hillsides to combine with ox and pig manure into a fertilizer compost for next spring's rice planting. That summer, villagers saw columns of soldiers scaling remote 3,000-foot heights where thick forest still stood, in search of rebels. The police evacuated and set fire to the dozen huts in Ahn Jom, the last hamlet up the valley, to deny its provisions to guerrillas. Some of the Ahn Jom refugees crowded into rooms in Im Ke Ri and Chu Gok Ri.

In August 1949, an old villager named Kim, cutting weeds for mulch above Im Ke Ri, heard young men scrambling up the slope. They ran sweating, panting past him, like game under pursuit. Soon policemen followed. He told them he didn't know where their quarry had gone. "This old bastard is a Commie, too!" one officer shouted, sticking his rifle in the villager's chest and pretending to pull the trigger. The others stayed his hand, but the old man was so shocked that he fell ill when he returned home and died several days later.

Old Kim had been away from his valley for sixteen years, working in a coal mine in Japan, and returned to Korea only after the war—one of almost one million Koreans who managed to come home from Japan, and a million others who returned from Manchuria, China and elsewhere. They were refugees in their own homes, many finding no work, adding to the millions of unemployed in southern Korea. Extra mouths to feed, American policy dislocations, guerrilla disruption, the loss of economic ties with the north— many factors pressed the people of Chu Gok Ri and the rest of South Korea deeper into desperation. If they had barley to eat, they were lucky.

But even in their daily struggle, the villagers never let go of dreams, especially the young. At the Yongdong middle school, Chung Koo-hun, now dignified and handsome at sixteen, finally was getting the real education he had hoped for. "I read *Romeo and Juliet*," he recalled, "and it was an entirely different world."

Shakespeare's long-ago world of impossible young love lay far from Chu Gok Ri. But in those days the teenaged Koo-hun did find himself caught helplessly in something that couldn't be. She was a village girl named Ke-soon. They crossed paths often in the dusty lanes of Chu Gok Ri, he running errands, she fetching water or laughing with girlfriends. They didn't talk to each other, the sexes didn't mix, but their eyes would meet and "speak" for an instant, and then he'd recover his senses. Falling in love was a foolish notion in young Koo-hun's Korea, and marrying someone from one's home village was worse than that. It was taboo.

At the right time, his family would settle on a suitable woman for him, from somewhere up the road. Until then, the young Shakespeare reader would have to forget this lovely girl. He tried to get Ke-soon out of his mind, only to find in the end that he was never far from hers.

MORE AND MORE NOW, THE OUTSIDE WORLD INTRUDED ON THE people of Chu Gok Ri. Eun-yong, demoralized by his Cheju Island experience, disgusted with police corruption and fearing for his family, decided in mid-1949 to resign from the police. Relatives who had expected him to grow rich on the usual police graft had been surprised to find Eun-yong in Taejon with holes in his shoes and his family eating barley. At a cousin's urging, he enrolled in a college in Seoul, hoping to become a lawyer or a professor. The cousin held out an even more impossible dream for him: to emigrate to America someday.

The police force that Eun-yong left behind was growing ever more violent. Summary executions of "communists" were routine. Bodies were dumped on doorsteps as warnings to others. By the spring of 1950, the dictatorial Rhee regime held an estimated 100,000 political prisoners in jam-packed jails, warehouses, any space that could be found. Tens of thousands of South Koreans, perhaps up to 100,000, were killed in the guerrilla war and repression of the late 1940s, according to later estimates.

The brutality was part of life in southern villages, an extension of the Japanese days. Chu Gok Ri villagers said the police, enforcing tax collections, hunting for anti-Rhee troublemakers, would gather people on the banks of the village stream, flog a few to intimidate all and slap even village elders in the face when their answers were unsatisfactory. "It was a lawless world where the police were the law," said Chung Koo-hong, a son of the 1919 village patriot Chung Hee-yong.

Back in Washington, some U.S. officials expressed misgivings about the ruthless, undemocratic partner they had put in power in Korea, but they were largely ignored in the growing anticommunist fervor in America, especially now that the Soviet Union had exploded its first atom bomb and the communists had triumphed in China's civil war. South Koreans were increasingly viewed as potential front-line shock troops in a global crusade. The U.S. government poured money and American military advisers into strengthening Rhee's 100,000-man army, which was led by men who fought for the Japanese, and in training his police force. The Soviets did the same for the North Koreans.

The Americans kept heavy offensive weapons out of Rhee's hands, since he had told them plainly he wanted to invade and reunite the north with his south. In bloody border skirmishes often provoked by the southern army, the two Koreas had clashed repeatedly along the 38th Parallel in mid-1949. As late as June 19, 1950, Rhee was asking Truman envoy John Foster Dulles for U.S. support for a cross-border invasion. For his part, the north's Kim Il Sung had taken a hostile, if at times vague, public line toward the "Rhee clique," declaring it would be destroyed. The northerners' early hope was that southern guerrillas would do the job.

For despairing southerners, some signs of hope appeared by the spring of 1950. The Americans had finally pushed through a plan for land redistribution, and election results that May promised to undercut Rhee's power. But it was too late.

A Korean proverb has it that "shrimp get broken backs in a whale fight." The anthropologist Osgood, in the timeless villages of a fading Korea, foresaw the catastrophe whose seeds the foreigners had sown. "For better or worse," he wrote, "the Koreans as a whole would have preferred to determine the course of events by themselves."

On Sunday, June 25, 1950, Sun-yong and the children had come up from the south to visit her husband, the law student, in Seoul. The young mother was dressing four-year-old Koo-pil and two-year-old Koo-hee to take them to church. Suddenly a commotion arose outside, shouting in the streets, a siren. Eun-yong and his neighbors gathered around a radio. "North Korean communists began invading across the 38th Parallel at four A.M. today," a nervous announcer read. For the first time in a millennium, Korean armies would fight each other in civil war. Somewhere north of Seoul, the backs of the shrimp were already breaking.

3

Hundreds of combat boots, buckled suede, scraped and shuffled up the hatchways of the USNS *Shanks*. Two-pound steel helmets and sheathed bayonets, fold-away shovels and M-1 rifles brushed and butted the bulkheads. On the troopship's decks, the 2nd Battalion of the 7th Cavalry Regiment was falling in. Heads were counted and then the combat-loaded Americans gazed out upon the Asian continent, at a dismal fishing port, at empty beaches trailing away into the haze, at green mountains marching inland through the clouds as far as their eyes could see, toward valleys, rice paddies, mud-walled villages, unseen places from which many of them would never return.

The summer sun, filtering through the overcast, still hung above the ridges when the *Shanks* anchored at 5:35 P.M. In drab olive fatigues damp with sweat, they stood by, awaiting orders, checking each other's gear, nervously joking, drifting in thought. For the coal miner's boy Ralph Bernotas, Korea's "heavy hills" looked like the rumpled slopes of Pennsylvania. For Pfc. James Hodges, the heat in Pohang Harbor was a Florida swelter. For his platoon mate Buddy Wenzel, collector of states, here was a whole country for his list—something new and, he told himself, only for a couple of weeks.

Away to the north, faint, distant, a war could be heard. Lt. Bill Kaluf, who had finally found a medical officer to clear his ears, picked up the occasional thudding boom from the direction of Yongdok, 25 miles up the coast, where U.S. Navy warships were firing their guns in support of South Korean troops struggling to hold the town. Aboard the *Shanks* nerves relaxed a bit as the Garryowens realized they would be landing unopposed, far behind the lines.

They still had to negotiate their first tricky descent into landing craft, on rope ladders swinging above 40-foot-deep waters. Packs went down first, followed by infantrymen. George Company's Sgt. John Ramirez watched the show. "Guys were hanging on for dear life. Up on deck the guys are laughing, and down below the guys are laughing. But not the guys in the middle."

The first of the 36-foot Higgins boats, loaded with dozens of men, was away at 7:23 P.M. The boats circled and then headed in, lined up abreast. The D-Day-style run to shore ratcheted up the tension again, but it eased at the sight of a familiar bespectacled face at the dock. Sgt. Snuffy Gray had landed at dawn that day, sent ahead with his regimental reconnaissance platoon.

After the stormy five-day crossing from Japan, the Garryowens had their boots on solid ground at last. Their new regimental commander, the ex-Pentagon comptroller Colonel Nist, soon drove off to get marching orders from 1st Cavalry Division commanders. Back aboard the *Shanks,* the Navy's watch officer noted in the log, "All's well."

BEYOND THOSE FAR MOUNTAINS, AMERICAN TROOPS WHO WENT into Korea before the 7th Cavalry were in desperate fights for their lives. A hundred miles to the northwest that day, a company of the 35th Infantry Regiment, almost surrounded by attacking North Koreans, had their backs against a swollen stream, and frantic young Americans were drowning in their panic to get across. Southwest of there on this Saturday evening, North Korean tanks rolled up against freshly dug-in troops of the 8th Cavalry, the Garryowens' sister regiment. It was the 1st Cavalry Division's baptism of fire in Korea, on the outskirts of the old crossroads town Yongdong.

The newly arrived 7th Cavalry still had hours of peace at Pohang, but it would be an uneasy, even bloody peace. The regiment's 2nd Battalion rode by truck to its overnight bivouac site in a field five miles southwest of town. On the way, these teenagers from the U.S. heartland were repelled and mystified by what they saw and smelled, especially the heavy use of human excrement, mixed with ash, to fertilize some fields. A junior officer, writing the regiment's official diary, noted that the men were amazed to see "half-naked" Korean women in the countryside, that they were sure "venereal diseases were as common as the common cold" in such a dirt-poor land and that "Japan was clean in comparison to this so-called Korea." In the steamy summer night, Korea seemed a strange, primitive place to these foreign troops, its odors overwhelming, its water infected, its mosquitoes maddening, its people silent, almost sullen, hardly welcoming. The Americans' spirits flagged, their nerves sharpened.

As the 2nd Battalion's five companies—E, F, G, H and Headquarters Company—haphazardly staked out bivouac spots, Lieutenant Kaluf realized his company commander, Captain Chandler, had not established a defensive position, with perimeter and password. "We just flopped down. It was a totally disorganized thing," Kaluf said. Over in his area, Snuffy Gray's men did have a password, "Texas," but they also had jittery trigger fingers. When Gray approached the perimeter that night after a short trip nearby, someone demanded the password, he gave it, and the response was an immediate flurry of M-1 fire. The platoon sergeant wasn't hit.

Up in the 1st Battalion area, the aim was deadlier. That battalion had moved immediately into defensive positions north of Pohang, backing up the South Korean troops fighting farther north for Yongdok. Out of the starless night, South Korean soldiers and refugees, pulling back, approached the battalion's lines. The confused Americans opened fire. One Korean soldier and one civilian were killed in the small-arms barrage, the first casualties inflicted by the 7th Cavalry in Korea.

That first bleak, chaotic night on the Korean coast was a portent. "They did not have the training," an aged Colonel Heyer, 2nd Battalion commander, later remembered. "They were just shipped in there without the training."

They were shipped without the equipment, too. Before departing Japan, the regiment wrote into the record that it was short on bazookas, mortar rounds, antitank mines, even binoculars, and the hand-me-downs from World War II were in bad shape, from machine guns to trucks. Obsolete radios would fail in combat. Some artillery pieces were inaccurate. Even the food was old, combat rations from the last war. Snuffy Gray felt obliged to steal five machine guns from the Army's Tokyo depot just before shipping out. At least this enterprising sergeant's men were battle-ready—except that his platoon, a reconnaissance unit, was issued no Korea maps.

The Garryowens, on their first night in Korea, were "curious and dubious as to what lay before them," the regimental diarist noted with bland understatement. Rushed across the Korea Strait after a few days of hurried decision making in Washington and Tokyo, they were told only that they would halt communist aggression with little problem. But what lay before these untested, thinly trained GIs was a long, cruel war unlike any that Americans had ever fought, under a supreme commander, MacArthur, who knew they were unready. They were "tailored for occupation duty, not combat," General MacArthur had confidentially told the visiting Army Chief of Staff, Gen. J. Lawton Collins, just four days before the 7th Cavalry Regiment shipped out.

There was one more sign the 1st Cavalry Division didn't know what to expect. It landed in Korea without fingerprint kits, personal-effects bags and mattress covers, the gear of a graves registration unit. It was unequipped to handle its own dead.

GENERAL MACARTHUR HIMSELF WAS CAUGHT OFF GUARD BY THE WAR that awakened him, with a telephone call, before dawn on June 25.

The muffled bell had rung insistently in his bedroom at the U.S. Embassy residence until the seventy-year-old general picked up. After a respectful apology for the early hour, a duty officer at the other end informed MacArthur that North Korean troops had struck across the 38th Parallel at 4 A.M. MacArthur later recounted his shock: "It couldn't be, I told myself. Not again!"—not another bolt from the blue, not another Philippines 1941.

Most of Tokyo's Little America slept late as usual that Sunday morning. The dance band had gone on past midnight at the General Headquarters Officers' Club. The day promised to hit a torrid 90 degrees, the hottest of the year. Many would head for the beaches. Early risers could check their newspaper for the latest on Jackie Robinson's bid to bat .400 for the Brooklyn Dodgers, or how Judy Garland was recovering from Wednesday's suicide attempt, or they could peruse the ads for newly arrived 1950 model cars, or scan the offerings at Tokyo's American movie houses. A GI and his girl could catch *Easter Parade,* with none other than Judy Garland.

Buddy Wenzel was looking for Sunday diversions at the USO downtown when a friend showed up with a *Stars and Stripes.* The military newspaper had rushed out an "extra" edition, and GIs gathered around to read it. KOREA AT WAR, declared the huge headline. Up at the Grant Heights housing complex, the McKowns were returning from the PX when a neighbor sergeant dashed out to give them the news. Bill and Lois, the young marrieds, had a lot on their minds—a fourteen-month-old boy and an infant girl. "Korea? I'd heard of it," McKown remembered. "It didn't excite me much."

The 7th Cavalry was soon sending Jeep patrols into Tokyo's back streets to roust men from their Japanese girlfriends' hooches. The brass were rounded up, too, though more discreetly. At a Sunday garden party at one American villa, word spread in brief, low conversations among General Headquarters staff officers, and one by one they slipped away to waiting cars that sped them to the Dai-Ichi building headquarters. There General MacArthur, like Sergeant McKown, didn't seem to know what to think.

The invasion caught the United States "flat-footed," an Army historian later wrote. "The nation had few forces immediately available and no plans for fighting in Korea." Just a year before, the Joint Chiefs declared Korea beyond U.S. strategic interests and withdrew the last U.S. occupation troops. Just five months before, Secretary of State Dean Acheson, in a major speech, excluded South Korea from the U.S. "defense perimeter" in Asia.

At first, MacArthur and his staff saw just another border incident. When its scale became clear as Sunday wore on, they fell back on the faith military advisers placed in the South Korean army. Earlier that week, the chief U.S. Army adviser in Seoul had assured Washington that "the South Korean forces could handle any possible invasion by North Korean forces." MacArthur, misled, took a relatively upbeat view of events across the Korea Strait well into Monday.

A high-level Tokyo visitor did not. The influential John Foster Dulles, a Republican internationalist and stern anticommunist, had been dispatched to Japan as a special envoy of the Democratic Truman administration to negotiate a U.S.-Japan peace treaty. Sensing MacArthur's inertia, Dulles cabled Secretary of State Dean Acheson: "Believe that if it appears the South Koreans cannot contain or repulse the attack, United States forces should be used even though this risks Russian countermoves."

Back in Washington, it had been a tense spring. That was evident in the headlines of Tokyo's *Nippon Times* in late June: revelations about Soviet atomic bomb spy rings, news of dozens of suspected U.S. communists being cited for contempt by the House Un-American Activities Committee. "There are now two worlds: the free world and the captive world," Dulles himself declared in a June 22 speech in Tokyo. Just five years after their joint triumph in World War II, American leaders were branding their Soviet counterparts a global menace. The tension even crept into popular culture: In the *Stars and Stripes* of that Sunday, June 25, comic-strip hero Steve Canyon had a nasty encounter with a Soviet submarine.

Above all, it was the "loss" of China in October 1949 that put Washington politics on a knife edge. The communist-hunting Republican Sen. Joseph McCarthy accused "subversives" in Acheson's State Department of abetting Mao Tse-tung's communists in their civil war victory. He assailed Acheson himself for defending alleged spy Alger Hiss, an ex-colleague. He labeled the Truman administration a virtual "bedfellow of international communism." With it all, but with little substantiation, McCarthy and others like him won headlines.

By the time Truman flew back to Washington from Independence, Missouri, that Sunday afternoon for an emergency meeting on Korea, he and his officials had been hammered for months for supposedly "coddling" communism. Acheson's staff had produced, overnight, a study paper weighted toward intervening in Korea. Thirteen senior U.S. officials convened over a fried chicken dinner at Blair House, the president's home during White House remodeling. Korea "offered as good an occasion for drawing the line as anywhere else," said Gen. Omar N. Bradley, chairman of the Joint Chiefs of Staff. Acheson strongly favored U.S. action, and Truman eagerly agreed. "If we let Korea down," the minutes showed the president saying, "the Soviet Union will keep right on going and swallow up one piece of Asia after another. . . . The Near East would collapse and no telling what would happen in Europe."

None of the top Pentagon and State Department officials dissented. One, Dean Rusk, described Korea as a dagger pointed at Japan. Now Far Eastern chief at the State Department, Rusk had been one of the two Pentagon officers who drew a line on a Washington map one midnight in 1945 and split the Korean people in two.

The Blair House group ordered MacArthur to expedite weapons shipments to the South Korean defenders and deploy air and naval forces to try to save Seoul. When the group met again the next day, there was serious talk of using American ground troops in Korea. Bradley now hesitated, but the momentum had taken hold. For a start, the group announced on June 27 a widening of U.S. air support for the South Koreans. At United Nations headquarters in New

York that day, the U.S.-dominated Security Council adopted a resolution urging members to "furnish such assistance . . . as may be necessary" to repel the northern attack.

Acheson's study paper, minimizing the Koreans' urge to reunite, said the North Korean invasion must be "a Soviet move," though one unique in the postwar period. The Kremlin must consider Korea "more important than we have assumed." The Soviets had never shown any intent to reunite Korea by force, however, and scholars later found that Kremlin leader Joseph Stalin, not wanting to confront the United States, only reluctantly acquiesced to Kim Il Sung's invasion plans after months of opposition. It is believed Stalin eventually sent pilots to help the North Koreans, but he never sent Soviet troops.

Washington's first announcements were kept low-key, with no hint that America was on the road to war. On Tuesday, June 27, the Army told reporters, "At the beginning, it is not contemplated that ground troops or Marines will be used." But MacArthur was receiving dire reports in Tokyo. The ROKs—the Republic of Korea army—were collapsing before the invaders. Seoul fell to the North Koreans on Wednesday, June 28, just three days after they invaded. The next day, MacArthur flew across the strait to get a look for himself. On June 30, back in Tokyo after eight hours on the ground south of Seoul, the supreme commander advised the Joint Chiefs in Washington that U.S. ground forces would be needed to drive the North Koreans back.

It was the middle of the night in Washington when the message arrived, but Gen. Joe Collins, the relatively new Army chief, rushed to the Pentagon to deal with it. He discussed it live with MacArthur by teletype and accepted the Far East commander's judgment. The early-rising president, ready for work by 5 A.M. at Blair House, immediately accepted it, too.

Without consulting the full Joint Chiefs, without submitting a war resolution to Congress, Truman was sending American soldiers to fight the North Koreans. But the press statement on June 30 played down what it called MacArthur's authorization "to use certain supporting ground units," and Truman seized on a reporter's suggested term for the U.S. operation in Korea. Yes, the president said, it was a "police action."

IN TOKYO, AMID THE ALERTS AND RUMORS OF LATE JUNE, AS TRU-man and Acheson discussed committing U.S. ground forces to Korea, the 7th Cavalry's commanders noted ruefully in their official diary that "training to date had not consisted of any battalion or regimental phase and only a limited amount of company phase"; that is, the units had never practiced battle maneuvers together. The 1st Cavalry Division artillery command acknowledged in its record that some gun crew members had never operated their weapons with live ammunition.

Once the word came from Washington, however, a gung-ho spirit, baseless as it was, took hold. MacArthur's intelligence chief, Gen. Willoughby, tartly told the 1st Cavalry Division commander, Maj. Gen. Hobart R. Gay, that if he didn't hurry his preparations, all he'd see when he got to Korea was "the tail end" of the 24th Infantry Division driving the enemy back north.

Right up to embarkation at Yokohama, the 7th Cavalry was organizing, down to the platoon level, with new sergeants drafted from other units, with men thrown together who had never shared a barracks or a beer before. In a final act, the men stuffed clothes and papers, letters and snapshots of girlfriends and buddies into secured footlockers—Snuffy Gray's purloined samurai swords went into one—to await their quick return. Whether because of theft or Army bungling, they never saw the footlockers again.

Writing home to his sister Juanita, G Company's James Hodges confessed he was worried, "although I try to convince Mother I'm not." Then the Florida runaway added, "I went over and increased my insurance to $10,000 dollars the 1st of July. If I do get bumped off the family will be sitting purty."

A few bunks away at McKnight Barracks, Hodges's friend Buddy Wenzel wanted to believe it would be quick and easy. "This was going to be a 'police action,' right?" Wenzel later said. "We were going to go over there and straighten things out and come back. So they told us."

But what these teenaged jitterbuggers, black marketers and spit-polished sentries were going to was a full-scale war, the first in U.S. history entered upon without the constitutionally mandated authority of Congress. More than that, it was the war that would institutionalize the Cold War for America, leading to four decades of huge military budgets, to perilous showdowns with the Soviet Union and to an even longer, costlier war for Americans, a generation after, in another corner of Asia. The rapid-fire decisions of late June overrode carefully debated U.S. positions taken on Korea in the previous year, and ignored a long-held U.S. military precept against fighting Asians on the Asian mainland. The decisions also seemed heedless of the deep unpopularity of the Rhee regime being defended in South Korea.

A "military superiority complex" was at work, a leading historian of the war, Clay Blair, later concluded. The glory of global victory in World War II, the seemingly boundless economic capacity of postwar America, the ultimate power of the nuclear bomb all combined to make any perceived challenge look surmountable.

"To back away from this challenge, in view of our capacity for meeting it, would be highly destructive of the power and prestige of the United States," Secretary of State Acheson, patrician son of a bishop, later wrote of the hasty days of decision in 1950.

As the *Shanks* crashed through the Pacific's waves with its cargo of seasick 7th Cavalrymen, President Truman was on the radio telling the American people that nothing less than U.S. national security was at stake on that poor, mountainous peninsula.

MacArthur, who wholeheartedly embraced the intervention, nonetheless wrote later, "I could not help being amazed at the manner in which this great decision was being made."

LIKE THE OLD WARRIOR MACARTHUR, THE YOUNG SOLDIER HARRY G. Summers Jr. was astonished to wake up to war. A corporal with the 24th Infantry Division, later a noted military writer, Summers knew his unit was a "hollow" force. "We were as surprised as Stalin and Kim Il Sung at Truman's orders to go into action in Korea," Summers wrote.

The 24th, in western Japan, was the closest U.S. division to Korea and got the first call. Two infantry companies and an artillery battery—promptly tagged "Task Force Smith" for their commanding colonel—were airlifted to Korea and piled into a train and then trucks for a wearying ride north to the war. Fresh from Japan's easy life, they bumped up the peninsula's central roadway, between endless white-clad columns of refugees and fleeing South Korean troops, detrucked 25 miles south of Seoul, and dug in on a ridge astride the main road, in a constant rain, to await the North Korean army. They numbered just 540 men.

The "military superiority complex" reigned in the 24th Infantry Division. "I remember distinctly MacArthur's headquarters telling us as we left Japan that as soon as the North Koreans saw us they would run," said Earl C. Downey, a young division officer at the time. From the start, however, the running, often a desperate headlong flight, was by Americans.

The Americans lacked not just numbers and equipment, but also intelligence about the enemy. Lt. Col. Charles Smith and his overconfident task force got that information on the job. From atop the scrubby ridge, at about 7 A.M. on July 5, Smith spotted eight North Korean tanks, Soviet-made T-34s, clanking down the road from the north. His artillery took them under fire, but the high-explosive rounds did nothing; his howitzers had almost no armor-piercing shells. When the tanks rumbled up abreast of them, the Americans fired their 2.36-inch bazookas, but the small rockets bounced off uselessly. Throughout, the North Korean tankers were firing their own 85mm cannon and machine guns, blowing the stunned, outgunned infantrymen out of their way, inflicting the war's first American casualties.

About thirty tanks poured through the gap and were followed by a massive attack by North Korean infantry, a six-mile-long column of advancing troops in mustard-colored uniforms who fanned out across the landscape before Smith's bloodied companies. The colonel ordered a pullback; it turned into a rout, as men dropped rifles, helmets and cartridge belts, abandoned the howitzers and fled cross-country through the muck of rice paddies and over hills.

This first contact slowed the North Koreans for a few hours, while other 24th Division units assembled miles to the rear. But in the end the loss of 153 of Smith's men dead or missing meant little, because in the coming days the rest of the division would also reel and break before enemy tanks. Soldiers gave it a name: "bugging out."

American arrogance toward the new enemy persisted, tinged with racism. One battalion commander referred to the North Koreans as "trained monkeys," the Army historian later reported. The *New York Times* military editor called them "an army of barbarians," the "most primitive of peoples." General MacArthur's intelligence chief, Maj. Gen. Charles Willoughby, labeled them "half-men with blank faces."

The men of the 24th Division quickly learned, however, that they had been misled: The northern troops, the Korean People's Army, were a formidable force, superbly trained and led, powerfully equipped. They had seven combat-ready infantry divisions and three newly activated ones, and an armored brigade with 150 T-34s, the Soviet main battle tank of World War II. They numbered 135,000 troops, including thousands who fought for the communists in China's civil war.

Against them stood a Republic of Korea army that counted 98,000 men on June 25 but was devastated by the surprise onslaught. It was now trying to regroup with its U.S. ally standing alongside. Many ROK soldiers were willing to fight and die for South Korea, and some units were inflicting serious damage on the invaders, especially along the mountainous east coast. Many others lacked the motivation the northerners showed, however, and many ROK army officers were incompetent and corrupt. The sight of South Korean soldiers, weaponless and leaderless, pouring south with refugees outraged the first American GIs to arrive. Language problems worsened things. In one incident, a group of U.S. soldiers, seeing South Korean troops preparing to blow up a bridge the Americans wanted saved, simply seized the explosives and threw them into the river.

Top U.S. officers shunned their South Korean counterparts. For their part, the ROK army cadre had lost some admiration for the Americans since U.S. Army advisers pulled out from frontline Korean units right after the invasion, the Koreans' hour of greatest need.

American soldiers almost universally pinned the crude word "gook" on all Koreans, whether enemy or allied, soldier or civilian. The *New York Times*'s Walter Sullivan reported that the U.S. troops' contempt alienated the local population from the outset. The Americans did not understand that many South Koreans despised the government the U.S. Army was defending. In fact, as the northern army swept down the peninsula, most South Koreans stayed put in their homes. But the tens of thousands who fled before the communists became a tide against which U.S. troop movements sometimes had to struggle.

It was a pathetic tide, often soaked by the early summer rains, their white garb spattered with mud, exhausted families trudging south with bundles of clothes atop their heads, bags of food and bits of furniture piled onto back A-frames, in pushcarts, or, for the lucky ones, on oxcarts. Bent patriarchs in their tall black hats, anxious housewives in high-waisted skirts, girls with babies strapped to their backs, the old and weak being carried, the young barefoot and bewildered, all trying to escape the fighting. In the two weeks after the Americans arrived, an estimated 380,000 refugees passed through the U.S.–South Korean lines toward safety, a safety often marked by hunger, sickness and uncertainty.

THE GIS OF THE 24TH INFANTRY DIVISION ENDURED HARDSHIPS, too, even when not under enemy fire. After months or years of routine in Japan, most of the Americans were not in shape for scaling the Korean hillsides in the humidity and mounting heat of the long July days. The terrain did not deter the enemy. "One of the big problems right now is the ability of the North Korean doughboy to take to the hills when the roads are blocked and get around our men," U.S. diplomat Everett F. Drumright wrote the State Department from the war zone in late July.

The Americans' Jeeps stuck in the mud. The men tumbled into the stinking sludge of rice paddies. Their rations were sometimes short, and drinking water was scarce. Local water felled many with dysentery. They got little sleep, consuming coffee and cigarettes to stay alert and alive. Under artillery fire, they learned to dig deep. But they also learned that a "million-dollar wound" could get a GI back to Japan by tomorrow. Some began shooting themselves in the foot.

After Task Force Smith's rout, "bug-out" fever spread through the 24th Division. In the next confrontation with the advancing North Koreans, a battalion of the 34th Infantry Regiment was ordered immediately to withdraw, and the men panicked, discarding weapons, ponchos, even their wet boots in their scramble south. Young Americans also stood and fought, but often were undone by their equipment or by weak officers. In the 21st Infantry Regiment, four light tanks blew their own turrets off when they fired their defective guns at the attackers. Radios didn't work in the rain; old bazooka rounds were duds. Infantry units were saddled with officers without infantry background, or nerve. One retired colonel recalled how, as a fresh lieutenant, he had to take over his company because its captain simply "quit."

The cost was heavy. In the first week, as many as 3,000 Americans were left dead, wounded, missing or captured. The vacant-eyed survivors grew used to the smell of blood filling the aid stations, the sight of vultures spiraling over battle sites, the sound of whimpering from men whose spirits were broken.

A 34th Regiment medic, Lacy Barnett, tried to describe the mindset of the GIs of July 1950: "Here they were, ill-equipped, some even with rifles with tags saying 'combat-unserviceable.' There were many times when American units went without food for days. In a combat situation you're under a hell of a lot of stress anyway, and to have such things occur you become more bitter—at your own army and at the refugees streaming down the road. By the end of July there was a bitter feeling among everybody."

Anger at all Koreans deepened. On July 13, a brief Associated Press dispatch from the front said "confirmed reports" had it that "Korean communists" were donning civilian white to infiltrate U.S. lines. The GIs were shooting at people in white seen along nearby ridges. "Korean curiosity is great. It is likely that many of the white-clad persons are farmers or refugees just taking a look," the article said. It did not say whether reported infiltrators were North Korean soldiers or southern guerrillas, nor did it cite specific cases.

The Eighth Army intelligence staff interviewed 24th Division officers about the perceived threat. Its report said almost all refugees were searched coming through the lines and "none was found to be carrying arms or uniforms." In fact, North Korean troops were easily circling around the 24th Division's road-bound units, whose numbers were too thin to establish a long, solid front line. But combat officers nonetheless "strongly suspected" North Korean soldiers were entering refugee columns and somehow picking up weapons and uniforms behind U.S. lines. No evidence was cited, but this fear of all Koreans began to tighten its grip on the beleaguered Americans.

By July 13, the tattered 24th Division's remaining troops were positioned south of the Kum River, a "moat" in front of Taejon, girding for an all-out attack on that key city. Army engineers had blown the bridges over the Kum, but the North Koreans didn't need bridges. The river could be forded in spots. At night, watchful for enemy crossings, the American defenders filled the sky over the Kum with bursting flares. At one point, hundreds of refugees began crossing the Kum and the top officer at the scene, fearing infiltrators, asked division commander Maj. Gen. William F. Dean to order artillery fire on the white-clad throng. But the general refused, one of his operations officers, Col. Forrest K. Kleinman, later reported. The war wouldn't be won by killing civilians, Dean said.

GENERAL DEAN MIGHT NOT ATTACK "PEOPLE IN WHITE" ALONG THE Kum River, but the U.S. Air Force would throughout the warfront, where it controlled the skies totally after July 18, last day of any North Korean offensive air action.

Air support had been erratic, even dangerous, for the defenders in South Korea in early July. Hundreds of tons of bombs had been mistakenly dropped on ROK army troops by American and Australian warplanes, the Australians having been enlisted by Washington to fight in Korea under an allied "United Nations Command." On July 3, hundreds of South Korean soldiers and civilians were killed south of Seoul by confused or reckless pilots. But the killing was not all accidental. In late June, MacArthur's headquarters ordered indiscriminate bombing behind North Korean lines by the U.S. Air Force, including areas where South Korean civilians still lived. Then in July, the U.S. military went further, ordering the strafing of refugee columns moving down roads toward U.S. Army units.

This violated the laws and customs of war. The prohibition against targeting noncombatants—in this case, citizens of an allied nation—is so basic a principle that it is part of customary, noncodified international law, but it also was spelled out in U.S. military pamphlets, which cited the 1907 Hague Treaty's admonition that "hostilities are restricted to the armed forces of belligerents."

In mid-July, the Korea exploits of the Air Force's 35th Fighter-Bomber Squadron won it a splashy cover story in *Life* magazine. Its pilots' after-mission reports, however, declassified years later, showed that their new F-80 jets, flying in at 400 mph from Japan, were not simply attacking enemy tanks, trucks and army units. "Some people in white clothes were strafed three to four miles south of Yusong," read one report dated July 20, 1950. A spotter aircraft, or controller, "said to fire on people in white clothes." In reports from other missions, pilots betrayed unease over the targeting, noting that groups they were ordered to strafe "could have been refugees" and "appeared to be evacuees." The unease spread up the chain of command in the U.S. Fifth Air Force, which had established headquarters in Taegu, in Korea's far south. On July 25, the Fifth Air Force's operations chief sent a memo to its acting commander, Brig. Gen. Edward L. Timberlake, that got unambiguously to the point.

"Subject: Policy on Strafing Civilian Refugees," it was headed. "The Army has requested that we strafe all civilian refugee parties that are noted approaching our positions," Col. Turner C. Rogers wrote. "To date, we have complied with the Army request in this respect." The memo, classified secret, took note of reports that North Korean soldiers were infiltrating behind U.S. lines via refugee columns. But the strafings "may cause embarrassment to the U.S. Air Force and to the U.S. government," Rogers wrote. He wondered why the Army was not checking refugees "or shooting them as they come through if they desire such action." He recommended that Fifth Air Force planes stop attacking refugees.

Fighter pilots flying from the U.S. Navy carrier *Valley Forge,* off Korea's far southern coast, had similar instructions. In an Action Summary for July 25, later declassified, pilots reported strafing a group of "people dressed in white . . . in accordance with information received from the Army that groups of more than eight to ten people were to be considered troops, and were to be attacked."

On that same day, also the day Rogers wrote his memo, U.S. planes attacked a huge gathering of refugees miles behind American lines, witnesses reported decades later. Police had ordered thousands of civilians from the roads and nearby villages to collect on a broad field beside the Bongchon stream, near Kimchon, site of the 1st Cavalry Division's rear headquarters, because of rumors that North Koreans had infiltrated the area. At 11 A.M., U.S. planes strafed and bombed the white-clad throngs, inflicting unknown numbers of casualties, witnesses said. The Air Force record, declassified decades later, shows an attack that day in that area deep in the rear that "destroyed 13 vehicles, damaged 6 vehicles, inflicted 125 troop casualties." The 1st Cavalry Division record noted no such North Korean troop presence near its headquarters.

It is not known how General Timberlake reacted to Rogers's

memo, or whether this hidden Army–Air Force dispute over attacking refugees was kicked further upstairs, to General MacArthur, the coordinating commander. The strafing went on even though Eighth Army headquarters in Taegu had issued a communiqué on July 21 declaring, "Red infiltration has been reduced to manageable proportions and can in short order be expected to approach zero."

The North Koreans, meanwhile, had driven the 24th Division from Taejon, crossing the Kum River at night at points where the U.S. defenses left gaps of up to two miles. One American regiment, less than 2,000 men, was scattered along a 30-mile frontage. Once again, the invaders simply outflanked the small, weak U.S. force; the Americans retreated south in disarray. William Dean himself, the commanding general, was captured. In the end, the two weeks from Task Force Smith to the fall of Taejon proved to be one of the great debacles in the annals of the U.S. Army. Of the 16,000 men who landed in Korea with the 24th Division, barely half remained, straggling southward. Historians eventually concluded with Clay Blair that the hasty U.S. intervention "was one of the most ill-conceived decisions in the history of the American military establishment."

But an influential voice at the Pentagon, Lt. Gen. Matthew B. Ridgway, a stalwart of the war in Europe and now a top Army deputy, told the military service secretaries that a withdrawal "could discredit U.S. foreign policy and undermine confidence in American military capabilities." The U.S. Army would stay in Korea, even if Washington was still unable to put much of an army there. The Truman administration, believing the North Korean invasion a possible diversion from planned Soviet military action in Europe, feared transferring troop units needed for Europe's defense. In the first major reinforcement of the Far East Command, units of the 2nd Infantry Division set sail from Washington State, but were not expected to reach Korea until the end of July.

Commanders normally would ease green units into combat gradually, but now it fell largely to the untested Garryowens and the rest of the 1st Cavalry Division, barely 10,000 men just arriving on the peninsula, to try to stop the North Korean drive in the southern heartland. They would take their stand in the ridge-lined area around Yongdong, a battleground since ancient times.

LEAD ELEMENTS OF THE GARRYOWENS' SISTER REGIMENTS, THE 5TH and 8th Cavalry, came ashore first at Pohang on July 18. "Well-trained units of the U.S. 1st Cavalry Division fanned out today from their newly established beachhead," a United Press dispatch trumpeted to American newspaper readers. But the "Cav" was a division of raw teenagers led by too few sergeants in the ranks and by men past their prime at the top. Like the 7th Cavalry, the 5th and 8th Cavalry Regiments were commanded by colonels too inexperienced and too old for the job; one was almost deaf. The division chief, Hobart "Hap" Gay, a man who swung a swagger stick and toted a shotgun in the field—"as though he was going bird-hunting," a staff officer said—had never led soldiers in battle. Similarly in the other front-line U.S. division, the officer in charge, Maj. Gen. William B. Kean, had never held a combat command. His 25th Infantry Division had teamed up with ROK army divisions to man the right flank of a ragged "front line" reaching from the east coast westward to halfway across the 160-mile-wide peninsula.

Gay, fifty-six, may have been the most prominent example of a ranking officer awarded a prestigious sinecure in Japan, command of a storied combat division, largely because of seniority and loyal service, not necessarily because of proven ability.

A onetime horse cavalryman, the Illinois farmer's son had spent years dealing with requisitions and supplies as a post quartermaster. When World War II broke out, however, he was tapped by George S. Patton, a polo-playing friend, to be his chief of staff in that legendary general's drive across North Africa and Europe. It was a heady job, but Gay never held a combat command requiring instant life-or-death decisions. He even lost his rear-echelon job for a time because supreme commander Gen. Dwight D. Eisenhower had grown unimpressed with Patton's comrade-in-arms. In Korea, Gay labored under two other handicaps, one of which, the loss of an eye in a 1929 polo accident, he had long ago accommodated. But the other would be telling in his first days of war: He had no experience of Asia, other than his nine months of occupation duty in Japan.

His two advance regiments were deployed to the town of Yong-dong on July 22, 1950, as remnants of the 24th Division retreated through the area by foot or truck. Yongdong County, the Americans learned, was a place of treeless slopes and narrow valleys. Its crowded rice-farming villages were as poor as any in Korea. Through Yong-dong town, equidistant from Seoul and the big southern port of Pusan, ran South Korea's main north-south highway and railroad.

In one respect, Hap Gay's troops were lucky: The exhausted North Korean 3rd Division, having seized Taejon, needed two days to rest, resupply and tend to casualties before sending its mustard-colored columns against the Americans again. But the defense plan from Eighth Army disturbed Gay, because it split the 8th Cavalry's two battalions, one to block the main north-south highway from Taejon, the other on the road approaching from the southwest. Gay would have preferred to tie their flanks together in a solid front. The 5th Cavalry, immediately to the rear, backed up the 8th Cavalry by stak-ing out positions in the hills along the main north-south road where it heads east from Yongdong before turning south again. The 5th Cavalry troops set up near a pair of villages called Chu Gok Ri and Im Ke Ri.

What also disturbed Gay were the endless white lines of refugees filing down the main road with the haggard, dispirited 24th Division and Korean troops. Some South Korean civilians, especially land-lords, government officials and policemen, were fleeing the com-munists in fear, but others were simply seeking shelter from the rain of artillery shells and air attacks.

The suspicions about the "people in white," the nervousness over infiltrators, were passed on to the newly arrived division and grew into distrust of almost any Korean. General Gay told reporters soon after arriving that he saw no need to coordinate troop movements with South Korean army commanders. He ordered the Korean national police out of his division sector. The Korean military police complained they couldn't monitor refugees because Gay's men kept stripping Korean MPs of their weapons. The troops' disregard for the Koreans showed itself in many ways—from denial of supplies to ROK units, to the chilling but not unusual sight of U.S. vehicles repeatedly running over the crushed body of a civilian killed on a crowded roadway.

The 1st Cavalry Division got its first taste of combat late Saturday, July 22, when North Korean tanks rolled south toward the 8th Cavalry Regiment's 1st Battalion. Armed with new, more powerful 3.5-inch bazookas, the Americans destroyed three of the T-34s, previously all but invincible. The attackers backed off.

The next day, as civilians streamed past out of Yongdong, division headquarters advised the 5th Cavalry command post to screen refugees closely because "from indications forward, many were armed." A communications log and an operations journal for that date, July 23, include some terse and cryptic entries from the 8th Cavalry as that forward regiment was hit repeatedly by North Korean artillery, mortar and tank fire, as well as infantry attack. Air reconnaissance reported "approximately 400 white shirts advancing along draw," said one entry. Another said only, "two platoons posing as farmers." A third said enemy troops were "believed" to be filtering into the 1st Battalion area, and they were "both civilians and nk trps [North Korean troops]." Another noted, "driving Korean refugees back."

The division war diary did not clarify whether these feared threats from "people in white" proved real. In fact, the diary, a unit narrative compiled later from various sources, did not mention these particular episodes at all. The next day's entry did describe one "reported" incident in which, it was said, a refugee's apparent pregnancy was found to be a concealed radio, which was said to have been used to advise the enemy on American positions. That July 24 diary entry also said many refugees turned out to be North Korean soldiers transporting ammunition and weapons in wagons and packs. But neither it nor the front-line regiment's log cited specific cases. Writing later in the 1950s, official Army historian Roy E. Appleman did not repeat that unsupported statement, although he wrote that the refugee crowds "undoubtedly helped" the North Koreans infiltrate American positions at Yongdong.

Pentagon observers who reached the front on July 26 called the reports of infiltrators disguised as refugees "unconfirmed." This Army observer team from Washington stressed more conventional, less risky "infiltration" tactics by the North Koreans in its report. "The frontages were enormous and precluded a continuous line of defense. This facilitated outflanking and penetrating operations by the enemy," they wrote.

At this point, three weeks into the U.S. intervention in Korea, as the 1st Cavalry Division struggled to hold Yongdong, decisions were made that may have led some attentive newspaper readers back in the States to pause and reflect on where their army was headed in this sudden war in this distant place.

On July 23, all Korean civilians were ordered out of the war zone, "to be sent to points far behind American installations," the Associated Press reported in a dispatch datelined "An American Advance Post in Korea." The article then added matter-of-factly: "In an area once cleared of civilians, anyone in civilian clothing may be shot." It said infiltrators disguised as civilians had been harassing American troops. "All Koreans, North and South, look alike to the Americans. Soldiers sometimes pot shot at suspicious white clad figures." The brief report also said American troops were shelling and burning South Korean villages to deny cover to enemy troops. "How many people stayed too long in their thatched roofed cottages is not known."

What was unfolding in the 1st Cavalry Division sector appalled Harold Joyce Noble, third-ranking U.S. diplomat in South Korea. A Korea-born son of missionaries, Noble had been decorated for bravery as a Marine officer in World War II. In July 1950 he was monitoring warfront developments for the U.S. Embassy and coordinating with the South Korean government. In a 1952 memoir, *Embassy at War*, Noble noted that civilians had already been ordered to stay in their homes—and not clog the roads—unless their safety was directly threatened. Now General Gay had ordered that all must leave their villages, but many peasants simply would not abandon their land, Noble wrote. "Thousands of men, women, and children remained in the division area, and they were not enemy agents." He called the "dogmatic" Gay's approach "absurd."

Even more fundamentally, any order to shoot civilians indiscriminately would violate the laws of war. A specific order came the next day, July 24. The 8th Cavalry log noted receipt of instructions from a liaison at division headquarters:

"No refugees to cross the front line. Fire everyone trying to cross lines. Use discretion in case of women and children."

The division war diary later made no mention of this order to shoot refugees, or of what its immediate consequences were.

Meanwhile, North Korean commanders had capitalized on the weaknesses in the 1st Cavalry Division line to loop around behind the 8th Cavalry's 2nd Battalion, cutting it off, while hammering the 1st Battalion with frontal attacks. On July 25, Gay's troops retreated from Yongdong, in some disorder, after suffering heavy casualties. One sign of the confusion: American advisers with the South Koreans reported the 1st Cavalry Division inflicted "numerous" casualties among the allied troops. "They are trying to straighten out green troops," the telephone message said of the division.

Three years later, corresponding with Army historian Appleman, Gay did not cite civilian-clad infiltrators in explaining his defeat at Yongdong, but rather "the thing the Division Commander most feared"—sweeps by enemy units around his unguarded flanks and through the gaping hole, seven miles wide, separating the 8th Cavalry's two battalions.

Douglas MacArthur's prized 1st Cavalry Division was faring no better than the hapless men of the 24th Infantry Division. Now it would fall to Gay's third regiment, the 7th Cavalry—the under-trained, understrength Garryowens—to move into the line. First they had to find a way to get there.

AFTER THEIR JITTERY FIRST NIGHT IN BIVOUAC NEAR POHANG, THE 7th Cavalry's 2nd Battalion waited hours on Sunday, July 23, before a South Korean train was found to transport them 100 miles north-west to the warfront. The men used the time to recheck and clean their weapons and stock up on the staples of war: eight-round M-1 ammunition clips for their cartridge belts, water for the canteen, C rations, rumors—of where they were headed, what they would face, when they might return "home" to Japan. "I was eager, I was eager," Ralph Bernotas said. But if any of them found a recent *Stars and Stripes,* the eagerness may have faded. The newspaper carried pictures of four U.S. soldiers captured by the North Koreans and slain, hands tied behind their backs.

The battalion's five companies, a trainload, finally set out from the harbor town at 6:30 P.M., some men in open gondola cars, the luckier ones in small passenger cars with wooden seats and a hole in the floor for a toilet. With multiple stops for water and other needs, the trip took 20 hours. The young soldiers, their bravado evaporating, sank into silence, thoughts of home and, mostly, sleep.

They awoke next morning to the strange new countryside of low earthen huts capped with thatch, of rice paddies steaming in the sun and waving green in the rare breeze. From the rocking train they caught glimpses of a dusty road paralleling the tracks, and of ox-carts, clumps of weary refugees, military trucks, men in uniform. "Seemed like everybody was heading back one way," said H Company trooper Ed Klinedinst. "And we were heading the other way."

The weather had cleared. The mud of early July was now the dust of late July, a grit that would plague the cavalrymen in the coming days, getting into their mouths, noses, ears and M-1 muzzles. Usually more than a foot of rain falls in southern Korea in the July monsoon, but July and August 1950 were abnormally storm-free. It remained humid, however, and was unusually hot, at times over 100 degrees. For the overloaded Garryowens, many out of shape, it would be an oppressive tropical purgatory. Soldiers collapsed from heat exhaustion from the first day.

The steam engine finally chugged up over the 600-foot-high saddle of Autumn Wind Pass, gateway for Japanese invaders centuries earlier, and on into Yongdong County and the war. The cool, crew-cut Capt. Mel Chandler of H Company warned his men aboard the train that disguised enemy soldiers might lurk among Korean refugees. This reinforced the impression some had from briefings aboard the *Shanks,* when they were told "this was guerrilla warfare," F Company's Herman Patterson said. "You won't see a soldier in uniform, or armor. I pictured civilians."

The battalion commander's own inexperience with war became clear in an odd moment on the train, when Lt. Col. Herb Heyer, the ex–Iowa postmaster, cautioned officers not to damage the farmers' fields in the area. "Here we are advancing into combat, and he's worried about this farmer's beans," platoon leader Bill Kaluf said. "He simply was not too aware of things."

At 2:20 P.M., July 24, the 2nd Battalion detrained several miles behind the Yongdong front. Men from the 24th Infantry Division, worn down, in filthy fatigues, some wounded, boarded the train for the return trip. The sight of the soldiers they were replacing shook the new arrivals. "They looked like totally beaten men. You could see it in their faces," Bill McKown said. "You're looking at this. 'What am I getting into?' " McKown was grateful he was a mess sergeant, not a rifleman.

Stories quickly circulated in the Garryowens' ranks about saboteurs, grenades, guns among the civilians. "We heard so many rumors," G Company's Joe Jackman said. "Everybody had that morbid fear: 'Here they come. They'll get in the rear.' " In North Korean–occupied Seoul, what they were hearing were tales of American brutality. That day a warfront report in the newspaper *Liberation Daily* concluded, "The Americans do not recognize Koreans as human beings."

THE 2ND BATTALION MARCHED FORWARD TO WHERE THE 7TH CAValry staff was setting up its regimental command post, about four miles short of embattled Yongdong. In his first combat command, Colonel Nist gave patrolling orders to Snuffy Gray, his tough reconnaissance platoon sergeant. "I remember standing there while he tapped on the map with the stem of his pipe," Gray said, "and he's tapping on three grid squares and he's telling me to take your platoon out and cover those squares. Three whole grid squares!" A staff officer later quietly scaled down the impossible assignment. "He didn't know anything," Gil Huff, regimental executive officer, later said sympathetically of Nist. The lower ranks were not so sympathetic. They began joking about "Nist's Nest" because the colonel made the men build up sandbag walls around his tent with each of the many command post moves.

Confusion arose at division headquarters, too, over how to handle refugees. Early on July 24, General MacArthur's command in Tokyo asked the divisions to report on how they were controlling refugees. Orders were already out declaring a shifting war zone off-limits to its civilian inhabitants, under the threat of being shot. Eight hours after the 1st Cavalry Division received the MacArthur query, word went down from division headquarters, as recorded at the 8th Cavalry Regiment, to shoot refugees—"fire everyone"—trying to pass through the front line. Then, just 15 minutes after that "shoot" order went out, the division sent a confused reply to the MacArthur query. First it said refugees were being collected and sent south, but next it reported that leaflets were being dropped on small villages telling their inhabitants to head north or "be treated as enemy" in the combat zone.

Hearing this, the Eighth Army staff further complicated matters by ordering the division to suspend leaflet-dropping until it had Eighth Army–approved leaflets. South Korean army intelligence at the same time reported to the U.S. command that "it is practically impossible to stop the refugees" fleeing from small and isolated villages.

The disarray prompted Eighth Army to schedule a high-level meeting for the next day, July 25, at its Taegu headquarters to work out a policy on refugee control, attended by top Eighth Army staff officers and representatives of the South Korean Cabinet. The contradictions were glaring even in an Eighth Army internal memo July 24 saying the staff consensus was both to "cease" refugee movements and to "control" them. In addition, the Air Force, which at the Army's request was already attacking refugee columns from the air, was not invited to the Taegu meeting.

Out on the dusty road leading to the south from Yongdong—it turns east there for nine miles to Hwanggan, the next crossroads town—the men of the 1st Cavalry Division were meeting the problem face-to-face, in long files of grim, white-clad villagers and townspeople, with babies or towering loads on their backs, fleeing the fighting enveloping Yongdong, dodging U.S. military vehicles withdrawing southward. Whatever confusion gripped headquarters, whatever bloody chaos was unfolding at Yongdong, refugees just to the rear were making their way southward.

"The civilians were so scared and they had the North Koreans behind them, and they didn't know where to go," said Tom Boyd of the 7th Cavalry Headquarters Company. "They were scared to death."

Late that night, July 24, as the fear of infiltrators swept through the 7th Cavalry, Lieutenant Kaluf would have another kind of encounter with refugees. He took a dozen-man patrol out on a flank of the 2nd Battalion to establish a security post. In the moonlight, they spotted the white clothing of a refugee group approaching down a road. He radioed the battalion command post and was told to shoot the civilians, Kaluf said. But on this he decided to use his own judgment.

"I had them fire on an area. We didn't touch the civilians. We let them come on through," he said. "We had enough enemy to shoot at in uniform without shooting civilians."

THE BATTALION, TAKING POSITIONS THAT FIRST NIGHT NOT FAR from the regimental command post, was still a few miles behind the Yongdong lines held by other troops. But "combat spooks," as regimental supply officer Maj. Lucian Croft called them, descended on the green infantrymen nonetheless. "When darkness came . . . all around soldiers started shooting," Croft wrote in a private memoir. "Tried to quell the panic. It was useless so I took cover and waited out the night."

The young riflemen startled at every sound. They wondered whether their left and right were occupied by friend or foe. They assumed anything in front was enemy. The crack and bursts of fire from the semiautomatic M-1s echoed through the blackness. "The kids were scared and they were firing all night long," said Lyle R. Gibbs, an E Company sergeant. "The kids were firing on everyone."

In the early daylight, the jittery teenagers of E Company saw their first dead man—one of their own second lieutenants. His body was brought down off their hill on a stretcher. "Somebody said he lit up a cigarette or something and somebody shot him," said Charles Leavitt, the company clerk. The young officer, who had only recently joined the regiment, was the Garryowens' first "killed in action" in Korea. Men in other companies heard from their officers about the lieutenant felled by his own men in Easy Company. In death, he became a lesson, but the regiment never noted this KIA, and at least one other casualty that night, as caused by friendly fire.

Events along the Yongdong-Hwanggan road now entered a period, July 25–29, 1950, when such evasions and contradictions in the official record, combined with the incomplete memories of old soldiers, leave gaps in any reconstruction. For one thing, the 7th Cavalry's communications log, a key document, vanished at some later point. As a result, the picture that emerges is a mosaic of bits of reality seen from many perspectives. From the distance of time, however, that mosaic blends into a singular whole, stark and black.

The record says General Gay, the division commander, rode up to the 7th Cavalry command post along the Yongdong-Hwanggan road at 8:20 on Tuesday morning, July 25, and told regimental commander Colonel Nist that his 2nd Battalion should be ready to move forward to cover the 8th Cavalry and 5th Cavalry Regiments in their retreat from Yongdong. The battalion did not move out until 6:50 that evening. The record does not specify where its companies took up positions, but 2nd Battalion veterans said they dug in on a hill above a long railroad tunnel paralleling the road. The only such spot, a 2,000-foot-long tunnel carrying the main-line tracks through a mountain's lower slope, lay about 3½ miles short of Yongdong. Major elements of the 5th and 8th Cavalry were still farther forward that night, toward Yongdong and the enemy.

The North Koreans entered Yongdong at 8 P.M. "and immediately took up defensive positions at the eastern edge of town," expecting a U.S. counterattack, Appleman's official Army history says. Meanwhile, something else was happening miles away to the

1st Cavalry Division's right. A regiment of the 25th Infantry Division that had been under North Korean pressure that day needed to execute a strategic pullback that night. To keep the U.S. defense line straight, Gay would have to withdraw his troops farther from Yongdong than he anticipated.

The hillsides were abrupt and the ground inhospitable for the 2nd Battalion, 7th Cavalry, too hard for many men to dig more than "scratches" in which to spend the night. At 10 minutes past midnight, battalion commander Heyer reported to Colonel Nist, "No enemy contact." At 1:20 A.M., Heyer reported the Yongdong-Hwanggan road clogged with refugees and said an unidentified vehicle, "possibly a tank," had passed his position.

The men were edgy. Ralph Bernotas, with Fox Company high above the tunnel, could hear the "clang, clang" of people and animals on the move. The eighteen-year-old corporal thought he knew what the North Koreans were doing. "They were running cattle, and I could hear all the commotion down through the valleys of pushing refugees ahead of their infantry," Bernotas said.

Off through the darkness somewhere, a battalion radioman, Sgt. Larry Levine, was on a two-man outpost when he was startled by a voice in the empty night saying, "Hey, Joe." He didn't know any "Joe." All the tense young trooper could think of were World War II movies and tricky Japanese infiltrators speaking English. He hunkered deeper in his hole.

Then, just 10 minutes after Heyer's last report, urgent word came from the regiment: Everybody up, everybody pull back. General Gay was adjusting the lines. But somehow the Garryowens' inexperienced officers got the impression the North Koreans had made a "serious breakthrough," as the regiment diary put it, on the right flank, where the 25th Division was making a planned withdrawal. Now the plan collapsed into a rout.

Shots rang out. Men streamed down the pitch-black hillsides, sometimes tumbling, twisting ankles, losing weapons, sometimes throwing them away. "It was like a madhouse. We just bugged out," said F Company's Herman Patterson. Officers also lost their nerve. Edwin Byles, the lieutenant who had seemed so troubled aboard the

Shanks, reached the valley floor with his men and then, when gunfire erupted, "just froze," F Company veterans said. Other officers also lost control, or at least lost their way.

Bernotas and others said they had crossed paths with a tank and North Korean soldiers. If some didn't actually see a tank in the darkness, they saw "balls of fire" unleashed by a cannon over their heads. Don MacFarland, the tailored Tokyo guardsman now carrying a 16-pound Browning Automatic Rifle with F Company, saw it differently: "We were actually firing on our own men. What outfit they were in, I don't know, probably from the Cav. We were firing on them and they were firing on us." If so, they most likely were 5th Cavalry or 8th Cavalry soldiers withdrawing down the road past the Garryowens' hillside positions.

Lieutenant Byles had disappeared, and young Corporal Bernotas sensed a need for leadership. He shouted to another corporal about setting up a defense line on the railroad tracks at the bottom of the hill, "and I remember this one cook coming up, and literally grabbing me and threatening me that I was going to get everybody killed," Bernotas said.

Some pulled back in an orderly way. Some didn't get the order immediately. For most, apparently, it was "every man for himself" as they groped rearward through the night, skirting past other men in uniform and white-clad civilians, any of whom, they felt, could be a threat. "We started running down the tracks, scattering like hell," said radioman Larry Levine. In Easy Company, clerk Charlie Leavitt picked up discarded bandoliers of ammunition as they scrambled away from Yongdong.

Some have unexplained memories. "They said stay off the road and low on the ground, so I was crawling with my machine gun. I didn't know what was going on," said G Company's Art Hunter. In the moonlight, he looked over into a field. "You could hear all these babies and all crying over in this field, and you could look over there and there was all this white clothing." A field full of dead civilians, the young Virginian decided.

The regimental war diary later said the 2nd Battalion came under attack this night, and blamed "enemy infiltration with refugees."

Appleman's official history dismissed this and called it a "panic" in the rear by an untried unit. In a seeming reference to it in his later correspondence with Appleman, General Gay said the battalion became "somewhat hysterical."

Finally H Company's Capt. Mel Chandler began picking 2nd Battalion men off the road to organize them. He led some 300 down the tracks, and by 8 A.M. on July 26 they had taken up defensive positions astride the main road, Chandler later wrote in a regimental history.

Stragglers still came in long after dawn, their sweating faces caked with dust from the haze kicked up by retreating vehicles. Officers sent a detail in Jeeps and trucks back up the road, and they returned with more than 160 rifles, machine guns and other weapons abandoned by the battalion.

THE RECORD SHOWS THE 2ND BATTALION, 7TH CAVALRY, POSITIONED that day, July 26, about 1½ miles west of Hwanggan, near a sturdy concrete railroad bridge. The Japanese had built the double-arched trestle to carry the main line over some water, a languid little stream that simply trickled across the nearby main road that paralleled the tracks.

A path from the dirt road, through a trestle archway, led to a cluster of farmers' mud huts a few hundred yards away, on the battalion's right. This hamlet, fringed by wet and lush rice paddies, was entered into the battalion's morning reports as "Rokin-Ri," one possible transliteration from the Korean alphabet. This was No Gun Ri, a name corrupted from a centuries-old one that signified "forest" and "deer." Little of either remained in the area.

After less than 48 hours at the front, the Garryowens were exhausted, unnerved, hungry and still unsure of what was going on. Rumors spread. Some heard that a "refugee woman with a radio," hidden under a baby, it was said, had been discovered nearby. Some heard talk that refugees tossed a grenade at men in the next company or the next battalion—somewhere.

The Yongdong "woman with the radio" report may have multiplied across the warfront. Gil Huff, the regimental executive officer, heard the story over and over. "I never saw one," he said years later. "But it makes a good story, a colorful story."

That previous night, while these teenaged troopers were clambering up Yongdong County hillsides, Eighth Army staff officers and Korean civilian officials were meeting in Taegu, far to the rear, to work out their plan for controlling refugees. In his makeshift office elsewhere at the Taegu headquarters, the Air Force's Colonel Rogers had written his memo urging the command to cease attacking civilians.

In the morning, at 10 A.M., July 26, the Eighth Army plan came down to the divisions by radio. The lengthy order detailed a program for eventually collecting refugees for organized movement south. But the key passage, for immediate action, lay in its first fourteen words: NO REPEAT NO REFUGEES WILL BE PERMITTED TO CROSS BATTLE LINES AT ANY TIME.

The temperature was rising this day in late July 1950. Above the cinders of the railroad embankment, the air rippled with heat. Around midday, off in the distance, over their gunsights, the infantrymen of the 2nd Battalion could make out a large patch of white. It was moving their way.

4

June 29, 1950
Osan, South Korea

They clung to each other atop the rocking train, the little boy and girl trembling with cold, the young mother and father pulling them closer as they rolled south in a drenching rain. The summer "plum rain" that nourishes Korea's orchards and paddies was this day soaking Korea's people, a white tide of refugees overflowing roads and fields, ferry slips and rail stations from the East Sea to the Yellow Sea.

Young parents Chung Eun-yong and Park Sun-yong, with their two small children, huddled low against the pelting headwind with hundreds of others, in family groups, blanketing the roofs of railroad cars clattering away from Osan, 30 miles south of Seoul. Each car was jammed to bursting with humanity, desperate and fearful. Law student Eun-yong and his wife were lucky. They had a place to go, his home village of Chu Gok Ri, and now they had a way to get there. The monsoon downpour would end at some point, and they would be far from the war.

The war had begun with the rainy season. In the darkness before dawn four days ago, Sunday, June 25, a hard rain was falling at the 38th Parallel when the North Korean army, led by tanks, struck across the line. Thirty-five miles to the south in Seoul, hearing news of the invasion on the radio, Christian convert Park Sun-yong had stuck to her Sunday plan, taking four-year-old Koo-pil and his two-year-old sister, Koo-hee, to church for services. Military trucks and Jeeps were careening through the city's streets, with loudspeakers blaring orders for soldiers on leave to return to their posts. In the quiet sanctuary of the church, the pastor led the congregation in prayer for the men of the South Korean military.

On the radio, the people of Seoul heard one story: "Our heroic soldiers are fighting and repelling them. All the nation's people are urged to remain calm and carry on business as usual." But in the mountains north of the capital, a different story was unfolding.

In the main attack, two North Korean divisions, more than 20,000 men with 80 tanks, were pushing down the "Uijongbu Corridor," a valley system leading straight to Seoul. Immediately south of the parallel, just one regiment of the Republic of Korea army stood in their way. That division's other two regiments backed up the first from positions miles to the rear. Many South Korean officers and U.S. military advisers were in Seoul for the weekend, and it took the high command several hours to recognize that a general invasion was under way and to order reinforcements up from deeper in South Korea. The northern armored force, meanwhile, was rolling over the outmatched southern defenders, who had no tanks or antitank mines—nothing at all—to stop the 35-ton T-34s. Other prongs of attack came down to the east and west of the main thrust.

North Korea told the world the invasion was a last-ditch effort to make Korea whole again, and a response to South Korean armed provocations. President Kim Il Sung took to the radio to declare, "The South Korean puppet clique has rejected all methods for peaceful reunification proposed by the Democratic People's Republic of Korea."

Monday, the second day of war, dawned clear and warm, and a hopeful Eun-yong set out for his law classes at Chung Ang College, only to find a notice there saying it was temporarily closed. He headed back to his rented room south of the Han River, across from central Seoul, where Sun-yong and the children had crowded in with him on their visit from his parents' house in Chu Gok Ri. On the way, he saw ten truckloads of soldiers, covered with grime after a long journey, singing as they rolled north to the war. The ROK army's 2nd Division was streaming up from the south for a counterattack up the Uijongbu Corridor, but the division was becoming disjointed, bogged down by slow transportation, and it failed to join the offensive, dooming the defenders' best chance to save the city. The ROK troops at the head of the mountain corridor had already begun a pullback around midnight Sunday. By Monday evening, flashes of artillery fire were lighting Seoul's northern horizon.

On Tuesday, hour by hour, panic set in at high levels in Seoul. At the U.S. Embassy, the staff burned documents in heaps on the street. Koreans thronged the building, begging for help in escaping the city and nation. President Rhee had decided the evening before to quietly evacuate his government to Taejon, 85 miles to the south, and left early Tuesday morning. Local radio first reported the government had departed Seoul, but then retracted that report, lulling some listeners into an unwarranted sense of security. As the day wore on, word spread of the failed counterattack. Thousands took to the southbound roads—government officials and their families, policemen, businessmen, landlords and others who would suffer under a communist regime, and uncounted thousands who simply hoped to escape the fighting. Many others stayed in Seoul, however, among them dozens of members of the National Assembly.

During the day, Eun-yong saw North Korean warplanes making repeated passes over downtown Seoul, until finally a U.S. plane appeared and chased them away. The dogfight convinced Eun-yong that the city was endangered and he should take Sun-yong and the children south.

It rained again Tuesday night. It seemed none of Eun-yong's neighbors went to bed; all were bustling in their homes or in the streets. His two children, agitated, refused to sleep. Then, sometime in the early morning hours, a tremendous explosion rocked the area and a bluish light filled the room. In the brilliant flash, Eun-yong saw the faces of Koo-pil and Koo-hee frozen in terror.

The main bridge across Seoul's great river, the Han, had been blown up. In a tragedy of military blunders, South Korean army engineers, following orders and a set schedule that, unknown to them, had been rescinded, blew the bridge at 2:15 A.M. They gave no warning to the throngs of civilians and retreating soldiers who were walking and riding, in bumper-to-bumper traffic, across the lengthy span. Hundreds were killed in the explosion, and many more fell to their deaths or drowned when surging crowds pushed them into the gap created in the bridge. The bridge demolition stranded ROK army units in Seoul with valuable equipment, to face likely death or capture by the North Koreans.

The blunders were not just Korean. Later that day U.S. Air Force planes, with orders to attack any military spotted on the north side of the Han, strafed and rocketed the South Korean 1st Division, killing and wounding many soldiers. Remnants of the division managed to cross the river west of Seoul.

At first light Wednesday, June 28, Eun-yong stepped outside and saw the roads alive with rivers of people headed south. On the radio, an announcer repeated the pleading message: "Citizens! Please stay at your jobs. Let's defend Seoul." But the law student and his wife gathered up the children and whatever else they could carry, and melted into the white-clad multitudes. "People overflowed the road, spilling onto cucumber, tomato and barley fields," Eun-yong said. "It was ragtag. Young men carried their baggage on their A-frames and their sick parents sat on the baggage. Women carried their bags and cooking utensils on their heads. Children walked along barefoot. We also saw some injured soldiers limping along, with their legs and heads bandaged over."

Units of the North Korean 3rd Division had entered Seoul on Tuesday evening, their tanks smashing open Sodaemun Prison and freeing thousands of jailed leftists. By Wednesday afternoon, the northerners held the entire city north of the Han. Civilians in red armbands, local sympathizers, urged their neighbors to come out to cheer the conquering army, but many people simply retreated to their homes, to look out from behind windows at the young victors filing down the streets in their mustard-drab uniforms, many still with camouflage foliage in their helmets.

Within another two days, less than a week into the war, the Korean People's Army controlled all the territory above the river, and the Republic of Korea army was struggling to regroup after having lost 44,000 of its 98,000 men, either killed, captured or missing. From generals to privates, uniformed men trudged down the main road along with the army of civilian refugees, streaming south past abandoned possessions, broken-down vehicles, exhausted families on the waysides. One small family among the thousands, Chung Eun-yong's, reached the town of Suwon, 20 miles south of Seoul, late Wednesday and spent the night at a school. On the radio, President Rhee was still urging people to defend Seoul.

The next morning, General MacArthur landed in the same town on his fact-finding flight from Tokyo. In a sedan that pushed north through the retreating throngs, the supreme commander rode up to the Han River with U.S. Army advisers and surveyed the scattered South Korean units holding the south bank. It was then, MacArthur later said, that he concluded the U.S. military should be brought in to stop the North Koreans.

As the famous American general flew into Suwon, the Chung family was departing, walking to Osan, 10 miles farther south. There they found a train ready to roll south, but already overloaded. The ex–police lieutenant, a slightly built but self-assured young man, managed to squeeze his family in among the people packed on the roof of a car. Soon after the train set out, the darkening monsoon sky opened up, emptying its clouds on the wretched refugees. Soaked through, shivering, they pulled into Taejon that night, 60 miles farther south, the city where Eun-yong once worked and where they could find real refuge at the home of his brother, a prison guard. Eun-yong learned from him that Rhee himself had fled to Taejon on Tuesday, a day before the president went on the radio urging everyone else to stay put in Seoul. On Friday, June 30, the day the first North Korean troops crossed to the south side of the Han River at Seoul, the haggard husband and wife and their two small children finally reached the thatched-roof home of Eun-yong's parents in Chu Gok Ri.

The village lay barely 100 miles south of the battle-torn capital city, but for the people of Chu Gok Ri, in their valley beyond their craggy little Sonang shrine, the war might as well have been 1,000 miles away. "Most of the ordinary people weren't ready for war," recalled the village's Chung Koo-hun, the tall, studious seventeen-year-old. "Even after it broke out, they just kept tending their fields."

FROM THE LIGHT GREEN OF SPRING, THE WET FIELDS OF RICE WERE deepening into the rich green of summer. The ever-present herons, snowy white, prowled the paddy rows in search of tiny fish and snakes. Down Chu Gok Ri's muddy lanes, front yard persimmon trees shed their flowers and showed their first green fruit, bees hovered over household hives, family cows tended to calves. Barefoot girls jumped rope while the boys roamed the summer hills. For the adults of Chu Gok Ri it was a season of hard work, like all seasons. The rice cycle governed the calendar in this Year of the Tiger, as it had every year for centuries, and the calendar told them it was time for the backbreaking task of weeding.

The cycle had begun early in the year when the villagers readied rice seeds for planting, soaking them in a salt solution, and prepared fields with manure. Each family then sowed its seeds closely packed in seed beds—the richest soil—to sprout and grow for several weeks. In mid-spring, the tiny stalks were transplanted to the more extensive paddies in weeks of arduous work carried out by groups of neighbors. To speed the long days, a village troupe traditionally supplied "farmers' music," with gongs, drums and oboes, sometimes improvising songs from country jokes, with mock-complaining lines—"How long will we have to do this?"

The early summer weeding was exhausting. Backs bent to the sun, paddy mud oozing through their toes, the villagers' knowing fingers felt for the weeds crowding their young plants, uprooted them and buried them upside down in the mud. The favorable

weather of 1950 promised a good harvest for the people of Chu
Gok Ri. But in good weather or bad, rice demands constant care.
"The rice grows hearing the footsteps of the farmer," according to
a Korean adage.

The farmers of Im Ke Ri, the neighboring village up Chu Gok
Ri's side valley, were weeding their way through the paddies one
day soon after the invasion when someone rushed up to report that
police had arrived to take away young villagers suspected of leftist
sympathies. The war had come to the valley.

One farmer, Lee Choong-keun, immediately sent his son into hiding, not because he was a leftist, but because he once helped a couple
of young guerrillas who came down from the hills looking for food.
Two young men in Chu Gok Ri got no such warning. Sohn Seok-
tae and Chung Chan-young were the villagers who, months earlier,
had been forced to join a "political rehabilitation" program after
being accused of giving food to a leftist guerrilla friend. Now that
war had begun, they were taken away by the police, never to be
seen again.

All over South Korea, villagers were disappearing from their
homes, as the Rhee regime rounded up "enemies," real or imagined.
The political terror of the late 1940s was continuing, bloodier than
ever. Killings were already occurring on the other side as well. Leftists freed from Sodaemun Prison staged "people's courts" in Seoul
and summarily executed national policemen and others they blamed
for their persecution. Those deaths behind the northern lines would
not be discovered and reported until months later.

The killings in the south were also carried out mostly in secrecy,
but they were too widespread to escape attention completely. In
early July 1950, O. H. P. King, an Associated Press correspondent,
reported that the national police chief in Suwon said police firing
squads summarily executed sixty alleged "communists" or "communist sympathizers" in the two days after MacArthur's much-
publicized visit to the town. King, in touch at the time with the U.S.
Army advisory team, wrote later that he was "shocked that American officers were unconcerned and not interested in helping me
ascertain the answers to the many questions the executions raised."

But the Suwon shootings were just a sampling of what was happening, and of what U.S. Army officers knew. After North Korean troops captured Taejon on July 20, a British communist journalist traveling with them reported in the London *Daily Worker* that they had discovered that the South Koreans had killed thousands of political prisoners in the Taejon area before retreating. The U.S. Embassy in London denounced the newspaper report as an "atrocity fabrication." The *Daily Worker*'s account would eventually be supported, however, by a U.S. military report and photographs, material classified "secret" and kept classified for almost a half-century.

The South Korean military police had trucked hundreds of political prisoners to a spot outside Taejon, shot them and dumped their bodies in long trenches. The killings were photographed by U.S. Army officers. A report to the Army intelligence staff in Washington by the U.S. Embassy's military attaché, Lt. Col. Bob E. Edwards, told the story succinctly: "Execution of 1800 (one thousand eight hundred) political prisoners at Taejon, requiring three days, took place during first week in July 1950." The accompanying photographs were grimly reminiscent of scenes from the recent Nazi holocaust, showing the terror on prisoners' faces beforehand and the tangle of corpses afterward.

Edwards suggested that the Taejon bloodbath was only one of many. He wrote that he believed that "thousands of political prisoners were executed within [a] few weeks after fall of Seoul to prevent their possible release by advancing enemy troops. Orders for execution undoubtedly came from top level." In another long-classified document, U.S. Embassy diplomat Everett F. Drumright said he and Maj. Gen. William F. Dean, in command of U.S. front-line troops, had protested the Taejon executions to top South Korean officials. Their intervention seemed to have little effect, because other documents unearthed decades later showed that wholesale political killings went on.

For the two Chu Gok Ri youths, along with thousands of others swept away by the Rhee regime, "rehabilitation" led to an unmarked mass grave somewhere in South Korea.

DAY BY DAY, THE WAR WAS UPENDING THE LIVES OF MILLIONS, NOT just in the south but in North Korea as well, where U.S. bombers began raining tons of explosives on the cities by mid-July.

Thousands of southerners every day trekked down South Korea's unpaved main highway, laden with bundles and boxes, trailed by children, sometimes by children carrying children. The road, at times of mud, at times of dust, ran through the crossroads town of Yong-dong and then east for several miles, skirting past Chu Gok Ri. For some travelers, that peaceful village was the journey's end, the safe harbor.

Even before the war, new people had come to Chu Gok Ri and its sister village Im Ke Ri, including some who had lost their homes when guerrilla-hunting police set fire to the nearby hamlet of Ahn Jom. Others, relatives close and distant, began arriving after the war broke out. The high school student Chung Koo-hun's cousins were among them, including Chung Koo-ok, a young woman who was the pride of the village, daughter of the 1919 village patriot Chung Hee-yong.

At age twenty, Koo-ok had managed to achieve an ambition rare for a Chu Gok Ri girl: getting an education. She had attended a one-year teachers' college and won a position at a grade school in a nearby village. A model for younger Chu Gok village girls, Koo-ok often wore a Western-style jacket over her teacher's uniform of white blouse and long black skirt. Her shoes were leather. She even had her hair permed. She was modern, smart, attractive. She would have been a prize for matchmakers, but Chung Koo-ok resisted the marriage overtures from other villages because a wife could never work outside the home and she loved her job and loved helping children. Even on school breaks home in Chu Gok Ri, when she threw herself into her books and papers, she made time to play and joke with village boys and girls, especially her eight-year-old cousin Koo-hak, Koo-hun's sickly little brother.

The schoolteacher's older brother, Chung Koo-il, twenty-three, had also made his way home to Chu Gok Ri from Seoul with the outbreak of war. The family of three sisters and two brothers, all tall and distinguished-looking, pinned its highest hopes on this eldest son and model student, a sophomore at the capital's Yonhee College.

This hardworking family, the only Chu Gok Ri family wealthy enough to have a tile roof on their mud-walled house, might strike the communists as ideological enemies, since the father was doing well in the dried-fish business. But the South Korean police outdid the communists in this particular "enemies" game. Unknown to the Chungs, the fishmonger's son Koo-il was on a police "watch" list—apparently for the offense, uncommon in his home village, of attending a university. For generations, under corrupt kings, colonialists and now President Rhee's beleaguered and unpopular right-wing rule, students had been viewed as troublemakers in Korea.

As July wore on and the war moved south, the homes in the peaceful valley grew more crowded and noisy under their thatched roofs. "Golden Girl" Yang Hae-sook's family of seven, in their cramped, century-old house in Im Ke Ri, took her father's sister and her husband in, with their four children, after they left their nearby home village. The aunt, Yang Mal-soon, was close to delivering a fifth child. To feed the brood, her worried husband brought along a huge sack of barley on his back A-frame.

One July refugee traveled more comfortably. President Syngman Rhee had hopscotched, by car and special train, all the way to the southern tip of the Korean peninsula within a week of the invasion, moving into an island beach home under Korean navy protection. Ordinary South Koreans were unaware how far from the front lines their president had retreated. They were also unaware that, back in Seoul, 48 legislators of the 210-member National Assembly, foes of Rhee's rightist autocracy, had pledged allegiance to Kim Il-Sung's northern Democratic People's Republic.

In mid-July, acknowledging his government's near-total dependence on the Americans, Rhee assigned overall command of the reeling Republic of Korea Army to MacArthur. The U.S. Far East commander, in turn, sent his Eighth Army chief, Lt. Gen. Walton H. "Johnnie" Walker, a short, stocky Texan with a reputation as a tough fighter, to the southern city of Taegu to lead U.S. forces in Korea.

Looking up from their paddies, the people of Chu Gok Ri were relieved to see trainloads of American soldiers and equipment heading up the main line toward the Taejon front, and U.S. Army truck convoys rumbling up the parallel highway, towing artillery. American jets screamed overhead—"shriekers," the startled villagers dubbed them. In their little wooden school, the children of Chu Gok Ri were assured by a teacher that the U.S. soldiers would quickly end the war by driving the communists back north, "where they belong."

Then, at the end of the third week of July, the traffic reversed. The North Koreans had driven the 24th Infantry Division from Taejon, and ragged remnants of U.S. battalions were withdrawing south. "The American defeats were a terrible shock," U.S. diplomat Harold J. Noble wrote of President Rhee's reaction at the time. "Like us he had thought our troops well-nigh invincible." On the central *matangs* of villages across Yongdong County, a morning's drive southeast of Taejon, clan elders traded rumors and fears. They knew the fighting was coming their way. Whistling southbound trains rolled past jammed with refugees, hanging from boxcar doors, sprawled perilously atop roofs.

In Chu Gok Ri and Im Ke Ri, the bone-tiring work of weeding and cultivation went on. The two small villages in a rugged green heartland, rich in people but poor in every other way, were a portrait in permanence—in their closely arranged homes and their intricately marked-out paddies, in the venerable hillside gravesites of ancestors, in the paths worn smooth by the feet of countless generations. For centuries, through typhoons, epidemics and famines, these communities had held together. Would they be abandoned now that Korean was set against Korean in the first civil war in a thousand years?

In the murmuring darkness of those summer nights, husbands and wives searched for answers: If we go, how will we feed the children? How can Grandmother travel? Where will we get money? Who will care for the paddies? Who will tend to the graves?

Some in Chu Gok Ri found an easy answer as the North Koreans neared. Suh Jong-koo, for example, a young man who worked for the government in Yongdong town, climbed over the Three Peaks Mountain behind Im Ke Ri and trekked to a more isolated village to stay with his in-laws. But almost everyone else remained, and remained torn. "We thought we would die of starvation if we left the village. But we also feared being beaten to death by leftists," said Koo-hun, whose father, like his uncle, was a dried-fish merchant. "To leave or to stay, both were dangerous for us. In the end, my family decided to remain."

ONE MIDSUMMER MORNING IN THIS YEAR OF THE TIGER, THE AMER-icans arrived in the valley. By the soldiers' reckoning, it was "0745, 22 Jul 50," as noted in the 5th Cavalry Regiment's operational log. A 5th Cavalry battalion set up a command post off the main road at the nearby village of Ha Ga Ri. Another battalion arrived at 4:30 P.M. They totaled more than a thousand men, with trucks and heavy weapons. Artillery units also moved in, and the Americans spread up the road to Chu Gok Ri, a mile away, some settling in along the streambed between Chu Gok Ri and the main road. The sharp smell of burned diesel and the grit of churned-up earth hung in the air around the village. The Americans pointed artillery in the direction of Yongdong, three miles farther up the road. They were troops on standby, assigned to back up another 1st Cavalry Division regiment, the 8th Cavalry, which moved farther ahead, through Yongdong, to deploy on its far outskirts to meet the oncoming North Koreans.

The villagers saw the Americans playing cards in twos and threes, or lounging beside the paddies watching and listening as the farmers sang their work songs, odd and incomprehensible to the American ear. Curious boys approached the foreign soldiers, knowing they might get some chocolate or other favors. But many of the Chu Gok villagers, having heard of the Americans' rough behavior, and espe-cially of things done to Korean women, kept their distance.

One who didn't was a young drifter and farm laborer named Lee Bok-hun, who went to the GIs asking for "cigarettos" or "gum," words he'd picked up somewhere. Villagers observed the Americans showing cigarettes to Bok-hun and using, in a broken attempt at Korean, a vulgar word to signify "woman." Just days from their Tokyo haunts, dropped into a traditional Confucian village in the Korean mountains, the Americans hoped to trade cigarettes for sex. Some of the rifle-toting Cav men apparently were determined to have it, whatever it took.

Two GIs were led by Lee to a house where a young woman of nineteen or twenty lived. They went inside, and "it was clear what they did," said Koo-hun, the tall schoolboy. He and a neighbor woman, watching and listening from over a wall, knew that a rape had occurred.

Village families grew frantic as the Americans, putting aside their duties or card playing, began strutting over to the paddies and huts in search of women. People secured their gates and doors. Grandmothers made girls wear dirty clothes and smear their faces with charcoal to make them repulsive. They hid them behind trees and shrubs when GIs passed.

"I hid in a big urn and Mother put the lid on the urn," remembered Park Hee-sook, who was a sixteen-year-old with high cheekbones and a long pigtail tipped with a red-and-yellow silk ribbon. "The GIs seemed to go wild whenever they saw women, whether they were old women or young girls. They tried to grab them." When soldiers bulled their way into village homes, she said, older women, enraged, waved scythes and threatened to emasculate them. "We girls didn't dare walk in the open." Then something else happened to anger the villagers, and to chill their souls.

Like most Korean villages, Chu Gok Ri had a burial society, a group that took care of the common equipment used for all funerals, kept in a small thatch-roofed shrine. Two American soldiers found this sacrosanct place and vandalized it. They hauled out the funeral bier, a brightly decorated platform on which the deceased's coffin is borne to the grave. They carried it here and there, playing with it, clowning. Seemingly bored, they threw it aside and then spotted a brass bell inside the shrine, the funeral procession bell, and toyed with that, ringing it repeatedly, so that its metallic knell, the sound of death in Chu Gok Ri, echoed over the village, filling those who heard it with a nameless dread.

BY SUNDAY, JULY 23, THE SOUND OF WAR COULD BE HEARD ON THE far side of Yongdong. The North Koreans' 3rd Division, which had seized Taejon three days earlier, had moved in from the north and was probing the lines of the newly arrived U.S. 1st Cavalry Division. The northern troops soon discovered a gaping seven-mile hole between the 8th Cavalry Regiment's two battalions at Yongdong, and found the U.S. flanks exposed. In fact, from Yongdong west to the Yellow Sea, a distance of 70 miles on the Americans' left flank, the North Koreans faced no resistance.

The 1st Cavalry Division's Gen. "Hap" Gay, in his first week as a combat commander, also feared enemy infiltrators were crossing his lines among refugees. On this Sunday, the division sent out an order describing a plan for evacuating civilians from the battle zone, with "controlled movements" of refugees to screening points. After that, U.S. news reports said, the Americans might shoot anyone in civilian clothes in the battle zone.

At noon, villagers remembered, an American Jeep drove into Chu Gok Ri and a U.S. Army officer jumped out, a Korean interpreter at his side. He told farmers taking a lunch rest in the shade that the village should be evacuated immediately, that Chu Gok Ri, a few miles from the front lines and set back just 200 yards from the main road, would soon turn into a battleground. He then climbed back into the Jeep and pulled away, apparently to alert other villages.

Some nervous Chu Gok Ri residents had already moved belongings to Im Ke Ri, a little more than a mile up their side valley's dirt track. The slopes around the smaller hamlet offered plenty of fruits, nuts and water. People might live there until the war passed through, just as peasants 350 years earlier pulled back into the folds of the mountains when Hideyoshi's Japanese invaders rampaged up the same road.

Now, as word spread from hut to hut, every family hurriedly gathered up what they would need, what they could carry: bags of barley and rice, extra clothing, sleeping quilts, cooking utensils, scythes and other tools for foraging for food. They tied squealing pigs and chickens on oxcarts. Some quickly dug holes in their tiny kitchen gardens or earthen floors and buried big pots holding ancestral tablets and other family treasures. Then they set out for Im Ke Ri, family after family, some five hundred of them, bags balanced on women's heads and lashed to the wooden A-frames on every man's back, bundles and household gear in carts or on the backs of family cows, hobbled grandparents and pregnant women lagging behind, small children wrapped tightly to their mothers' backs. The sturdily built teenager Chung Koo-hun carried little brother Koo-hak atop the bag on his A-frame because the eight-year-old was recovering from malaria and was too weak to walk.

Moving a village family was onerous: Someone had to carry the big cast-iron pot for cooking rice, the heavy mortar for pounding barley, and other cumbersome items. Many took bulky, padded winter blankets, knowing they might have to sleep outdoors. Some grumbling farmers wondered aloud why they would flee communists who, according to rumor, promised equal property for everyone.

Reaching Im Ke Ri, up the narrowing valley, they knew the village had far too few huts to hold them. Families sought shelter in sheds, under big trees, in caves. Some thought the houses too exposed anyway. The Yang family of Im Ke Ri—"Golden Girl" Hae-sook's family—left their crowded old home and claimed a hiding place in the small gold mine behind the village, a black, forbidding hole in the hillside, unseen from the valley floor. Hae-sook's father carried her grandmother there on his backframe, and thirteen-year-old Hae-sook, little brother Hae-chan and the rest of the Yangs settled in among the resident bats with six other families.

On a nearby slope, a poor rice-growing family from Chu Gok Ri excavated its own hole. Chun Soon-pyo, who had served with the Japanese military in the Pacific war, dug an air-raid shelter with his younger brother, then covered the opening with tree branches and spread rice straw mats on the dirt floor. Their temporary home was big enough to hold all nine family members, including Tae-sung, a baby boy whose name meant "Great Success."

Chun and his wife, in their first dozen years of marriage, had produced only three girls, and two had died. Choon-ja, now ten, had watched as her two younger sisters writhed through the feverish agonies of smallpox, the fearsome scourge villagers dubbed Son-nim, "Respected Guest." She watched as her distraught grandmother prayed and sacrificed to the *samshin,* the mountain gods, for mercy. It was to no avail. The girls were buried on the hill behind their house. Her parents doted on the survivor, Choon-ja, but she knew they wanted a son above all and would keep trying. Finally, some months before the war, a boy was born. "They handled him as if he was a piece of gold," Choon-ja recalled of the overjoyed family. "It was as if we were the only family in the world that had a boy."

Now, in their hillside shelter, the baby's ever-protective grand-mother watched over him as the family prepared to wait out the war. They planned to survive mostly on a home concoction called *misookaroo,* a powder made from roasted barley for mixing with water. To the lively little girl Choon-ja, wondering what new things awaited them, it was a lark. "It was like camping out," she said.

The afternoon heat that Sunday built white billows of cumulus clouds high into the sky. When rain poured down that evening, it caught some Chu Gok Ri peasants, inexperienced refugees, poorly protected. The flash and thud of big guns, reflecting off the sky's low cover and resounding off distant mountains, struck new fear into the villagers. One in particular, Chung Eun-yong, had a spe-cial fear.

The ex-policeman's family, like many, had been unable to find a room when they trekked up from Chu Gok Ri, and spent the night in a shed housing a small millstone. Their bags, like many others, had to be left outside and were soaked in the rain. Along with Sun-yong and the two children, the group included Eun-yong's parents and two younger brothers, and the wife and four children of his third brother, the Taejon prison guard who had already gone on to the south.

Eun-yong's parents and wife were deeply worried by rumors ref-ugees brought from the north that North Korean troops were round-ing up policemen in conquered areas and executing them. Eun-yong himself had heard about such kangaroo courts from a young man who fled Kaesong, north of Seoul. In the cramped, damp shed that night, as the rain outside pelted the persimmon leaves, Sun-yong quietly read her Bible and then told her husband the entire family should flee south.

In the morning, the start of a rain-free but steamy late July day, Eun-yong talked to his father about going south, but the old man resisted. The family, especially the children, should not undertake such a hard journey in the heat of summer, he said. His father told Eun-yong, with Sun-yong's support, that he alone should go. "Don't worry and just go," the elder Chung said. "Even if they're communists, the North Korean soldiers won't harm children, women or old people."

The twenty-seven-year-old law student, once a young man so determined and sure, was torn with indecision. "I was not comfortable with the idea of leaving my family," he said, but he felt they would be safer among neighbors and a secure food supply in his familiar home valley. He felt, too, that if he stayed with them, they might soon be permanently without a husband and father. He decided to leave. His mother prepared a small backpack of rice, spare clothes, soy sauce, a bowl, spoon and chopsticks.

With a deep bow to his parents and a gentle squeeze of Sun-yong's hand, he set off. He had barely passed Im Ke Ri's hollowed-out big tree, a landmark at the village entrance, when four-year-old Koo-pil came dashing after him, begging his father not to go. "Please take me with you," the boy said, as his mother came and scooped him up.

It was a difficult moment. The bond of intimacy between father and son is the greatest bond of Confucianism. Now, at a dangerous time, Eun-yong was leaving his son, the bright boy who had shined from the start, learning to speak at an early age. At the traditional first-birthday celebration, Koo-pil had been bedecked in customary finery of "rainbow" sleeves and silk "Good Fortune" hat, and had posed, a little man, before his own small table bearing writing brush, coins and bow and arrow, traditionally arrayed to represent a child's future. Grandparents, uncles, an aunt were delighted, and Eun-yong was filled with pride. "He was a smart boy," he said. "I had a lot of expectations for him." He indulged in a luxury for the party, hiring a photographer to take a picture of his gaily dressed son.

Now that photo of their first-born lay with other family keepsakes in a buried leather box beneath a shed at their Chu Gok Ri home, and a grim Eun-yong, having parted from his wife and son, was soon striding onto the main road, heading away from the sounds of the Yongdong fighting. He joined the strung-out columns of refugees following the road east, then south.

Around noon, a few miles along, Eun-yong decided to take a rest away from the burning sun. He stepped off the road and into the cool shadows of the concrete railroad trestle near the hamlet of No Gun Ri. The little double-arched bridge was a local landmark, built by the Japanese when they added a second track to the main line in the early 1940s. Eun-yong splashed his face with water from a small stream that ran under the soaring, echoing arches, sat a few minutes, then finally felt a chill and went on his way.

Less than a mile farther along, just before the town of Hwanggan, he ran into a bottleneck, a refugee checkpoint set up by South Korean police who inspected the luggage and identities of the hundreds of civilians pressing southward.

While Chung Eun-yong shuffled along in this queue, and then finally walked on through Hwanggan, a train pulled past him in the opposite direction. It carried the 2nd Battalion of the 7th Cavalry, the U.S. Army regiment known as the Garryowens, at the end of a tiring rail journey from Korea's east coast. Lt. Col. Herb Heyer, Capt. Mel Chandler and the battalion's more than six hundred other officers and men were arriving at Hwanggan to aid their sister units defending Yongdong, nine miles up the road.

Back at Im Ke Ri, as nightfall spread over the valley, the Chung family settled into a hillside shelter they built from tree branches, sleeping on a floor of leaves. Young mother Sun-yong's heart grew heavier, hearing the thunder of war nearby. She saw red streaks crisscrossing and a glow in the northwest sky, and wondered whether villages were burning out there, where Shimchon lay, the home she left five years before as a hopeful bride, a young woman "rescued" by a serious young stranger.

IT WAS ON THE MAIN NORTH-SOUTH ROAD NEAR SHIMCHON, FIVE miles northwest of Yongdong, that a battalion of the 8th Cavalry had first clashed with the North Koreans two nights before. By this night, July 24, fires set by U.S. and North Korean artillery and by American air attacks were raging across the Yongdong front; by the next morning, Tuesday, July 25, the forward American troops were trying to extricate themselves from a North Korean trap, from an enemy whose soldiers seemed to advance from every direction.

By the morning of July 25, too, 1st Cavalry Division and other U.S. military commanders, worried about reported infiltration by civilian-clad North Koreans, had issued orders that were at times clear, at times confused over what to do with the South Korean refugees trying to escape the fighting.

On July 23, the orders had gone out to evacuate civilians from the battle zone, after which anyone in civilian clothes might be shot. The next day, Monday, orders came from the 1st Cavalry Division headquarters for front-line units to shoot refugees—"fire every-one"—trying to cross their lines. Then, within minutes, the division telephoned higher headquarters to report both that it was shepherd-ing refugees southward and that it was dropping leaflets warning villagers to head north or be treated as enemy. A division operations officer, Lt. Col. J. P. Powhida, offered still another version of what was happening in late July. "Communists in Allied territory were giving false information to villagers to start them on their way along the narrow rocky roads," he said in a training bulletin issued months later in Washington.

The Air Force, meanwhile, at the Army's request, was following a policy of strafing refugees; Navy pilots had been told to attack any groups of more than eight people; and on Tuesday, July 25, the Air Force's Col. Turner Rogers would write his memo warning of the potential "embarrassment" of blatant U.S. killings of noncom-batants.

At Im Ke Ri, Monday night passed sleeplessly for many as they listened to the artillery duels and worried what the day would bring. In the morning a few families set out for the south through a high pass in the 2,500-foot mountains beyond the village. Most remained, including many who spent the day tending to their paddies.

Wispy columns of smoke drifted over the valley, from the cooking fires of grandmothers and housewives. In the late afternoon, a small plane flew in and circled low over the village, so low that people could see the helmeted pilot. Children waved. About two hours later, at dusk, a truck bumped up the dusty path to Im Ke Ri and about ten American soldiers in olive-drab fatigues jumped out, carrying rifles, villagers recalled. An officer, through an interpreter speaking Japanese, told men idling under the village "big tree" to gather up everyone. They had to leave and head south.

The news heartened some but disturbed others. After their experiences of recent days, many recoiled from the Americans. Park Sun-yong, without her husband, was greatly relieved. "They were like a savior," she said of this promise of safety. The Chung family began collecting its things; Sun-yong took care not to forget her Bible.

Some had to be called home from the fields to join the evacuation. Many barely had time to pack. Ten-year-old Chun Choon-ja's father came to their makeshift shelter and told them to gather their belongings. They were following the Americans. "I was happy," Choon-ja said. "I thought that if I went to the south, I'd see big towns. I always wanted to see big towns. I didn't know what a war was. I didn't know what being a refugee meant." On this night, already dark, not all went happily. Some villagers, including old and sick people, tried to stay in their homes. The Americans dragged them out. The Yang family was among them.

Yang Ho-yong, Hae-sook's father, was a certified "loyal son." A local administrative office had once presented him with an award, a tradition in those days, for exemplary fidelity to his parents. But this loyal son faced a dilemma when he came up from the paddies to the gold mine to tell the family they must leave. His elderly mother announced that she was too frail to go.

Troops of the U.S. occupation army parade through Tokyo's Imperial Palace Plaza on July 4, 1948. The 1st Cavalry Division's police and ceremonial duties in Japan kept its soldiers from receiving adequate training for wartime. *(AP WideWorld Photos)*

Pfc. James Hodges ran away from a sharecropping family's hard life to join the army at sixteen, lying about his age. He never came home from Korea. Many in the U.S. occupation army were underage and school dropouts. *(Courtesy of Decar Hodges Wenzel)*

"I didn't have a care in the world," a 7th Cavalry Regiment trooper said of Tokyo's good times. Fox Company buddies included (second row) Cpl. Ralph Bernotas (center) and Pvt. Don Down (far right), and (first row) Pfc. Dan Brumagen (far left), Cpl. Al Clair (second from right) and Pfc. John Boehm (far right). Brumagen and Boehm were killed early in the Korean War. *(Courtesy of Alfred Clair)*

The rice-farming village of Im Ke Ri, South Korea, in the 1960s, one of two home villages of most victims of the No Gun Ri killings. *(Yongdong County Office)*

Park Sun-yong, cradling son Koo-pil, is at lower left at this 1946 picnic. Her husband, Chung Eun-yong, is behind and above her right shoulder. Koo-pil was killed and Sun-yong wounded in the No Gun Ri carnage. "I knew that I was never going to have another happy day in my life," Eun-yong said of the moment he learned what had happened. *(Courtesy of Chung Eun-yong)*

Min Young-ok stayed behind when her husband, a prison guard, fled the invading North Koreans. She and two of her four children, including son Koo-sung, shown with her in March 1950, were killed by U.S. troops at No Gun Ri. *(AP WideWorld Photos)*

Chung Koo-il, seen here as a student in the late 1940s, pleaded futilely in English with American soldiers to halt the killing at No Gun Ri, witnesses said. Four members of his family were killed. He escaped but then vanished. *(Courtesy of Chung Koo-hong)*

In Japanese-style uniforms, seniors at a Yongdong middle school gather in March 1950. At the far left, middle, is Chung Koo-hun, who escaped from the No Gun Ri killings and returned to rescue his younger brother from among the dead. Their mother and one-year-old sister were killed. *(Courtesy of Chung Koo-hun)*

First Cavalry Division units disembark at Pohang on July 18, 1950. South Korea's rugged terrain looms in the background. The first U.S. units sent to fight in Korea were understrength, poorly equipped and often led by officers with no combat experience. *(AP WideWorld Photos)*

Troops come ashore at Pohang. After the 7th Cavalry landed on July 22, 1950, the regiment's daily record said the troops were "curious and dubious as to what lay before them." They were told to expect a guerrilla enemy in civilian clothes. *(AP WideWorld Photos)*

Hundreds of thousands of South Korean civilians fled their homes to head farther south after the North Korean army invaded. These refugees stream down a road away from the central city of Taejon on July 19, 1950, one week before No Gun Ri. *(AP WideWorld Photos)*

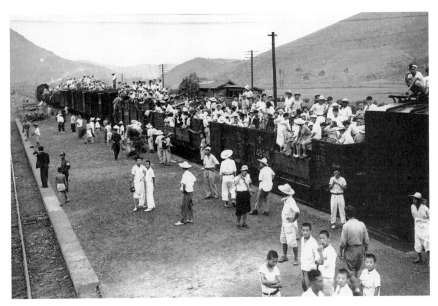

Refugees in traditional white blanketed the cars of South Korean trains headed south. In a monsoon rain, Chung Eun-yong's family rode atop a jam-packed rail car to reach their home village, Chu Gok Ri, in late June 1950. *(AP WideWorld Photos)*

0745	1st Bn	Enemy patrol working around N flank. Enemy troops concentrated E flank. Notified 2nd Bn.
0800	S-3	27th Inf Regt under attack.
0800	Air	Tanks moving SE on road from OKCHON (Square 1050-1490) (Div)
0800	TAR	Enemy dug in (1 Co?) (1070.9-1470.9) YONG DONG.
0900	2nd Bn	Co E sighted 300 NK's yds in front of Co E position. Arty FO contacted obs plane. If confirmed, will use arty. Will keep contact with us. Notified S-3.
1000	G-3 Ln	No refugees to cross the front line. Fire everyone trying to cross lines. Use discretion in case of women and children.
1020	Div Arty	Suspected Korean carrying radio at 1073.5-1475.4.
1020	HW	Road block at White motor pool. Est 1 Plt w/auto wpns. Recommen ded tanks. S-3 sent 2 tanks and 16 Rcn plat to eliminate them.
1015	Air Ln	Troops, horse & truck arty being concentrated in KUMSAN (1040.(1460.6) B-26 strike to be made. (Div)

At 10 A.M. ("1000") on July 24, 1950, two days before the No Gun Ri killings, 1st Cavalry Division instructions told troops to fire on refugees trying to cross the front line. U.S. commanders feared North Korean infiltrators. The communication is recorded in the 8th Cavalry Regiment journal, once secret, now declassified. *(U.S. National Archives, College Park, Md.)*

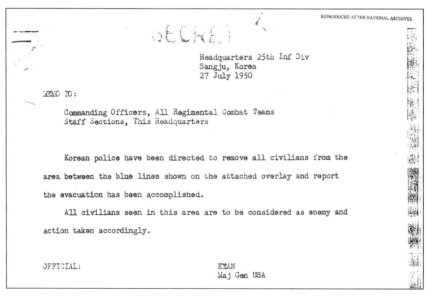

SECRET

Headquarters 25th Inf Div
Sangju, Korea
27 July 1950

MEMO TO:

Commanding Officers, All Regimental Combat Teams
Staff Sections, This Headquarters

Korean police have been directed to remove all civilians from the area between the blue lines shown on the attached overlay and report the evacuation has been accomplished.

All civilians seen in this area are to be considered as enemy and action taken accordingly.

OFFICIAL:

KEAN
Maj Gen USA

On July 27, 1950, Maj. Gen. William B. Kean ordered his 25th Infantry Division to treat civilians as enemy in the war zone, since civilians were to have been evacuated. In relaying the command, declassified documents show, his staff said civilians should be "considered as unfriendly and shot." *(U.S. National Archives, College Park, Md.)*

Maj. Gen. Hobart R. Gay, 1st Cavalry Division commander, said he was sure most white-clad people on South Korea's roads were North Korean guerrillas. Gay ordered a bridge blown up while refugees were crossing, killing hundreds. *(AP WideWorld Photos)*

FIFTH AIR FORCE
APO 970, Unit 1

25 July 1950

MEMO TO GENERAL TIMBERLAKE

Subject: Policy on Strafing Civilian Refugees

I. THE PROBLEM:

1. To determine the policy for guidance of all Fifth Air Force units in regard to strafing of civilian refugees on the highways.

II. FACTS BEARING ON THE PROBLEM:

2. It is reported that large groups of civilians, either composed of or controlled by North Korean soldiers, are infiltrating U. S. positions.

3. The army has requested that we strafe all civilian refugee parties that are noted approaching our positions.

4. To date, we have complied with the army request in this respect.

III. DISCUSSION:

5. Our operations involving the strafing of civilians is sure to receive wide publicity and may cause embarrassment to the U. S. Air Force and to the U. S. government in its relation with the United Nations.

6. It appears that such civilian groups are marching on the highways through U. S. ground positions. It is not understood why the army is not screening such personnel or shooting them as they come through if they desire such action. Further, it is felt that more suitable targets are available for the air effort, the destruction of which would be of more value to the army in the long run.

IV. RECOMMENDATIONS:

7. For the protection of the Air Force, it is recommended that a policy be established whereby Fifth Air Force aircraft will not attack civilian refugees, unless they are definitely known to contain North Korean soldiers or commit hostile acts.

8. It is further recommended that we inform the Army Headquarters.

TURNER C. ROGERS
Colonel, USAF
D O/S Operations

In a classified memo the day before No Gun Ri, the Fifth Air Force operations chief noted that U.S. planes were attacking civilian refugee groups at the Army's request (paragraphs 3 and 4). The "strafing of civilians . . . may cause embarrassment to the U.S. Air Force and to the U.S. government," he wrote. *(U.S. National Archives, College Park, Md.)*

A 1960 photograph of the five-foot-high culvert near No Gun Ri where many surviving refugees fled after their group was attacked by U.S. planes on July 26, 1950, as they rested on the railroad tracks above. Up to one hundred were killed in the strafing, survivors said. Ground troops opened fire on civilians in the culvert, American and Korean witnesses said. *(Courtesy of Chung Eun-yong)*

A 1960 photograph of the No Gun Ri trestle. Refugees not killed by the first attacks were led into the eighty-foot-long underpasses. Three days of American gunfire then left the sandy floor covered with up to three hundred dead, mostly women and children, survivors said. Some ex-GIs estimated one hundred or fewer were killed; some said hundreds were killed. "We just annihilated them," a former machine gunner said. *(AP WideWorld Photos)*

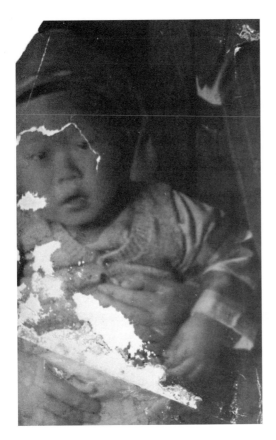

Ex-policeman Chung Eun-yong buried family keepsakes at his Chu Gok Ri home before fleeing. U.S. troops then set the village houses ablaze. On his return, Eun-yong found these photographs damaged by the heat: son Koo-pil (left), killed at No Gun Ri, on his first birthday; Eun-yong (below left) and his future wife, Sun-yong (below right), as teenagers. *(Courtesy of Chung Eun-yong)*

Men of E Company, 2nd Battalion, 7th Cavalry fire a machine gun at targets across the Naktong River in a photograph dated August 26, 1950. Twelve days earlier, as G Company's Art Hunter held a similar machine gun position, the batallion repulsed a North Korean attack from across the river. *(U.S. Army, Center of Military History)*

1625 hours	Baker 3 - Patrol went out over ridge and valley to behind the left flank of Swing Red. Returned and saw no enemy. Brought in 2 civilians. Desire that civilians be jacked up and turned.
1625 hours	Peter 1 patrol reached destination and returning.
1630 hours	Scrappy 2 - Send all refugees back to Regt by truck.
1655 hours	Shoot all refugees coming across river - from Scrappy 6.
1657 hours	Shuttle all men back to Scrappy; 2 men and children continue to walk from Scrappy 6. Patrol N & W at Redball route above wide line 48.
1658 hours	Baker and Charlie notified of Stop Refugee order.

A declassified battalion journal in the 8th Cavalry Regiment shows that at 4:55 P.M. ("1655 hours") on August 9, 1950, the regimental commander—code-named "Scrappy 6"—ordered troops to shoot all refugees crossing the Naktong River. Many were killed by U.S. forces along the river in mid-1950, Korean witnesses said. *(U.S. National Archives, College Park, Md.)*

In August 1950, 1st Cavalry Division soldiers watch a mass of South Korean refugees wade across the Naktong River to safety. The U.S. military's treatment of refugees was unpredictable. At times they were shot, but on August 6 the division screened 5,500 civilians and allowed them across the river. *(Carl Mydans/TimePix)*

until next time O
Your loveing Bud
James
P.S.
Ask the preacher for
a prayer for all George
my gong for we are
about to move into Bloody
territory.

In an August 28, 1950, letter to his sister, Cpl. James Hodges asks for prayers as G Company prepares to move into "Bloody territory." It was his last letter. *(Courtesy of Juanita Hodges Royal)*

First Cavalry Division riflemen in a firefight at a rail yard in Pyongyang after U.S. troops entered the North Korean capital on October 19, 1950. Within weeks, the Chinese army intervened and rolled back the American offensive. *(AP WideWorld Photos)*

Troops take to boats in the 7th Cavalry's costly assault on the Hwachon Dam on April 11, 1951. When F Company was ordered to the boats, Sgt. Ralph Bernotas thought, "No way we're going to get out of this. We're sitting ducks." Then, at the last minute, the attack was suspended. *(AP WideWorld Photos)*

Cpl. Suey Lee Wong in March 1951. Wong joined the 7th Cavalry months after No Gun Ri and heard about the refugee killings from old hands. *(Courtesy of Suey Lee Wong)*

Lt. Col. Gilmon A. Huff in the early 1950s. Huff led the 7th Cavalry's 2nd Battalion through some of its toughest fighting. "He always said soldiers as well as civilians were the pawns of war," his daughter recalled. *(Courtesy of Susan Huff Rush)*

At James Hodges's funeral in 1952, Buddy Wenzel (left) joins James's parents Eula Mae (second from left) and Cauley Hodges, and grandmother Mattie Yoman at the gravesite. Wenzel later moved to the Hodges farm—"kind of taking the place of James." *(Courtesy of Decar Hodges Wenzel)*

A Chung family gathering in 1953. Three years earlier, eleven members of the extended family were killed at No Gun Ri. Park Sun-yong is at center, holding a new baby daughter. Two small nieces who survived No Gun Ri are to her left and right. Husband Eun-yong is at upper left. In front of Eun-yong are (in white) his brother Kwan-yong and (in black) the "1919 patriot" Chung Hee-yong. Three other No Gun Ri survivors are at upper right: Chung Koo-hun, the tall youth in school uniform; Chung Koo-hong, in uniform to his right; Kim Bok-hee, below and between them. *(Courtesy of Chung Eun-yong)*

Yang Hae-sook (seated) in 1955, a year after receiving her artifical left eye at age seventeen. She poses with cousin Yang Bong-nam, also a No Gun Ri survivor. "I've lived my life in tears," the "Golden Girl" wrote many years later. *(Courtesy of Yang Hae-sook)*

Sixteen-year-old Park Hee-sook shouted the only English she knew, "Hello, hello," and was spared by American soldiers at No Gun Ri. Her parents, sister and baby niece all were killed. Returning to the tunnel several days later, she found a "scene from hell." She is pictured here at age thirty-eight, in 1972. *(Courtesy of Park Hee-sook)*

As a private first class, Art Hunter killed dozens of North Korean soldiers and earned a Silver Star. But other killings would haunt him all his life. Like many combat veterans, he found help in the Veterans Affairs program for post-traumatic stress disorder. *(Charles J. Hanley)*

Buddy Wenzel married Decar "De" Hodges, his dead buddy James's sister, in 1955. Nightmares and flashbacks to No Gun Ri and other events in the war left him, like many comrades, deeply troubled. "Some of the wives did stick with their husbands," Wenzel said. "My wife did." *(Charles J. Hanley)*

Chung Koo-hak in 2000. The "last survivor" of No Gun Ri, the eight-year-old boy with the mutilated face had been rescued by guilt-stricken older brother Koo-hun. *(AP WideWorld Photos)*

Park Sun-yong, at age seventy-two in 1998, wipes tears while recounting the death of Koo-pil, her four-year-old son, at No Gun Ri. *(AP WideWorld Photos)*

Chung Eun-yong at age seventy-seven in 2000. He made the search for the truth of No Gun Ri his lifelong quest. By taking on the U.S. government, friends told him, he was like a "praying mantis trying to stop an oxcart." *(AP WideWorld Photos)*

Chun Choon-ja at a memorial gathering at the No Gun Ri trestle in 1998. The ten-year-old's mother, grandfather, uncle, two aunts and baby brother were killed. "They had to do what they were ordered to do," she said of U.S. soldiers. "It's the government that must be blamed, and the high-ranking people and the kind of war they chose to fight." *(AP WideWorld Photos)*

It was unthinkable for Yang to separate from his mother. In that case, he told her, the entire family must stay. She finally relented, and the son once again placed his mother on his wooden pack frame, lifted her onto his back and, this time, took her down the hillside. Hae-sook, thirteen, carried her small brother on her back. Her mother balanced a bulging bundle atop her head. When this large group—with two aunts and an uncle, cousins, brothers—reached the Yangs' house in Im Ke Ri, they hesitated once more, unsure whether to proceed. Then soldiers appeared, shining flashlights into the huts, and forced the Yangs, at bayonet point, to get moving.

"American soldiers came into our rooms without even taking off their boots," remembered younger brother Hae-chan, then ten years old. "They poked their weapons into the blanket that we huddled under together." When the Yangs looked out beyond their gnarled old pear tree, they saw other villagers falling into line on the road. They joined them: grandmother, "Golden Girl," pregnant aunt and all.

Once the long, pitiful procession got under way—hundreds of people, parents loaded down with baggage and crying children, ox-carts piled high clanging in the darkness, some families with little more than the white cotton or hemp clothes on their backs—the American GIs grew impatient with their slow progress and began prodding them with rifle butts, cursing loudly, checking watches repeatedly. For some in the refugee column, more distressing still was what happened before they set off, when soldiers separated out at least twenty young men and took them away. What was planned for these sons and brothers?

As the Koreans moved down the narrow valley path toward Chu Gok Ri, they saw U.S. soldiers dug into the hillsides between the two villages and planting big antitank mines along the way—in the mistaken belief, some later surmised, that the rough valley track, a cul-de-sac, was a "through" road that could bring the North Koreans in from another direction.

Even before reaching Chu Gok Ri, the refugees could smell smoke. Then they saw the flames, their homes ablaze, and U.S. soldiers hurrying away, loading up their trucks. American commanders were adopting scorched-earth tactics to deny the advancing enemy any shelter or sustenance. The thatched roofs had made an easy job of it for GIs' cigarette lighters. The rock and tree of the Sonang, the village's guardian spirit, stood forlorn in the flickering shadows.

Such catastrophe had not befallen the families of Chu Gok Ri for many generations. In despair, and in fear of worse happening, they trudged on, each family slowed to the pace of its slowest member, parents calling children closer to their sides in the late-night gloom. The throng stretched out as it mounted the main road—the road they once took to market and to school, the road from Sunyong's wedding, the road that would take them now east to Hwanggan, and then on south. Along the way, groups from other villages would come and go among them.

The Yang family was one of the biggest, numbering at least fifteen. A pregnant cousin, Min Eun-soon, had joined them with her small child. The pregnant aunt, Yang Mal-soon, had her four children in tow and was herself laden with a bag of clothes. Her husband, Park Ne-eung, still carried the sack of barley on his back.

Suddenly, the sounds of war were upon them. They heard sporadic gunfire and blasts both far and near. Lives apparently were being lost somewhere in the darkness. Some recalled refugees being killed tripping over wires that set off explosions—American mines or booby traps. "I saw cows killed the same way," said Park Hwa-ja, one of Aunt Mal-soon's children. "This happened after we traveled out of Im Ke Ri and approached Ha Ga Ri."

As the slow caravan neared Ha Ga Ri, the village off the road a mile east of Chu Gok Ri, the refugees unknowingly passed just yards from a ditch where two dozen young men cowered in terror of the noises and flashes around them. These were the "suspects" rounded up hours earlier at Im Ke Ri. Without explanation from the Japanese interpreter, the Americans had marched these village youths up the main road, then ordered them over the parallel railroad tracks and into a ditch at the foot of a hill. They sensed something terrible was planned for them, and villager Kim Bok-jong appealed to the interpreter.

"What are you trying to do? There must be some misunderstanding," Kim told the Japanese. "We're not communists. We're innocent villagers. Some of us work for the government." Kim himself worked at a government agricultural center. "Please tell this to the American soldiers."

At first reluctant, the interpreter finally talked to the GIs. He then turned back to the Koreans and told them to lie face down in the ditch. "Don't look up. If you do, the soldiers will shoot you. Stay here until ten in the morning and then you may return home." After a terrifying night hunkered down in the hollow, the young men emerged to find the villages empty.

THE MAIN REFUGEE GROUP HAD PRESSED ON, UNDER GI ESCORT, AND around midnight they came abreast of Ha Ga Ri. Truck headlights illuminated the area, an apparent assembly point for the Americans. Suddenly soldiers were pushing the villagers off the road, down an embankment to a gravel streambed. Some old people and children tumbled down the steep slope, villagers recounted, and a bulldozer pulled up and tipped oxcarts off the road, to make way for American vehicles.

As American guards watched, the refugees bedded down beside the stream and tried to rest, but the din and lightning of war made it impossible. American howitzers positioned in a field close by boomed through the night, fireballs flashed overhead, and the road above vibrated with a steady stream of U.S. Army trucks headed away from Yongdong in clouds of dust.

The villagers tried to stay low, to stay silent. Park Hee-soon, sister of the pigtailed girl Park Hee-sook, was helpless to control her baby's wailing, and her father became furious, saying the noise would get them all killed. Finally the grandmother took the child from the unpracticed new mother, who had fled her Yongdong-area village when her husband was seized for army service.

A pale half-moon dropped behind the mountains before two in the morning. Gunshots and explosions—of grenades or mines or other devices of war unfamiliar to these peasants—cracked and thundered in the blackness. Suddenly their own neighbors were becoming targets. "People who strayed away from the group were shot and killed," said Chun Choon-ja, the little round-faced ten-year-old whose excitement had turned to terror. Two older villagers, Chung Jin-myong and Park Jong-dong, both around twenty at the time, said the victims were people who went off to relieve themselves. Unknown to them, the village families had been led by the Americans, at gunpoint, into the middle of an American retreat.

The official Army record showed that the two battalions of the 5th Cavalry Regiment that had arrived July 22 were still positioned at the Chu Gok Ri valley on the night of July 25, the night the villagers were rousted and evacuated. Sometime on July 25, a third unit, the 2nd Battalion of the sister 8th Cavalry Regiment, pulled back through Yongdong and eastward past Chu Gok Ri after being badly mauled by North Korean troops southwest of Yongdong. Stopping at Ha Ga Ri, where the refugees were, they were beaten, bitter Americans, having seen comrades killed in their first encounter with the Koreans. The North Koreans occupied Yongdong by 8 P.M. on July 25, taking defensive positions on its eastern edge, the official U.S. Army history reported. This was 3½ miles west of where the refugees spent the night at Ha Ga Ri.

Around 1:30 A.M. on Wednesday, July 26, as the moon disappeared, the 1st Cavalry Division ordered all units to pull back still farther from Yongdong, to align its front with the withdrawing 25th Division on its right. In the darkness, the Chu Gok Ri refugees were hearing the trucks of 5th and 8th Cavalry elements heading east.

Two miles east, the 2nd Battalion of the 7th Cavalry Regiment, in its first full day at the front, had fanned out over the hills to support and relieve the retreating sister regiments. But the 1:30 A.M. order to pull back produced what the Army historian called the "panic" in that 2nd Battalion. It was accompanied by exchanges of fire, possibly with other retreating Cav troops, although 7th Cavalrymen maintained they were attacked by North Koreans, miles from the reported enemy line.

The sun rose at 6:25 A.M., at the end of a frightening night for the villagers. They looked around and found their American guards gone. They could see Americans in the hills, but things were eerily quiet. Then they discovered that a half-dozen of their number had been killed in the night—whether by gunshot, grenades, exploding mines, they were not sure.

Shaken by what they had been through, desperate to get as far from the war as possible, the villagers slowly gathered up their things, climbed to the road and resumed their trek. Along this eastbound segment of the road to the south, they were flanked on their immediate left by the parallel railroad track and, beyond that, an abrupt wall of barren slopes rising to 1,000 feet or more. On their right, fingers of rice paddy land stretched in among hillsides and pine groves that gradually rose toward jagged peaks.

They stumbled upon more terrible, unexplained sights. Slipping and falling at one point, the seventeen-year-old Chung Koo-hun lifted himself up and saw a woman's hair spread through the dirt. Looking closely, he realized it was a body, her head crushed by a heavy vehicle, "like the flattened body of a rat run over by a tire." His cousin Chung Koo-hong recalled seeing three bloated, blackened bodies along the road that morning. Another villager, Lee Byong-hoi, saw a dead baby, with "dust settled on her face." They shuddered and pushed on.

As the morning lengthened, the midsummer heat grew intense. In their rice-straw sandals and baggy white garb, under towering loads, they walked on, stopping to readjust packs, haul weary children to their backs, slap faltering livestock. "It was terribly hot," said Park Hee-sook, the sixteen-year-old. "I always seemed to be lagging behind. I huffed and puffed to catch up." Some children sweltered under extra sets of clothes mothers had layered on their bodies. Koo-pil lost a shoe and his foot was soon bloody. His grandfather picked up the tearful four-year-old and carried him.

Two miles up the road, near a hamlet called Seo Song Won, they came to a U.S. Army vehicle—a truck or an armored vehicle—blocking the way. Soldiers waved the Koreans off the road and toward the empty railroad tracks. The Americans were rough with some of the slow-moving elderly, and again loaded oxcarts were toppled into roadside ditches, villagers said.

After climbing up on the railroad embankment, the refugees pushed ahead down the double-tracked right-of-way, only to be stopped again by American soldiers who searched their things, jabbing bags with their rifles and bayonets, and taking away chicken knives, scythes, saws and other sharp implements they found.

They were two Korean villages, perhaps six hundred people in white—weary, afraid, bewildered, and hot, irritable and hungry. At this rate it might take until dusk to cover the almost three miles to Hwanggan. Other refugees were backing up behind them, in a dense column stretching 200 or 300 yards back. Less than a mile ahead they could find the cool shadows of the railroad trestle near No Gun Ri, an inviting rest stop. Instead, detained again by the Americans, families began spreading out beside the tracks to find some wispy shade beneath the acacia trees and scoop out some crushed barley to cook for a midday meal.

There they rested for the long journey to come—the pigtailed Hee-sook and her nervous sister; the pretty schoolteacher Chung Koo-ok; the sprawling Yang family, with the loyal son and unhappy grandmother, with Hae-sook ever watchful over the boys; Choon-ja and the "success" baby, Tae-sung; the tall, idealistic student Koo-hun; and the heartsick Park Sun-yong, with her four-year-old and two-year-old and well-worn Bible, and with her faith that Eun-yong, who found her once and saved her, would find her again.

The sun was high. In the glare, through the haze of heat, the villagers could see American soldiers in the hills around them.

PART II

THE BRIDGE AT
NO GUN RI

5

July 26, 1950
No Gun Ri, South Korea

Cicadas filled the heavy air with their shrill insect drumming. Herons flapped lazily, long-necked, from paddy to abandoned paddy. Scattered clouds floated by. It was a good day for flying. "Visibility unrestricted," American fighter pilots reported at midday.

The villagers, war refugees barely three miles from their smoldering homes, exhausted and fearful, had set down where the steep slopes of White Horse Mountain, rising 1,750 feet on their left, came down to meet a gentle bend in the main-line railroad. Several hundred yards ahead, the empty tracks crossed over the small double-arched concrete trestle near No Gun Ri, and then stretched on to Hwanggan. That town lay beyond the 600-foot-high ridge to the villagers' right front.

Not far off, one hundred yards before the railroad bridge, a brook trickled down the slopes to run beneath the tracks via a five-foot-high culvert that cut crosswise through the railroad embankment. It was to this spot that little Chun Choon-ja hurried with a split gourd to fetch water for mixing with *misookaroo* for her family's meal. Her mother, staying behind, was breast-feeding baby Taesung. Nearby, the many Yangs also mixed mud-colored *misookaroo*. In all the turmoil of the night and morning, they had eaten neither dinner nor breakfast.

Heat rose in waves off the railbed. People tethered their cows to bramble bushes and squeezed in under the sparse shade of the six-foot-high acacias. On the hillsides here and there, green-uniformed Americans popped in and out of sight, sometimes raising binoculars to their eyes. Others were near the tracks, keeping a watch on the Koreans.

These were not the same GIs who had led them from their homes. One had a radio pack on his back and a second used the handset to talk to someone, villagers remembered. An Asian-looking soldier trailed them, Chung Koo-hun said, and the teenaged villager appealed to him. "I said in Japanese, 'Please help us.' He seemed to sympathize. He said, 'I'm sorry for you poor people,' and he went away, as if he couldn't do anything for us. I had a bad feeling about what was going on."

The Americans hurried off. A light plane was flying overhead, engine droning, circling low over the refugees. "They must be counting us," villagers told each other. "They're trying to decide how many trucks they need to take us south."

Hungry babies cried, and restless children shouted. Men opened their shirts to fan themselves with woven bamboo. Grandmothers, fretting, tried to rest. The cicadas hummed their eternal song.

FIFTY MILES TO THE SOUTHEAST, IN TAEGU, JOHNNIE WALKER'S Eighth Army staff had hastily established its headquarters in the gray wooden buildings of a local college campus. One roof sprouted tall antennas, and on this day an important message was radioed to General MacArthur in Tokyo, at his Far East Command offices overlooking the willows and swans of the Imperial Palace moat.

REFERENCE YOUR RADIO CITE 58460 DATED 23 JULY 50, General Walker's message began.

The evening before, July 25, staff officers at Eighth Army had met with South Korean officials and put together their outline of steps for dealing with refugees, to guard against possible enemy infiltrators and keep the roads free. At ten this morning, July 26, the sketchy plan—for "controlled movement"—had been radioed to the two front-line divisions, the 1st Cavalry and the 25th Infantry. Now the Eighth Army chief was updating his supreme commander in response to MacArthur's query about refugees three days earlier.

THE FOLLOWING ACTION HAS BEEN TAKEN BY THIS HQ TO CONTROL AND INTERROGATE ALL REFUGEES, the Walker message reported. NO MOVEMENT OF REFUGEES WILL BE PERMITTED THROUGH THE BATTLE LINES OF OUR FORWARD AREAS. Areas designated by American commanders will be evacuated, it said, and it went on briefly to list points of the plan.

Walker then concluded: REQUEST LEAFLETS BE PREPARED AND DROPPED BY YOUR HQ BY AIR OVER AREAS FORWARD AND REAR OF BATTLE LINES TO ASSIST IN THE TIMELY DISSEMINATION OF THIS INFORMATION. LEAFLET AIR DROPS TO BE ACCOMPLISHED UPON CALL OF THIS HQ.

The message was timed off by Eighth Army with military precision, at 1200—exactly noon.

SOME OF THE REFUGEES AROUND THE TRACKS RECALLED A LAST DIStinctive sound: soldiers blowing whistles.

In the next moment all such sounds were drowned out. A whine from over the horizon, from the direction of Hwanggan, grew instantly to a roar. Heads turned, looked up. From among the broken clouds American planes were dropping down toward them.

Ten-year-old Choon-ja was at the brook and culvert when she heard it and looked up, when the ground suddenly shook wildly and everything lifted into the air in an unearthly, deafening thunder, dirt and gravel from the railbed, bags and bushes and white clothing blasted upward, with people and parts of people. Again and again the earth rocked, and Choon-ja's ears "went numb," and suddenly midday was midnight amid dust, dirt and falling leaves, and planes again and again roared in, unleashing bombs or rockets, firing machine guns. "The ground was shaking and both my legs shook like walking on a small boat," Choon-ja said. "I couldn't see a thing, like walking in darkness."

From every direction, in every direction, people were running, panicked, helpless, not knowing what was happening, children with hands over their ears, adults dragging children by their arms. Some scratched into the ground trying to hide. Others lay bloody and silent, dismembered, strewn about. Still others lay sprawled crying pitifully for help. Cows screamed. The limbs of people and animals rained down. As he lay on the ground, teenager Chung Koo-shik felt something hot land on his back. It was the head of a baby.

"It looked like heaven crashed on us," Choon-ja said. "I threw away the water and ran to my mother. I found her moaning, breathing her last gasps. Part of her head was gone." Tae-sung, the "Great Success" of a poor peasant wife, lay at her breast. The horrified grandmother pulled the bawling baby away. "Small fireballs flew everywhere," Choon-ja said. "I heard the 'ping-ping' sounds of bullets flying past me. People fell around me. I ran this way and that, trying to run away from the explosions. I cried. I couldn't find my father. Suddenly there seemed to be no one I could recognize."

Villagers said "fireballs" from some kind of heavy weapon came from the hills, that soldiers on the ground had opened fire on them. The planes, two to four, flew off. But the killing went on. Families, every few feet, were being torn apart bit by bit, life by life.

Yang Hae-sook was saved by her mother, who somehow dragged the thirteen-year-old "Golden Girl" and two of her brothers, ten-year-old Hae-chan and six-year-old Hae-yong, under an acacia tree, where she covered them with her body and skirt. But their grandmother, the reluctant old woman who wanted only to cling to Im Ke Ri, had been blown to pieces. The pregnant cousin, with bullets in her legs, crawled over to Hae-sook's mother, terrified, crying, "Aunt! My son has his eyes open but he's not making a sound!" The baby was dead. His wide-open eyes stared out in frozen wonder, and the children gaped, dumbstruck. Nearby, Hae-sook's uncle, cowering behind his barley sack and trying to shield a daughter, suddenly cried out. Hae-sook recalled her shock: "He was flipping over in pain. I saw the intestines coming out of his belly. They were blue. He screamed three times and then he was silent." Struck by the same bullet, his thirteen-year-old girl lay under him, also dying.

Freeze frames of horror were burned forever into young survivors' minds. The seventeen-year-old student Chung Koo-hun, unscathed under a thick quilt, looked up through the smoke and saw people climbing a nearby hillside, only to be cut down by American soldiers' fire. One eight-year-old girl struggled out from beneath her mother to find a large hole in the woman's head and to see her father writhing, dying. Another survivor would never forget the sight of a dead man's legs pointing up toward the sky.

Park Hee-sook darted back and forth, the pigtailed sixteen-year-old first following one panicked group, then another, as gunfire rattled around them. Then she saw her sister, the nervous new mother, lying on the tracks. "Blood was spurting from a hole in her left breast, and her hips and legs were shaking and convulsing," Hee-sook said. "She said, 'Water, water.' I cannot forget her eyes, the way she looked at me. Did she know it was me? . . . I found a small pool of water in a ditch. I cupped the water with my hands and brought it to my sister. I fetched water one more time and when I tried to give it to her, she stopped breathing. She died just like that."

Craters now dented the embankment, its rails twisted grotesquely in the air. Wounded lay moaning, baggage burning beneath thick smoke that hung everywhere. A cow bellowed in agony, ablaze with the bags on its back. Ten-year-old Hae-chan saw such infernal sights, but sister Hae-sook no longer could. Her right eye was clotted shut with blood. Her left eye was gone.

An explosion beside them at the acacia tree had flung a "fireball" into the girl's face, a flash that struck her like a big stone. She recovered to find her eye blown out. Hae-chan saw it dangling below his sister's face, "bigger than a fist," hanging on gossamer threads. "My eye!" the girl screamed. "My eye!" She begged a neighbor woman to pluck it off, but the woman took fright and ran. Finally Hae-sook grasped it in her own fist. She yanked it, broke it off herself, and then the tall, conscientious thirteen-year-old, the "Golden Girl" who wanted dearly just to go to school, threw her eye away.

SOME GIS COULD SEE, SOME COULDN'T, FROM THE SCATTERED HILL-side positions of the 2nd Battalion, 7th Cavalry. For some it may have been almost a mile away, through the haze of heat. But others knew what was happening. Some were involved.

"They come down pretty low. You could see that star on that plane real easy—about three planes," said Eugene Hesselman, a corporal and Captain Chandler's clerk in H Company. "They dropped a bomb. That's where a lot of the people got hit with shrapnel. . . . A lot of them got killed."

After two nights at the warfront, shooting at phantoms and retreating from rumors, these untested infantrymen were now getting their first close look at an air strike. They didn't know what to make of it. Hesselman thought it was a mistake. He said Captain Chandler himself had asked for a strike, but against North Korean artillery far up toward Yongdong, not on the refugees. "They were kind of shortening up the zone and hit them. They hit us, too, some of our troops." But there was nothing that looked like artillery or tanks among the refugees, and other GIs saw no mistake. "I thought it was intentional," said Herman Patterson, a rifleman who watched from a hillside foxhole in F Company.

The attack fit the policy the Air Force was pursuing at the Army's request, to "strafe all civilian refugee parties that are noted approaching our positions," the practice that Col. Turner Rogers, in his secret memo to the generals on Tuesday, just a day earlier, warned would embarrass the United States before the world. It also fit the instructions to Navy pilots: Attack any group of more than eight people.

Hap Gay, the 1st Cavalry Division commander, evidently supported such strafings. At division headquarters this very day, Wednesday, July 26, the general praised the "wonderful" Air Force support he had gotten. "God has been good to us on the weather," he added, and when asked by reporters about "heavy refugee movements" spotted by air reconnaissance, the general, in his fifth day as a combat commander, replied that he was sure most of the white-clad people on the road were North Korean guerrillas.

Eighteen miles northwest of Gay's schoolhouse headquarters, in the blood and fire near No Gun Ri, Pfc. Delos Flint would have told the general otherwise. The F Company rifleman, one of the GIs caught in the strafing, remembered pushing into a low, narrow culvert with terrified refugee families, probably the one where Choon-ja fetched water. "It was like a hornet's nest in there. . . . It was civilians just trying to hide," Flint said. Then somebody started shooting in at them. "One of my buddies got hit. Shot off part of his privates. Hurt him bad. We was in there hours. Then we come out little by little."

ONE CIVILIAN TRYING TO HIDE IN THE CULVERT WAS A THIRTEEN-year-old with a special burden. In the blinding showers of gravel and shrapnel, Park Chang-rok, an Im Ke Ri boy, lost track of his parents. His little sister was still with him. He clapped the four-year-old to his back and ran straight for the small culvert, a place he knew from visits to his grandparents at No Gun village. He was the first to find it, then others piled in, covered with dirt and blood. Bursts of gunfire suddenly rattled through the tight, 200-foot-long passage. "The ricochets were ear-splitting," Chang-rok said. "Pieces of concrete hit my face."

Above, in the chaos around the tracks, Chun Choon-ja ran aimlessly, sobbing, her mother dead, her father missing. She heard a shout, "Choon-ja!" It was her grandfather, unharmed, his rice-straw mat harnessed neatly to his back. He grabbed her. They stumbled down the embankment to the culvert. "There were already a lot of people, maybe fifty people, when we got there," she said. "Some seemed to be dead already. As we hugged in there, I saw the flashes when bullets hit the concrete wall." The confined space shook from a blast, possibly a mortar round. They felt they had to get out, or die.

"My grandfather held my hand again," Choon-ja said. Rushing

back out into the harsh afternoon sun, the ten-year-old saw her white skirt soaked red with other people's blood. She saw a woman sprawled dead, an infant wailing next to her. She ran beside the embankment, along a ditch toward the big tunnels, the tall openings under the No Gun Ri trestle. Bullets flew on all sides. She somehow became separated from her grandfather. "I was crying and following whoever was in front of me."

Chang-rok ran with his little sister on his back. "I still remember big bullets kicking up dirt right in front of my eyes. People running in front of me were hit and fell," he said. "I tumbled and crawled over the dead people, and I don't know how I made it to the big tunnels." Choon-ja made it, too, and ran straight through one of the two towering underpasses to the other side. There she found her grandfather, face down in a small sandy flat, his rolled-up mat still tied to his back. The old man had tried to reach the road and was cut down by American gunfire coming from still another direction. The little girl sank deeper into shock: "The American soldiers played with our lives like boys playing with flies."

FOR MOST OF THESE TEENAGED AMERICAN INFANTRYMEN, ONLY days from the taxi dancers and neon streets of Tokyo, it was the first time they had fired their weapons in Korea. The barracks inspections, the manuals, the field training in Japan didn't prepare them for this kind of war, in this strange land, among strange people. The recruiting sergeants never told them. Hollywood war movies gave no hint. Buddy Wenzel, the dropout who found his "out" in the Army, had no idea what he might be asked to do someday.

"Word came through the line, open fire on them," Wenzel recalled. "They were running toward us and we opened fire." The Koreans seemed "confused," he said. "We understood that we were fighting for these people, but we had orders to fire on them and we did." The mind of this young man, the sad boy who raised two small sisters back in New Jersey, was then and there, at No Gun Ri, imprinted with its own freeze frame: of a little girl caught in the sights of his M-1. "I think I shot her."

A "little girl" claimed her place in others' memories, too. "She came running toward us. You should have seen guys trying to kill that little girl with machine guns," said James McClure, who was in a 2nd Battalion reconnaissance squad. "She was crying and she ran back into that mess, and I guess the mortars got her."

For Ralph Bernotas, what lodged in the mind was the distant sight of a "fountain" of white clothing, of refugees' bodies "splashing" into the air with the impact of shells. "Seeing that mortar fire coming in on that mass of people was very hard to take," said the altar boy from the coal country.

Not every man remembered the "fountain." Not every man remembered the little girl or small culvert. During these days dug in before Hwanggan, soldiers were in different foxholes over many hundreds of yards of twisting terrain, with different views, different jobs, different comings and goings. Some in the 660-man battalion may have seen little of the refugee killings. Some may have seen other refugees who approached U.S. lines at No Gun Ri before the Chu Gok Ri group, or the next day. Blank spots of memory, the disappearance of records, the reluctance of many veterans to discuss those days—all contributed to gaps and inconsistencies from the American perspective. In the end, however, the soldiers' memories from July 1950 at No Gun Ri fit neatly with those of the Korean survivors into a mosaic of wholesale death whose backdrop, whose official design, none forgot. As Bernotas explained, "Our orders were not to let any refugees through any line at all."

SCORES OF SURVIVORS SCATTERED SAFELY AWAY INTO THE HILLS OR fields after the air strike. Chung Koo-hun, the tall student lying low, was one of the last to leave the tracks. He ran back in the direction of Yongdong and ducked into another small culvert to hide. But American soldiers flushed him out and sent him back toward the trestle.

Smoke drifted over the deathly landscape. Soldiers converged on the scene, villagers recalled, checking bodies with a nudge of their boots, gathering people on the tracks, on the adjacent hillside, in the small field between the tracks and road, and herding them toward the trestle. Parents carried children. People supported wounded relatives who could walk. Sobbing, or in silent shock, they slowly shuffled toward the cavernous tunnels under the bridge. "On the way I saw baggage and dying cows and human bodies scattered about," Koo-hun said. "I saw limbs torn apart. I even saw heads separated from bodies. It was dark because of the smoke and dirt cloud and debris. I stumbled on bodies. I could only see a bit of clear sky to the south. Then I heard gunshots again, and I hurried into the big tunnels."

The teenaged villager had seen something more as well, before the GIs caught up with him. When he first ran from the scene, he said, he heard shots, looked back, and saw what appeared to be soldiers shooting point-blank at wounded who could not move to the tunnels.

The girl Chun Choon-ja was at one point part of a group rounded up by GIs. "The soldiers had us kneel down with our hands on the back of our heads and look at the ground," she said. "When a few people raised their heads and pleaded for help, they threatened to hit them with the butts of their rifles and threatened to shoot."

The Yangs lay bloodied, the mother crippled with leg wounds, daughter Hae-sook virtually blind. The father had disappeared. Ten-year-old Hae-chan watched as soldiers approached the family with bayonets fixed to their M-1s. "They touched us with the tips of their bayonets and motioned to us to get up and move," he remembered. "Go! Go!" their mother told the children. "Hurry!" But they cried and refused to leave her, and finally the four of them, with their wounded six-year-old brother hobbling along, began to move.

"Mother used a stick with one hand and Hae-chan held Mother's other hand. He also held my hand," Hae-sook said. "We began moving. Mother couldn't stand up, so she dragged herself on the ground. We moved over the tracks and bodies that way. I kept tripping over bodies because I couldn't see well. Before we moved out of the shrubs, I opened the other eye with my hand. Then I saw the baby with his eyes wide open. My mother said, 'Leave him there. He's already dead.' "

They moved so slowly that the boy Hae-chan, terrified, thought the soldiers behind them would shoot. He all but dragged his mother and sister, past the burning bushes, past the broken bodies of neighbors, past the violet wildflowers. Finally, painfully, they crept into one of the trestle tunnels, and descended into hell.

The vaulted ceilings of the two concrete underpasses were forty feet high. Each underpass was twenty-two feet across and eighty feet long. The shallow stream ran mostly through the tunnel on the eastern, Hwanggan side, with a bit trickling through the other. The dry streambed in that western underpass served as a path from the main road to No Gun Ri, whose huts sat three hundred yards away. The western tunnel held most of the people, both dead and alive. Some Koreans at the trestle had already been shot, especially by soldiers dug in on a low rise about two hundred yards away, across the main road.

When she entered the tunnel, after leaving her dead sister on the tracks, Park Hee-sook remembered seeing babies crawling around dead or unconscious mothers. "It was already a living hell there." Park Sun-yong staggered into the underpass with her Bible and two small children. She had survived with a shrapnel wound in her right arm. The children, Koo-pil and Koo-hee, and her husband Eun-yong's parents had survived, too. But Sun-yong could see the horror had not ended. "The entrance to the tunnel was so thick with bodies strewn everywhere, I could hardly walk without stepping on them."

Inside, it was bedlam. Frantic villagers cried out children's names. Boys and girls screamed for their mothers and fathers. Family groups crawled to the safest spots, away from the road, shoving and pushing for space on the jam-packed sandy floor. Choon-ja's grandmother finally glanced out toward the road and saw a man's body with a straw mat on its back. "There's my husband!" she wailed, but she dared not go to him.

Gunfire rang through the tunnel sporadically through the afternoon, villagers said. "I couldn't get my senses back. You couldn't even raise your head," Sun-yong said. "It looked like the Americans were shooting at us out of boredom," said Koo-hun. Some refugees were shot trying to climb back up the embankment to fetch food from abandoned bags. Some were shot when, desperately thirsty, they ventured outside for stream water.

Across the road, in an American foxhole up the low slope, a

young Korean looked on helplessly. Big brother Park Chang-rok, with his four-year-old sister clinging to him, was there with a machine gun team that opened fire repeatedly on people around the railroad. "I pleaded with them not to shoot," he said. "I rubbed my hands together, and I jumped up and down. I told them my parents were not bad people. But, of course, they didn't seem to understand me."

Chang-rok had been saved by the soldiers. After running from the small culvert, the thirteen-year-old scooped out a hole in the sand near the trestle, put his sister in it and lay on top. "My parents used to tell me I should always take care of my little sister," he said. Two GIs passed by, rifles at the ready, and poked him with the barrels. The boy got up, hands together, begging for their lives. "I thought both of us were dead because I saw people killed by GIs," Chang-rok said. But the sight of two children stacked in a hole seemed to surprise the soldiers. Instead of shooting, they gestured for the boy to go with them. "I threw my little sister on my back and followed them to the small hill across the road, facing the tunnels," and to safety.

Such acts occurred here and there amid the bloodletting. U.S. Army medics came to the trestle at one point on Wednesday, the day the shootings started, to treat and bandage wounded, villagers said.

Another small group or two of soldiers also appeared outside the underpasses that afternoon, the Koreans said. The besieged refugees stirred and a few went out to beg for the villagers' lives. Urged by elders who stayed behind, university student Koo-il took the lead the first time. Koo-hun, the tall seventeen-year-old, stood back and watched. "According to my cousin Koo-il, who spoke a little English, the soldiers told him that they were shooting at us under orders," Koo-hun said. When he returned to the tunnel, villagers remembered, Koo-il told them, "We are now all dead." His sister, schoolteacher Koo-ok, later went out and she "held the soldier's arm and begged, but they pushed her aside and went away," after first taking a good look into the tunnel, Koo-hun said. Villager Suh Jong-ja, then nineteen, also remembered a Japanese-speaking soldier telling one old woman they were firing under orders.

Inside, it was suffocatingly hot. The refugees' thirst was overwhelming, particularly for the wounded. The villagers lay, more than three hundred of them by their own estimate, huddled in groups, some dead, many alive, some dying. They tried to keep quiet amid the drone of flies.

With all the bursts of fire, survivors' memories did not agree on when the first big barrage began—around dusk that day, later that night, early the next morning. But they remembered seeing sparks on the hillsides—fusillades from .30-caliber machine guns and M-1 rifles—and then a rain of death.

Hae-sook, unseeing, heard the bullets flying "like bees around me" and heard them striking her neighbors "like beans in a frying pan." Hundreds of deadly rounds rang echoing, ricocheting off the concrete walls. Tracers, the fiery bullets machine gunners use for aiming, spun overhead or slammed red-hot into bodies. Gunfire came from both ends of the underpasses, villagers said. When it started on one side, the terrified refugees rushed toward the other. When it came from there, they crawled back over bodies again. Each time, fewer and fewer moved.

Heavy shelling also shook the tunnels, the villagers said, and possibly a new attack by warplanes—"terrible explosions, day and night," Sun-yong said. When the mortar or artillery rounds hit, said Koo-hun, "I thought the tunnels would collapse on us." People closer to the entrances were blown apart. One girl, hiding under a blanket, was struck by something heavy and sat up. It was a dismembered leg.

Survivors clung close to the inner wall. They clawed into the sandy floor and began to build barricades of bodies. One woman placed traditional offerings of rice and water before her on the tunnel floor and prayed for mercy. Dreadful sounds and mad scenes played out across the blood-soaked sand. Deep into the night, with so many dead or wounded, survivors could hear one wounded villager calling his daughter's name over and over, "Jong-boon. Jong-boon." As he bled to death, with his last breath, he still called the girl. Jong-boon had escaped during the bombing.

Survivors grew terrified that any sound or movement would draw more fire. When the motherless baby Tae-sung, still in his grand-mother's arms, would not stop crying, others hissed hysterically, threateningly at Choon-ja's family. The half-crazed father grabbed his "Great Success" from the old woman, tried to leave the tunnel, but retreated when gunfire rang out. Witnesses said he then went to the other underpass and dropped the howling infant, the son he always wanted, face down into the stream. The baby jerked a few times, then lay still.

In a trench far across the road, the stranded thirteen-year-old Park Chang-rok sat in wonder at what he was seeing and hearing around him, and at the men behind the guns, big men, Americans who seemed like normal people. "They didn't appear to be people who would kill fellow human beings."

IT WAS REPORTED IN THE AMERICAN PRESS ON THIS JULY 26 THAT U.S. Army Reserve medical officers were not volunteering for Korean duty in the numbers needed. The war was not stirring doc-tors' patriotism. A *New York Times* article noted a special problem emerging among the young soldiers in Korea: "Reports from the fighting area advised medical officers that cases of psychoneurosis were expected to run higher than, as a spokesman put it, 'in other operations.' " For all July, more psychiatric casualties would be evacuated than seriously wounded men.

On the front line at No Gun Ri, men remembered fellow soldiers recoiling in their foxholes, revolted, from what they were seeing or doing. The shock wasn't limited to the enlisted ranks. At the 2nd Battalion command post, close behind the line positions, battalion commander Herb Heyer seemed shaken when the order was passed down to fire on a refugee group, one of his communications cor-porals remembered. "I was within ten yards and I could tell by his face that there was nothing that he liked about it," said James Crume. "It was an emotional thing, I'm sure. He would just lie back—sit back—there on the side of the hill and shake his head."

Crume remembered a refugee group in the open being hit by

battalion mortar rounds, but radioman Larry Levine, a staff sergeant at Heyer's command post, remembered an hours-long "standoff" with refugees at the trestle, after which an order came down around dusk—from the 1st Cavalry Division or higher, Levine believed—to eliminate them. First mortars were fired, he said, and then "a feeding frenzy took place, once it started. . . . Guys were shooting because they hadn't shot before, and they had permission to shoot. . . . It's like, 'Hey, shoot at anything that moves out there.' "

Down among the machine gunners and mortarmen of H Company, Mel Chandler, the congenial captain who had never seen combat, had gotten on the radio to battalion to ask what to do, his clerk Gene Hesselman said. Then, "I remember Chandler saying we got to get rid of all of them. He couldn't on his own. Evidently the division give it to him because he said, 'Let them have it.' "

Rifleman Joe Jackman, in G Company, remembered refugees coming under fire in the open—"running around like bees were after them"—possibly after the initial strafing. It came down the line, he said: "Open fire!" He also recalled the sound of the refugees. "Christ Almighty, they were just screaming. Who wouldn't scream? The fear—I thought, 'Jesus Christ, what the hell are we into?' "

"We was holding that railroad bridge to keep them from coming across that," remembered Melvin Durham of F Company. "But those people—there was women, children, old people—we had to eliminate them. . . . Our orders was to start opening fire and when we did, there wasn't nothing standing but a couple of cows. We fired for about an hour, an hour and a half."

Fox Company's Delos Flint, having escaped from the culvert, wanted no part of killing civilians. "I wouldn't fire at anybody in the tunnel like that. . . . It was unnecessary to kill them. . . . A lot of guys, the orders just went in one ear and out the other." Others also remembered men refusing to fire. But many GIs—confused, angry, hearing rumors on their second full day at war—did not hesitate. "If you let refugees through, you get shot in the back," said Norm Tinkler, the nineteen-year-old machine gunner. "We was just kids, and I was scared. . . . I ricocheted them in there. I knew how to shoot. Oh, I could see about that much of the wall that was going through the tunnel, and I put it on that." But Tinkler was torn, too. He said he prayed, "Please God, if I make it home alive, don't let me have sons, because I couldn't bear for a son of mine to go through this."

From a distance, Cpl. Tom Hacha of the 7th Cavalry's newly arrived 1st Battalion saw tracers bouncing through the underpass, fired by one of the 500-rounds-a-minute machine guns. "To me it was like one of these mistakes where, 'Jesus, stop it, turn it off.' It was like somebody was firing out of fear, just shooting. I knew that people were being killed there. The refugees, they tried to get out but they couldn't. It was a terrible shock."

Mortarmen, machine gunners and riflemen blasted away from their ragged holes on the dusty, barren hillsides, in the 7th Cavalry's first big encounter with the "gooks" in Korea. "We just annihilated them," Tinkler said. "It was about like an Indian raid, back in the old days."

The burly Pfc. Delos Flint, who had been trapped with the "people in white," was half Cherokee Indian. He felt differently. "If you ever saw them," he said, "they were wonderful people."

LONG AFTER THE SUN SET BLOODY RED, AS THE MOONLIGHT FLED the darkening tunnel that night, Kim Ke-soon came to Chung Koo-hun. The teenaged village girl whose eyes had met his in Chu Gok Ri's pathways was not supposed to talk to young men, let alone come so close. "Ke-soon came to me and hugged me," Koo-hun remembered. "It was something unimaginable."

In this place of mangled flesh and suffering, she was on a mission of hope. "She told me that I should try to get out because I was a man," he said. "She said we were going to die whether we stayed or tried to get out. She said men should try to get out and tell people what happened." Other women were telling their husbands and sons the same. In their clumsy *hanbok* skirts, with children, the women would never get far, but stealthier young men might—and possibly find help.

About ten younger men stripped off their white clothes and smeared their bodies with camouflaging mud. One father gave his son the family deed and family lineage book. One son refused to leave his father. The men crawled out the opening on the No Gun Ri side, away from the main road. Later, as the night deepened, other men, and some women, slipped away. Not all survived.

Koo-hun left behind the sick eight-year-old brother, Koo-hak, he had carried on his back. "I thought I was a coward to leave my brother and family in there," he said. "But I hoped for the best." Fear and cowardice, duty and devotion, self-preservation and guilt— ultimate emotions tore at the hearts of the villagers. One young man, Chun Choon-ja's newlywed uncle, chose to remain with his bride. When it was over, they found him sitting with her in the underpass, hugging her protectively. Both were dead.

In a momentary lull before the young men escaped, after the horrifying first barrage, the surviving refugees suddenly heard a woman moaning, panting in pain, then shrieking. Villager Cho Nam-il's wife was in labor on a blanket on the tunnel floor, with her mother-in-law as a midwife. Finally, with a long sustained cry, she delivered a boy. Then the gunfire erupted again, and the woman's father-in-law was wounded in the shoulder. Moving toward him, the mother-in-law was struck and killed instantly by a bullet. The fallen old man begged to be taken home to die. His son, the new father, lifted him onto his back and summoned his wife. She cried out that she had been wounded in the wrist and couldn't take the baby. The young man hesitated, then finally told her to leave the child. The three slipped out into the night. The baby whimpered and struggled on the floor, but eventually grew quiet and still.

A second woman also gave birth under the trestle, the wife of thirteen-year-old Chang-rok's cousin Park Chang-ha. The father was shot dead as he tried to climb to the tracks to find food for his wife. The mother, Han Soon-suk, and her newborn were killed soon after. Other women also would be found dead with their babies under the trestle. Some infants were lifeless; a few clung to their mothers' breasts and to life.

"IN GENERAL THERE WAS LITTLE ACTION ALONG THE ENTIRE FRONT," Eighth Army headquarters reported this day from Taegu. But Gen.

Johnnie Walker, privately, was deeply worried, especially by the poor performance of the 1st Cavalry Division. He personally called Tokyo to seek permission to withdraw his headquarters even farther back, to the southern port of Pusan.

To bolster the faltering Army, the U.S. Air Force's young F-80 jet pilots were "scorching the earth," unleashing tons of bombs and streams of lead over South Korea during the day and returning to their bases in Japan to spend the night with their families. As the terror was unfolding hourly at the No Gun Ri tunnels, wave after wave of fighter-bombers attacked Yongdong, seven miles to the west, the town where the North Koreans had stopped, and where Chu Gok Ri villagers had sold their rice and firewood, where the Chungs had their dried-fish shops, where Chung Koo-hun and others went to school, where farmers' children might find musicians and clowns, where the Salvation Army ran a hospital.

An Associated Press reporter, flying overhead, reported that Yongdong "no longer exists as a city. It looks like Nagasaki after the atom bomb. . . . Yongdong has probably been here for 4,000 years—and never known such silence." The fires raged into the night. In Yongdong's streets and burning homes lay bodies of South Koreans who had not tried to flee south.

IN THE FIRST GRAY LIGHT NEXT MORNING, THOSE LOOKING ACROSS the tunnel floor were both blessed and damned. They were alive while most were dead. But they might be next.

The half-blinded Yang Hae-sook and her younger brother Hae-chan helped their wounded mother move deeper inside the tunnel, up against the wall. The ten-year-old boy, son of a loyal son, some-how dragged and shifted body after body to build a wall around his mother. The children's aunt, Yang Mal-soon, very large in the eighth month of pregnancy, had barely survived the first night with severe wounds. In her dying agony, she asked her nine-year-old girl to strangle her with her cloth belt. In the end she simply faded. The daughter, Hwa-ja, was carrying her four-year-old sister that second day when "I heard bullets whistling by my ears, and then half of her head was gone." She laid the little girl down. The Yang family was being destroyed, one by one.

Heavy nighttime fusillades of machine-gun fire gave way in daylight to potshots and flurries of bullets that kept the survivors pinned down. Anyone who moved risked drawing fire. The heat and the stench among the swelling, putrefying bodies and puddles of blood were overwhelming. Hunger ravished the survivors. But thirst, more than anything, moved them. The water trickling through the western tunnel had pooled behind the mounds of dead and grown viscous with blood. When Hae-chan tried to bring water to his mother, "I found the surface thick with blood. When I pushed it aside, it cracked like a mud cake."

The pigtailed Park Hee-sook had watched that first afternoon as her father and then her mother were killed. She heard her dead sister's baby daughter crying, somewhere. "I am sure she died of starvation." The sixteen-year-old clawed away at bodies, pulling aside arms and legs to hide herself beneath the dead. "I could hear blood flowing down, the sound of blood gurgling out of the bodies," she remembered. Her throat was burning; she gulped down what she found on the floor. "I drank like a mad person. . . . The horrible thing was that blood kept flowing down from the bodies above me. So I couldn't really tell whether I drank blood or water."

After some hours, when it grew quiet, Hee-sook finally wriggled her way free, and walked unsteadily to the tunnel entrance. "I could see a lot of soldiers on the hills," she said. "I said, 'Hello, hello.' That was the only English word I knew. I said more loudly, 'Hello, hello.' I cried and began explaining that both my father and mother were dead. I didn't care whether they understood me. Then I said, 'Hello, hello' again."

An American looked at her through binoculars. He beckoned her to the hill. "Soldiers climbed out of their foxholes and looked at me." She was coated in blood, from long pigtail on down. She screamed and cried that they had killed her parents, and pounded on them with her fists. "They couldn't understand, but they knew where I came from. They just looked at me, at what they had done."

Hee-sook was saved, as were some others. In the deadly chaos of the first afternoon, Chun Choon-ja, the motherless ten-year-old, was swept up in a wandering group of about ten refugees that, for some reason, was summoned by soldiers instead of shot. They filed across a low earthen dike between rice paddies and reached the hillside foxholes. "They gave us something to eat, maybe chocolate, but I didn't eat it. I just cried. My mind and my eyes kept turning back to my grandfather," Choon-ja said.

The merciless shooting went on, too, and on the second day American warplanes returned to No Gun Ri, survivors said. They remembered the pilots dropping bombs or firing rockets at the trestle, and making repeated machine-gun strafing runs—"as if the planes flew through the tunnel," one said.

In the deafening noise and the clatter of splintered concrete, in the dusky shadows of the concrete arches, young mother Sun-yong lay weak from hunger and crushed with grief. Just a month earlier, she and Eun-yong had risked a perilous ride on this very railroad to get their two children to the safety of Yongdong County. Now her husband was lost somewhere in this war, and she had only one child left to protect, because Koo-hee, the two-year-old, was dead.

Koo-hee had begun wailing hungrily, her face red, on the first afternoon. Her grandmother picked the child up and, confused, distraught, walked outside. "I don't know why she went out," Sun-yong said. "Everyone who stepped out was killed." Gunfire rattled. A bullet pierced little Koo-hee's neck, killing her. The grandmother dropped the baby and struggled back inside, wounded in the shoulder and buttocks.

That night, Sun-yong's father-in-law and her husband's two younger brothers slipped out of the tunnel. The grandfather said he believed the Americans might cease firing if they saw only women and children. Sun-yong tried to flee, too, with four-year-old Koo-pil and the Chung family's houseboy. They didn't get far. Bodies blocked their hillside path and they rushed back inside, shaken.

Her boy's hungry cries grew more insistent. Lives were bleeding away around her, and her circle of family was dwindling. Her sister-in-law, Min Young-ok, wife of Eun-yong's brother the prison guard, at some point died in a pool of blood, with her baby boy beside her fatally wounded. "I began praying," Sun-yong said. "I became determined to save my remaining child." She decided to try to escape again the second night, to rejoin Eun-yong, wherever he was.

They moved slowly away from the tunnel. The fifteen-year-old house servant, Kim Hong-ki, carried Koo-pil on his back. "Aunt Park seemed hardly able to walk," Hong-ki recalled. It took them hours to move a few hundred yards in the direction of Hwanggan, hiding from gunfire, searchlights and flares. Then, when they were climbing a hill, gunfire rang out again. She heard Koo-pil cry, *"Eum-ma!"*—"Mama!" He was standing, his legs ripped by bullets, and Hong-ki was running back down the hill. She tore cloth from her skirt and bound the boy's legs, and then prayed. Koo-pil kept asking for his father.

As a faint first light came from the east, she began carrying him up the hill again. "I didn't walk far when I saw an American soldier," she said. "The soldier was carrying his rifle." Desperately, in Korean, she begged him not to shoot, said they weren't bad people, they weren't communists. "But he fired at us. It was like some big hammer slamming my body. I fell back and all consciousness seemed to flow out of me. . . . I thought this was the end of my life. Then I heard Koo-pil saying, or maybe I imagined I heard him, *'Eum-ma, Eum-ma.'* I lifted myself a little bit and looked back. Blood was spreading from the small body of my child."

He had been hit in the chest. "I saw the thin hair trembling in the breeze on Koo-pil's forehead," she recalled. "I lay still, my mind blank. Two soldiers came over, a fat one and a tall one. They looked down at us and talked to each other. Later more soldiers came and they wrapped my son in a white bag." She heard shoveling. "They took me to an ambulance. That day I saw the two faces of America. I just don't know what got into their heads to kill my boy like that. I just don't know. The Americans must have gone crazy."

Sun-yong carried something else with her from the tunnels, her Bible, and she would always believe the soldiers saw it and decided to spare this blood-spattered woman, lying there with her dead boy, muttering the Lord's Prayer in Korean. The young mother, finally delivered from evil, had been asking her Lord to take her, too.

"TO THE PATRIARCHS, PRIMATES, ARCHBISHOPS . . ." ON THE DAY the killing began, Pope Pius XII, by happenstance of fate, summoned a kind of vision of No Gun Ri. "Let us all remember what war brings, which, alas, we know from experience; nothing but ruin, death and every kind of misery," the pope declared in "Supreme Grief," an antiwar encyclical issued July 26 in far-off Rome. "Such murderous and inhuman weapons have been introduced and developed as can destroy not only armies and fleets . . . but also innocent children with their mothers, those who are sick and the helpless aged." The "rulers of peoples," the pope wrote in his severe Latin, bore a special responsibility to dispel the dark clouds of war.

In Washington on the day the killings began, the rulers were focusing not on war, but on dollars and cents. Truman's economic advisers reported "the highest levels of peacetime prosperity ever achieved." But the president cautioned that the new war "will be costly." Americans should be prepared to pay higher taxes, he said.

In the Far East, the chief prosecutor of the war, Gen. Douglas MacArthur, flew to Korea from Tokyo on that second day, July 27. Alarmed by General Walker's plan to retreat further, he went to Taegu to tell his Eighth Army chief that his unsteady divisions must stand. Then, to the press, MacArthur praised the front-line commanders for "superior efficiency" and the Air Force for having "done everything possible for them to do." Turning to South Korean officials, the American supreme commander grandly assured them, "We are going to take care of your country."

Closer to the front that day, the 25th Infantry Division's Gen. William Kean—also in his first combat command, like the 1st Cavalry Division's Hap Gay—declared South Korea's "people in white" a target for his troops. Three days earlier, the instructions had gone out in Gay's neighboring division to "fire everyone" trying to cross U.S. lines. Now Kean issued an order to all his units, accompanied by a map, saying that civilians were to have been evacuated from an extensive area—the entire war zone—and therefore "all civilians seen in this area are to be considered as enemy and action taken accordingly." Logs showed his staff relayed this as "considered as unfriendly and shot."

Kean, like General Gay, feared that North Koreans were using refugee columns on the roads to infiltrate behind his lines. On this same day, however, in a repeat of what happened at Yongdong, North Korean troops simply poured over the countryside into a large gap between the two American divisions and attacked the 25th's left flank, somewhere off to the right of the 7th Cavalry at No Gun Ri.

The 7th Cavalry's other battalion, the 1st, had moved into the line next to the 2nd Battalion by Wednesday evening, July 26. Now, on July 27, the two battalions were receiving sporadic long-distance artillery and mortar fire from the North Koreans, but the regiment generally reported "all quiet on both battalion fronts."

BY FRIDAY, JULY 28, THEIR THIRD DAY IN HELL, THE SURVIVORS were mostly children, burrowed under dead parents, grandparents, brothers and sisters, or under someone else's family, starving, parched, lapping up whatever liquid they sensed around them, in a waking nightmare but alive—because of guardians living and dead.

In a furious barrage the second night, a thirteen-year-old boy named Chung Koo-ho and his sister were pressed protectively against the tunnel wall by his mother. Shrapnel gouged his left arm and leg. Then he heard his mother moaning. In the darkness, he found she was wounded many times. By morning, she was gone, facedown in the sand. But through the night this peasant woman did the only thing left to a dying mother. "She was a devout Buddhist," Koo-ho said. "She kept muttering to Buddha. In her dying breath, she was praying for a good life in the next world for herself and her two children."

An eight-year-old Chu Gok village girl, Kim Sung-ja, lost consciousness amid the bullets and shrapnel. "I don't know how much time had passed. When I tried to get up, I could hardly move. I was underneath my mother's body. When I struggled, other survivors pulled me out. My mother was holding me, and that apparently saved me."

A shard of sound told little Sung-ja she was alive. "I woke up hearing the water flowing and the birds chirping outside." After two dry days, it rained on Friday in Korea.

AFTERWARD, SOME SOLDIERS BELIEVED THEY HAD BEEN FIRED ON from beneath the trestle. "Every now and then you'd hear a shot, like a rifle shot," Cpl. Gene Hesselman said. "I just heard people talk about it," said George D. Preece, a sergeant in Captain Chandler's H Company. "Whether that's right or not, that's what I heard."

But any such shots, veterans acknowledged, may have been ricochets of American bullets fired from the tunnels' other side. Some GIs never heard gunfire from the underpasses and never heard about it. "No, no one ever said anything about them firing out on the troops," said G Company's James Elkins. "To say they was firing out, I don't know," said F Company's Melvin Durham. "We was laying down such a barrage out there no one could tell."

There were no guns among the refugees, the Korean survivors insisted. The record supports them: The regiment's war diary included no such report, even though any weapons captured or enemy killed would have been the first for the newly arrived 7th Cavalry. In fact, the official diary mentioned nothing at all about the events at No Gun Ri, unless they were disguised in a line on July 26 about 2nd Battalion operations—"Mortar fire and patrols eliminated the threat of guerrilla activities from nearby villages"—or in another line on July 28, when the 1st Battalion reported that the enemy was "forcing mobs of civilians ahead of their troops into the line of fire." Those entries, in a diary compiled after the events, were not further explained. Concluded one who was at No Gun Ri, career soldier George Preece, "It must have been covered up." The regimental journal would have included minute-to-minute messages to and from No Gun Ri. But that communications log was the one that disappeared at some point.

During this three-day period, the North Korean enemy moved cautiously toward the 7th Cavalry line. Army intelligence reported the enemy front line was four miles up the road from No Gun Ri at midnight, July 26, according to declassified documents. By the third night of the trestle shootings, July 28, the North Koreans had only moved forward to within 2½ miles of No Gun Ri and the Americans, the intelligence reports said. North Korean documents captured later confirmed this slow movement, putting the advancing troops on the road two miles from No Gun Ri the night of July 28.

On the morning of Friday, July 28, 1st Cavalry Division headquarters showed impatience with the 7th Cavalry's performance. The division chief of staff called regimental commander Col. Cecil Nist and ordered him to "get patrols out to your front and flank and contact the enemy and maintain this contact." That night, however, the 7th Cavalry sent a written message back to headquarters: "No important contact has been reported by our 2nd Battalion."

CHUNG KOO-HAK, THE EIGHT-YEAR-OLD NO LONGER PROTECTED BY big brother Koo-hun, floated in and out of consciousness. To the end, his cousin Koo-ok, the teacher, watched over the spindly, sickly boy. At one point, she put him on her back and headed out of the tunnel to try to escape, but was driven back by gunfire. For her, the end was not far off.

"My cousin and my mother and I sat together facing each other and put a blanket over us and huddled," Koo-hak said. "I don't remember how much time passed, but I suddenly felt something like hot water flowing down my face and then I lost consciousness."

Later, Koo-hak said, "I remember seeing a village woman I could recognize sitting on the other side, leaning her back against the concrete wall. She seemed to have lost her mind. She didn't move at all and her eyes were fixed on something far away. When she slowly adjusted her eyes to me, she said something about my face, something like, 'Poor child, what happened to your face!' . . . When I struggled and managed to get up, I felt dizzy. I felt like I was a giant eight feet tall. The world seemed to swirl around me. I had to sit down. I crawled to the water but when I tried to drink water, it fell through my face and I could hardly drink at all."

ON SATURDAY, JULY 29, HARRY TRUMAN FINALLY GOT AWAY TO THE USS *Williamsburg,* the presidential yacht that had waited for him for many days, all polished teak and brass, at a Potomac River dock. The president boarded the sleek 244-footer for a bachelor weekend of river cruising, report reading and the usual poker games. Beforehand, Truman got his daily briefing on the war from Gen. Omar Bradley, the Joint Chiefs chairman. Nothing would surface later in the surviving record indicating the president was ever informed that the U.S. military, under orders, had begun attacking South Korean civilian refugees.

The hardworking Truman needed a rest. He'd hardly had a break since his fateful decision before dawn 29 days earlier to intervene with American troops in a war in far-off Korea. But his nemesis was not resting this weekend. Back home in Wisconsin, in a speech to 4,500 hunters and fishermen at a lakeside picnic, Sen. Joseph McCarthy delivered a slashing attack on Secretary of State Dean Acheson once again for helping "mastermind disaster for America and victory for communism in the East."

The Truman administration must mobilize the world for an armed crusade, the Republican demanded, and he asked, "Why must the State Department insist that only the lives of American boys be used? Why cannot other peoples of the earth be used also to help create the necessary seawall of blood and flesh and steel to hold back the communist hordes?"

HEAPS OF DEAD NOW BLOCKED THE ENTRANCES TO THE NO GUN RI underpasses. Bodies spread out on the sandy tunnel floor. Others were strewn on the flats outside, on the path up to the rail embankment, on the tracks—swelling in the sun, food for insects, carrion for birds. Under the trestle, the energetic buzz of flies replaced the sound of cicadas on the hills.

The human wreckage of two villages lay there: Hae-sook's and Hae-chan's big brother and little brother, their pregnant aunt, their stubborn grandmother, Choon-ja's mother and fallen grandfather, the baby "Great Success," Hee-sook's sister and parents and baby niece, Koo-hee and Koo-pil, his father's pride, the baby Cho, born and died in the tunnel, the teacher Koo-ok who begged for everyone's life, the girl Ke-soon who met Koo-hun's eyes. All lay there, and many more.

Precise numbers would never be determined, but decades later survivors compiled a list of the names of some 200 dead or missing. They estimated that actually up to 400 were killed—100 in the strafing and 300 under and around the trestle. Possibly 200 escaped during the initial chaos or from the tunnels, they believed. On this Saturday, July 29, 1950, perhaps two dozen remained alive, silent, some unconscious, under those walls of blood and flesh.

THE RECORD SHOWS THE 7TH CAVALRY PULLED BACK IN THE EARLY morning hours of July 29 even though the regiment and the rest of the 1st Cavalry Division were "under no immediate enemy pressure," as the official Army history noted. That pressure would begin soon enough. The young Americans were moving on to trials of fire and sacrifice that many would not survive.

Along with their machine-gun tripods and entrenching tools, their ammo belts and C-rations, the green Garryowens, in their fifth day of war, took away from this place east of Yongdong their own lasting freeze frames, their own personalized nightmares. Ralph Bernotas, for example, remembered that after the mortars "splashed" the refugees, they were "a mass of white. . . . They all blended together, like newspaper on top of newspaper." Pfc. Lyle Jacobson, from G Company, finally got a good look as the men climbed over the trestle embankment to head south. "There were quite a few slaughtered there. . . . But you didn't know until you got down there and seen all the bodies at the mouth of the tunnel."

Survivors said several GIs stopped in front and fired their rifles into the tunnels, emptying their clips into the still darkness. Later the first North Koreans, in their mustard-colored uniforms, moved warily up the road toward No Gun Ri, reaching the area just west of Hwanggan in early afternoon, according to U.S. intelligence. The smell of wholesale death drifted through the air.

SEVENTY MILES TO THE SOUTH THAT DAY, ANOTHER U.S. ARMY UNIT was also withdrawing. The stranded 1st Battalion, 29th Infantry Regiment, was groping its way through the Chiri Mountains, pursued by an unseen North Korean division. Along the way, the hard-pressed Americans joined with hundreds of South Korean refugees, who guided them, who helped widen a mountain trail for their vehicles, who slept under their protection at night. Refugees and Americans alike finally crossed to the safety of a new defense line being formed around the Taegu-Pusan region.

At least 750,000 refugees had poured into this "Pusan Perimeter," the southeastern quadrant of South Korea, perhaps half of them crowding into Taegu, the Eighth Army headquarters city. One among these milling, uprooted thousands was a slender, intense young law student, an ex–police lieutenant, who had found a sleeping space at the Taegu jail where his brother, a prison guard, was staying.

Chung Eun-yong had heard something barely coherent but frightening about No Gun Ri from a nephew, the teenager Chung Koo-shik, who had escaped and made his way south. Now Eun-yong couldn't sleep. His mind raced. His guilt grew daily. He must find Sun-yong and the children. The young husband, the bridegroom who once placed so much hope in an easy morning's passage from Shimchon to Chu Gok Ri, would soon be embarking on a long and almost hopeless journey, one that would last a lifetime.

PART III

THE ROAD FROM
NO GUN RI

6

August 13, 1950
Samni-dong, South Korea

The Naktong River rushes down from the rocky Sobaek Mountains, flattens into a wide muddy ribbon and eases south toward the sea, skirting terraces of rice and groves of apple and pear, hugging humpbacked hills and meadows of tall reeds, and dividing Korea's far south, in its winding way, into two parts, east and west.

Private First Class Art Hunter sat by his machine gun on the east side of the Naktong, on a little rise beside an apple orchard under a sky of midnight blue, and peered out toward the dark quiet river. It lay less than a thousand yards to his front, beyond a dry bottomland of rice stalks. Over on the west bank, across the 200-yard-wide stream, an invisible enemy looked back. For the young Virginian and the rest of the Garryowens, the Naktong could never be wide enough.

It had been 15 days since the 7th Cavalry's teen-aged infantrymen pulled back from No Gun Ri. Few had talked about what happened there. Their days and nights had been too full of fear and fire, on the run, pursued by enemy tanks, trading blind shots in the dark with probing North Korean units, killing and being killed, until finally they reached and crossed the river and dug in, exhausted, to await the final battle. Hunter had seen and learned a lot about war since July 24, his nineteenth birthday, the day the Garryowens arrived at the front. He had even learned about war's absurdities: The Army postal service delivered a birthday cake to his foxhole, all the way from his mother's oven in Lynchburg.

The Naktong River was unusually shallow in August 1950 because of the dry summer. It had dropped three feet in just the past few days. In spots, a man could wade across through murky chest-high water. The North Koreans had other methods as well. Far off to Hunter's left, the unseen enemy, under cover of darkness and unknown to the Americans, had completed an "underwater bridge," a sunken causeway of rice-straw bags filled with rocks.

As the moonless night stretched into early morning, the nervous assistant machine gunner sensed a flicker of movement out of the corner of his eye, in the paddies to his left, not far from a twisted pile of girders that had been a bridge, a gateway to safety, but was now a lifeless jumble of steel.

ELEVEN NIGHTS EARLIER, ON AUGUST 2, 1950, CIVILIANS BY THE thousands crossed that narrow bridge at Tuksong-dong, joining South Korean soldiers and men of the U.S. 24th Infantry Division pulling back over the Naktong at a spot just 55 miles from the peninsula's southeastern corner at Pusan.

The refugees were a shuffling stream of white, 60 feet above the river's waters, women clutching babies, children barefoot and frightened, old men riding piggyback. Some led oxcarts hastily loaded with the baggage of lives shattered by sudden war. Carroll F. Kinsman, a sergeant with the 14th Combat Engineer Battalion, was impressed at the loads women balanced on their heads. "One was carrying a sewing machine up there," he recalled.

The stories had spread about infiltrators lurking among columns of refugees approaching the Naktong crossings. One even had it that innocent-looking Korean children were acting as artillery spotters—the supposed reason enemy shelling was so accurate. Kinsman and his men were posted on the bridge to screen the fleeing civilians. "I stayed up all night searching the refugees," he said. They found nothing.

Shortly after midnight, trucks loaded with the men of the 21st Infantry, a regiment of the haggard, beaten 24th Division, rumbled across the bridge to head south, downriver, to take positions behind the new Naktong line. The last defending unit, the ROK army's 17th Regiment, withdrew over the river just before the sun rose at 6:32 A.M., led by Col. Richard Stephens, the 21st Infantry's commander. His driver, Cpl. Rudy Giannelli, brought the colonel's Jeep to a halt on the far side of the bridge, where Stephens climbed out to talk to 14th Engineers officers.

Eighth Army headquarters had ordered all units to withdraw behind the river by this date, Thursday, August 3, and to blow up the Naktong bridges behind them, denying the crossings to the enemy. The 14th Engineers had taken two days to wire the Tuksong-dong bridge with 7,000 pounds of TNT. Now the Eighth Army deadline was pressing.

Stephens notified the engineers that the last of his forces had cleared the 650-foot span; they could do their job. But refugees still trudged across. An engineer officer ran onto the bridge, firing his pistol in the air to warn the Koreans away, and then dashed back. The white-clad throng followed, beckoned by the safety of the other side.

The declassified record shows that North Korean units had not yet been sighted near the river at Tuksong-dong. But the young soldiers who were there suddenly sensed something terrible was about to happen. "They wouldn't stop. They were abutment to abutment. . . . They were average folks, ladies, children and old men, carrying their baggage on their heads," recalled Pfc. Leon L. Denis. "There are people!" Pfc. Joseph Ipock remembered shouting to someone. "We were told to scatter," Kinsman said. "Next thing I know they revved up the generator and threw the switch and the bridge went." Recalled driver Giannelli, "It lifted up and turned it sideways and it was full of refugees end to end. . . . You saw the spans of steel flying and you knew they were killed."

The charges had been set not only below, on the bridge supports, but above along the roadway itself. The deafening blasts pulverized bodies and showered them, and their shredded white clothing and bits of baggage and wood and oxen, into the river flowing listlessly below. The Americans roared off in their vehicles, not looking back. They knew hundreds had died, said Kinsman, Denis and Giannelli. "The Tuksong Bridge was blown at 0701 hours," an adjutant later noted in the 14th Engineers' war diary. "Results, Excellent."

TWENTY-FIVE MILES UPRIVER FROM TUKSONG-DONG, AT THE TOWN of Waegwan, another road bridge spanned the Naktong. As daylight faded later this same day, August 3, that bridge still stood, as Maj. Gen. Hobart R. Gay watched the last of his grimy, weary 1st Cavalry Division troops roll across to the east bank. Thousands of frightened refugees converged on the crossing.

The previous twelve days had been "not too glorious" as his division faltered and then fell back before the skillful, determined North Koreans, Gay later acknowledged to the Army historian. In the 7th Cavalry Regiment, the withdrawal itself, from the area of Hwanggan and No Gun Ri, showed how unready the green soldiers were for glory.

As 7th Cavalrymen filtered southward from the hills around No Gun Ri, a few jittery recruits had been left behind in the predawn to cover the withdrawal of A Company, 1st Battalion. Soon North Korean tanks clanked up the road from Yongdong in the darkness, fired their cannon toward battalion positions and then disappeared. One of the rear guard, rattled, moved among the foxholes whispering for another man. The second suddenly stood up. "A shot went off, and I turned and he yelled and went down," recalled A Company's Tom Hacha. The first had shot his buddy, the shadow in the darkness, "right in the middle of the chest." He was a big farm boy. They couldn't handle the body; they left it behind. "Killed in action," was all the company report noted.

Hour by hour as they pulled back, walking, sometimes riding trucks, the 7th Cavalrymen began to learn more about the unending dreads and instant terrors of war. Red, white and green flares popped in the skies as North Korean units hunted their American quarry. Artillery shells crashed somewhere around them, from somewhere unseen. The teenaged troopers, well disciplined in obeying orders, instinctively looked to their commanders to save them. But even their officers sometimes betrayed them with inexperience. In the early-morning darkness of July 30, some 24 hours after beginning the pullback, H Company's mortar platoon lieutenant had his men arrayed and dangerously exposed on the forward slope of a hill three miles east of the No Gun Ri trestle. Commencing fire when they spotted enemy tanks, the mortar-tube flashes became an easy target for the North Koreans. A first tank round killed the platoon lieutenant and three privates. More tank fire followed, and nine other H Company men were wounded. Not only was the platoon unwisely positioned, but 2nd Battalion officers, hearing the approaching tanks, had spread word that it was the sound of American bulldozers working on the road.

The men were beginning to accept the carnage around them, but they still were shocked, Buddy Wenzel by the paralyzing sight of a medic's head blown off by a heavy round ("I stood there frozen"), others by a nightmarish scene in which an officer mercifully killed one of his own men after he was horribly wounded by an incoming mortar round. The crew-cut boys who had caroused on the Ginza together and exchanged their sisters' addresses, who had scammed and spit-polished through their days in Tokyo, were now seeing barracks buddies carried off on bloody stretchers. Each was building a picture gallery of horrors in his mind, but also of heroism.

After his mortar platoon was decimated, H Company commander Capt. Mel Chandler put himself in an exposed position and, with a last telephone line to the rear, directed artillery fire onto the advancing tanks. For eight hours, under fire, the newcomer to combat fell back on his Fort Benning infantry training to knock out tanks and stall the North Koreans.

The sight of a thick-armored T-34 tank chilled the Garryowens' blood; they had little to stop them. But late on July 30 one of the deadly new bazookas, 3.5-inch rocket launchers, reached F Company, and Ralph Bernotas's squad leader, Cpl. Al Clair, decided his men ought to try it out on tanks still firing on the 2nd Battalion from up the road.

Bazooka man John Boehm—at age twenty-nine, "Pop" to his buddies—was leery of the unfamiliar weapon, and so Bernotas took it over, leaving his M-1 with Pfc. Boehm. Then Clair, Bernotas and two others crept through the darkness, along the cover of a railroad embankment, to within fifty yards of two tanks. They had only four rockets and had to work quickly before the North Koreans spotted them. Clair loaded the first and tapped Bernotas's head. The Pennsylvania deer hunter squeezed but it wouldn't fire. They groped in the darkness and finally found and released a safety on the brand-new bazooka. Bernotas aimed and fired. It was short. The tanks fell silent, wary. Then the North Koreans opened up again, and the two GIs loaded a second rocket. "I elevated it a little bit, and boom! I was right on it," Bernotas said. "The tank—blew it to hell. It kept exploding all night." The little team beat it back to their own lines, more than 1,000 yards through the sunrise mist, to cheers from F Company troopers.

Such small victories would steadily transform MacArthur's praetorian guard into a seasoned combat force, but not before many more hard days of retreat and then defense on the Naktong. Digging in each night, inching backward to the south each day, the Garryowens grew used to the tactics of "How Able," hauling ass, that defined the GI experience of mid-1950. The rain showers that began at No Gun Ri lingered on, and fog spread over the mountain peaks as the Americans withdrew through Autumn Wind Pass, over muddy, slippery roads, behind ambulances and litter Jeeps carrying their wounded and dead. One was Pop Boehm, who had been killed with Bernotas's rifle useless in his hands, a cleaning rod jamming its barrel.

Along the way, platoons were assigned to set fire to villages and everything else they could find, leaving a scorched-earth path of destruction for the North Koreans. Kimchon, a city of 50,000, was set ablaze by 1st Cavalry Division engineer troops on August 2. Its nighttime glow was visible for miles. What remained were columns of refugees, weary and frantic, families that had been separated, lame old people, children crying for food, all moving toward the Naktong. Soldiers remembered fields "covered with clothing" that would suddenly come alive in the mornings, to flow south again in long files of white.

The Americans, unnerved and filthy, embittered by war's ugliness and misery, grew more hateful toward the people they supposedly had come to protect. "The refugees are cursed by American soldiers, who know they harbor enemies who cannot be distinguished from the mass of innocent," United Press reported on August 3. Although General Gay's intelligence staff reported only that guerrillas were "suspected" among refugees and cited no confirmed cases, the division commander himself argued to reporters that refugee infiltrators were "the North Koreans' most potent weapon."

As the Americans approached the Naktong, they were not pursued closely by the enemy divisions, depleted of both manpower and tanks in the five-week-old offensive. The enemy main forces were reported at least 15 miles away on August 3 as people in white flowed over the Waegwan bridge. But American commanders felt pressed by the Eighth Army timetable, and the bridge was set for demolition that day, explosives rigged to the supports of one of its 200-foot-long spans.

Gay had a rear guard attempt to hold back the thousands of refugees thronging the far shore, but every time the soldiers would make a last run over the bridge's 15-foot-wide roadway, waves of civilians would follow. Corresponding with the Army historian after the war, Gay said he saw no alternative. "It was nearly dark. There was nothing else to be done. The Division Commander gave the order to blow the bridge," Gay wrote of himself. "It was a tough decision because up in the air with the bridge went hundreds of refugees."

A second Naktong bridge had been destroyed, again with Korean women and children, old men and young men, killed in an instant or dropped into the river 40 feet below to drown in its muddy waters. For American soldiers already safely across, watching from the riverside paddies, it was another sight lodged in the gallery of memory. But the deaths were not officially noted in any Army unit document.

ON AUGUST 3, NOW ACROSS THE NAKTONG, THE GARRYOWENS' 2ND Battalion—the riflemen of E, F and G companies, the machine gunners, mortarmen and recoilless riflemen of H Company, the clerks and scouts and radiomen of Headquarters Company—got their gear together and trucked 25 miles southward, to dig into a defensive line near the first blown bridge at Tuksong-dong. Art Hunter's G Company settled in around the apple orchard in front of the hamlet of Samni-dong.

In less than two weeks at war, the 1st Cavalry Division's 11,000 troops had suffered almost 10 percent casualties: dead, wounded and missing. In the 2nd Battalion, the wounded included Wenzel, riddled with shrapnel on July 30, and Bernotas, shot through the wrist on July 31. Both were evacuated to Japan, and both wondered whether they were out of combat for good. The battalion had a new commanding officer, the battle-hardened Lt. Col. Gil Huff, who had been the 7th Cavalry's executive officer. "Whiskey Red," as men began calling him, took over from a devastated Lt. Col. Heyer. "Herb's tired," Huff remembered hearing from regimental commander Col. Cecil Nist. Heyer was brought to the rear and the regimental staff.

The men hunkering down on the Naktong's eastern banks believed either they would be evacuated from their toehold in southeastern Korea or the full force of the U.S. military would come to their rescue. "You don't have much to worry about," James Hodges, Wenzel's G Company buddy, wrote his sister Juanita on August 10. "Everybody over here is confident that this thing will be over in a couple or 3 months." But the North Koreans, moving troops toward the Naktong in the night, had their own ideas.

"We must get to the enemy's rear. . . . We must envelop and anni-
hilate all of them," a North Korean regimental commander wrote in a
lengthy battle plan, later captured, as his fresh 10th Division mar-
shaled in the hills across the Naktong from Colonel Huff's battalion.

The envelopment began early on the morning of August 12, when
North Korean troops slipped across the river and through a gap on
the battalion's left flank and doubled back against H Company's
forward positions. Some of Captain Chandler's men were shot in
their foxholes from behind. It took hours of counterattack and artillery to repel the infiltrating enemy, and in the end the 101-man
H Company, hit hard again, lost seven men killed and twenty-three
wounded. Chandler himself and No Gun Ri machine gunner Norm
Tinkler were among those evacuated with wounds.

Two mornings later on the right flank, Art Hunter was seeing
flickers of movement in the darkness, enemy infiltrators creeping
forward through rice stalks and pea patches. As a third soldier ran
off to alert the company, Hunter and his machine-gunner partner
opened fire with their air-cooled .30-caliber gun, and in seconds the
Tuksong-dong front exploded with small arms and mortar fire and
the crisscross streaks of tracers from both sides.

The machine-gun team's intensive fire began to cut down enemy
soldiers, but then the weapon jammed. The gunner scrambled back
over the crest of the rise just behind them, to find a cartridge
extractor, he said. Hunter, alone, picked up his M-1 and began firing. Looking around, finding no help, he believed the company had
pulled back and left him. North Koreans kept coming. Bullets ripped
past his head. He'd rather be killed than captured, the young 7th
Cavalryman decided, and he stood up with his rifle and fired off clip
after clip. George Company riflemen, taking cover on a back slope
30 feet behind him, were amazed to hear him shouting into the din:
"Garryowen! . . . Garryowen!"

George and other companies were collapsing in spots but reor-
ganizing in others. Mortar fire zeroed in on the North Koreans.
Outgoing artillery shells whistled over Hunter's head. His partner
never returned, but Hunter went to work on the machine gun, using

the heel of a pistol to dislodge the ruptured cartridge. He began firing again but ran out of ammunition. He grabbed an expended, 20-foot-long ammo belt, the kind that fed bullets into his gun, and tossed the fabric strip up on the crest behind him, where his platoon sergeant tied on a full box of ammunition. He dragged it down to his exposed position, loaded and fired on. Over and over, as the sun floated up over the eastern ridges, Hunter pulled more boxes down the slope and turned back to the business of killing strangers in mustard-drab uniforms. Their bullets never touched him. They counted 32 boxes of ammunition used by Art Hunter—more than 9,000 rounds. When it was over, after American tanks rolled up to blow away pockets of holdouts, "That was when I was able to sit down and get a little shaky," Hunter recalled.

The August 12–14 defense by the 2nd Battalion was a crucial victory on the Naktong line. If the North Korean 10th Division had broken through, Taegu and Eighth Army headquarters lay just 14 miles away.

The killing didn't end when the smoke of battle cleared. Battalion commander Huff sent platoons combing through the riverside pea patches and paddies, hunting for stranded and wounded North Koreans, and killing them. "You go down there, Sergeant, and you clean out those goddamned gooks," the recon sergeant Snuffy Gray remembered the colonel telling him.

Heavy-winged vultures, clouds of huge black flies, the stench of bodies rotting in the sun took possession of the Naktong bottomland. The 7th Cavalry claimed 1,500 enemy dead in the three-day fight. About 150 lay in front of G Company's positions, many credited to Art Hunter. The Americans, too, paid a price: G Company alone suffered seven men killed and twenty-seven wounded.

The "2nd of the 7th Cav," the men who bugged out at Yongdong, had redeemed themselves. *Stars and Stripes* ran photos of the heroes, one showing Lyle Jacobsen and other ragged G Company troopers picking apples in the orchard. "I have never commanded a better group of soldiers, who fought any better or more bravely," Gil Huff later wrote of his men on the Naktong. "It was all on-the-job training," Snuffy Gray reflected. "And by the time we knew what we were doing, we lost fifty percent of our men. But those who remained had become damned good soldiers."

ONE OF THE MOST PERILOUS U.S. MILITARY OPERATIONS EVER undertaken, it became known as the Pusan Perimeter, a southeastern corner of Korea running 85 miles north to south, generally along the Naktong, and 60 miles east to west. It was thinly held, not by a continuous defense line, but at strong points—hills, road junctions, river fords—manned by understrength units, sometimes a mile apart. To fool the North Koreans, combat engineers kicked up storms of dust with bulldozers and heavy trucks, the ruse of a big army ever on the move.

For the GI in this last-ditch defense, just a month from the comforts and pleasures of Tokyo, soldiering had become misery. The area around Taegu is the hottest in Korea, its midsummer temperatures topping 100 degrees. When it didn't rain, the thick dust clogged weapons and coated sweating bodies. When it did rain, the soldier was soaked through. If he managed to nap, it was on a poncho thrown on the floor of a watery hole, amid malarial mosquitoes.

Because the Army's food pipeline sometimes broke down, Japan's beer-loving palace guards became lean, hungry men and boys. Tinkler said he had dropped to 156 pounds from 200-plus by the time he was wounded August 12 and shipped from Korea. The C-ration box became the GI's staff of life: toilet paper, cigarettes, powdered coffee, tinned biscuits, canned fruit, small bars of chocolate and soap, and beans and franks or another of eleven "meat items."

His gear grew lean with the soldier: fatigue shirt and pants, steel helmet, combat boots, his weapon and his web belt—with canteen, first-aid packet, bayonet, entrenching tool and ammunition clips attached. Up the steep hills, on long patrols, the soldier learned to travel light. At times the Eighth Army's strained supply system even let these sparsely supplied men down. A passing Korean stole the combat boots of a sleeping Don MacFarland, an unusually small size 5. MacFarland had to keep on the move, patrolling with F Company for two weeks in stocking feet—"I fractured two toes running off a damned hill"—before the quartermasters came through with a new pair.

In their memories, six summer weeks besieged on the Naktong grew into an eternity—of two-man listening posts at the river's reedy edge, of the chaos of sudden attacks, of silent patrols into the enemy's midst. The patrols across the Naktong, usually squad size, were risky but necessary, to observe North Korean movements and sometimes bring back a prisoner to learn more. The squads paddled small boats or waded across the river, penetrated a mile or more, and always avoided firefights if possible. The stealthy work took a steady toll. Men drowned when boats overturned; one twelve-man patrol from the 2nd Battalion never returned from the far shore.

On their first patrol, in early August before the heavy fighting, Cpl. Al Clair's F Company squad heard moaning in a house in abandoned Tuksong, by the destroyed bridge, and found a boy of about ten who had been shot through the shoulder. "The boy had a gaping wound, full of maggots. He couldn't have lasted long without treatment," Clair said. Their medic cleaned and dressed the wound, and the men left the boy some food and water. In the days to come, other patrols stopped by to check on the child, until finally he was strong enough to be brought safely across the river.

The enemy patrolled the American side as well. The Naktong days were the worst of the war, said MacFarland, and the worst of the Naktong was the morning on a listening post when he turned and saw a North Korean coming down on him with a knife. "My squad leader fired a shot from behind me and killed that guy."

The Garryowens measured time not by dates, but by the death of a buddy, a trip to the rear, a letter from home. They daydreamed about fried chicken, about clean sheets, about women. From the August 6 *Stars and Stripes,* they saved a photo of "Miss Morale," an unknown starlet named Marilyn Monroe. Later that month they ripped out a very different photo to keep in their helmets: a picture of twenty-six dead GIs found with hands tied and shot in the back by their North Korean captors. Already full of the vengefulness of war and a hatred of Koreans, the hard young men on the Naktong now had it certified in black and white. "We take no more prisoners," they told each other.

Men broke down, from pressure and fear, in these stifling afternoons of buzzing cicadas, or on overnight outposts beneath bursting flares. The medical corps reported the rate of psychiatric admissions among GIs in the intense Pusan Perimeter fighting soared to the equivalent of 258 per 1,000 troops per year in August. Combat veterans told doctors they found the fighting tougher than in World War II. Men bugged out, showing up unauthorized somewhere in the rear. Men shot themselves in the foot. Men wondered what it was all about. "When you see buddies killed, guys alongside you killed—what the hell are we here for? Police action?" Wenzel remembered thinking. As Lois McKown and other wives and girlfriends anxiously followed the news back in Tokyo or the States, Bill McKown recalled, "most of us were wishing, 'Why don't they get us out of here? What are we doing here to start with?' "

On August 20, James Hodges wrote his sister that he hoped to be back in Japan by the end of September. "I stayed in Tokyo so long until it seems like home," the Florida runaway wrote. He told Juanita the chaplain had visited G Company that day, a quiet Sunday. Then, before scrawling his signoff, "Love, James," the shy younger brother finally gave his sister a glimpse into his dread. "We can really use God's help over here."

The first help the Garryowens and other hard-pressed units received came in the form of Marines and regiments of the 2nd Infantry Division, thrown into the Naktong battles in early August. By early September the combined U.S. and South Korean armies behind the Naktong outnumbered the 70,000 North Koreans by about two to one.

American military might was converging on a scrubby, rock-bound corner of Asia that the Joint Chiefs of Staff had dismissed barely a year earlier as strategically unimportant. Now the chiefs had endorsed full-scale war in Korea, and they were rewarded by President Truman in early September when he announced he would ask Congress to finance a huge, three-million-member military to face down what was increasingly described as a threat of global communist conquest. Truman's Navy secretary, Francis P. Matthews, even called publicly for a preventive world war against the communist nations, saying Americans thereby "would become the first aggressors for peace."

At the State Department, the influential George Kennan, who helped formulate Washington's anti-Soviet "containment" policies, was deeply troubled by the incendiary rhetoric. "It implied that we could not adopt an adequate defense position without working our people up into an emotional state," he later wrote.

FROM THE NAKTONG FRONT IN EARLY AUGUST, BRITISH JOURNALIST Christopher Buckley reported that the war in Korea was "exceptionally ruthless." The savagery was not confined to one side, but American newspaper readers and radio listeners might have thought so.

The celebrated CBS newsman Edward R. Murrow, leaving the Naktong front in mid-August, sent a radio report to New York saying the U.S. military was creating "dead valleys" in South Korea, and wondering whether the South Korean people would ever forgive America. His network, CBS, refused to broadcast it, infuriating Murrow. News organizations were operating under a self-censorship system that forbade criticism of the U.S. military; those who violated it could lose access to warfront coverage.

Murrow didn't detail what he had seen, but many valleys in South Korea were being "killed" during those days, usually out of sight of reporters. Journalists even visited the 7th Cavalry on July 27, while the No Gun Ri killings went on, but there is no indication they ventured beyond the regimental command post, two miles from the trestle. Likewise, no outsiders were watching when the 2nd Battalion, according to veterans, killed other refugees in the days to come. In one cryptic message, an Army chaplain reported on July 28, "First Cav is taking action against the civilians . . . by the use of bayonets and other means of force." A division artillery unit noted in its war diary for July 29, "Anyone seen is considered enemy."

The Americans were leaving behind a trail of civilian dead and a charred landscape. The rockets and napalm bombs of U.S. warplanes burned down scores of villages and towns. "Effectively worked over, particularly after the 25th, were 48 villages and towns," read the classified July report of the Air Force's airborne controllers. One jet pilot reported a controller directed him at mission's end to set a South Korean town afire with his rockets "rather than carry them home." Another four-plane mission flying along the Kum River, near Taejon, reported, "Saw only 2 fishing boats and strafed them. Resulted in occupants diving overboard."

Fleeing such devastation, reaching the Naktong, long columns of refugees found the bridges destroyed. At one point, an estimated 200,000 displaced people were spread on the western bank, stranded, caught between North Korean and American guns. Three days after he blew up hundreds of refugees at the Waegwan bridge to keep it out of North Korean hands, General Gay finally sent troops and South Korean police across the Naktong in boats to screen and allow 5,500 civilians to cross to the east side. This desperate group had gathered around a large crude sign: AMERICANS, WE ARE NOT COMMUNISTS. North Korean army units had still not reached the river in Gay's sector.

Another three days after that change of heart, however, commanders' fears and deadly solutions were again distilled into an order, this time preserved in a battalion log. "Shoot all refugees coming across river," read the straightforward message on August 9 from Col. Raymond D. Palmer, commander of the 8th Cavalry, the Garryowens' sister regiment.

That's what American troops did, both veterans and Korean witnesses said. Air Force P-51s, propeller-driven fighters, flew routine missions up and down the river "interdicting" refugees, stitching the west bank with lines of .50-caliber machine-gun fire. Men of the Garryowens' 2nd Battalion even began shooting refugees who did not try to cross, but merely appeared on the far shore, veterans said. General Gay himself ratified the indiscriminate shooting on August 29, as North Korean pressure built along the river. "Saber 6"—Gay's code name—"orders all refugees to be fired on," the divisional artillery staff noted in its log. Gay declared refugees to be "fair game," another log showed.

Lives were extinguished on a scale both large and small. On August 16, the Air Force sent 98 heavy bombers to carpet-bomb a 27-square-mile area across the Naktong, dropping 960 tons of bombs, in hopes of randomly hitting enemy troop concentrations. In one village alone, Sachang, northwest of Waegwan, about 130 civilians were killed in the bombing that afternoon, survivors said. Unknown numbers of other villagers and stranded refugees were killed elsewhere in the zone. Days earlier, in a daylong siege on August 11 in the 25th Infantry Division's sector, American troops fired on villagers sheltering in a local Confucian shrine, killing about eighty, survivors later reported. Aerial bombing and strafing and indiscriminate fire from U.S. ground troops killed hundreds of South Korean civilians during August 1950 around the Pusan Perimeter, Korean witnesses said. The devastation prompted the Army's public relations office in Washington to message Tokyo about "rumors that there is promiscuous bombing in Korea." The declassified record shows the Pentagon strongly recommended that the command stop reporting villages bombed in its communiques, and instead call them "military targets."

The killing could be intimate, too, one on one. As the Garryowens evacuated villages to their rear, inside the Pusan Perimeter, Sgt. Lyle Gibbs in E Company was sent on a special mission. "They wanted a village emptied, and there was a woman left there," he said. "Get rid of her," he was told. "I went down and tried, but I was not going to shoot her." Then "some young kid" was sent, who killed the woman, Gibbs said.

For some Garryowens, such killing became casual. "They didn't know anything about these people. They were acting like little kids who had gotten away from their mothers," Gibbs said. Many men abhorred what they saw. Some reviled a particular 2nd Battalion sergeant as "Baby Killer." But the killing, both authorized and unauthorized, went on, and little hint of it could be found in American newspapers. "Most reporters were afraid to print what they witnessed in Korea, given the Cold War atmosphere of the time," historian Bruce Cumings eventually concluded.

When the Tuksong-dong bridge was destroyed on August 3, two leading U.S. reporters were there. Hal Boyle of the Associated Press and W. H. Lawrence of the *New York Times* had been held back from the blast site, then went forward and interviewed Corporal Giannelli, Colonel Stephens's driver. Both quoted Giannelli as reporting that the engineers tried to keep the refugees back, and that "when the smoke settles there wasn't anything standing at all." Giannelli said he went further, telling them the refugees "kept coming across . . . and were on the bridge when they blew it." That was clear in his account, he recalled. But, as published, the AP and *New York Times* articles did not report the deaths; they simply did not address the refugees' fate.

"KOREA, 28 AUG. 50, DEAR SIS . . ."

James Hodges's letters to Juanita were hurried notes, arriving in Florida smudged with the red clay of Korea. But in late August he managed to fill three small pages. He asked after the family. "As for me," he wrote, "I am living." He said G Company had been alerted to move out. He asked her to send him two pints of Canadian Club; he didn't like whiskey, but all the guys were getting some. He signed off, "Your loving Bud, James." Then this nineteen-year-old GI, the singing boy on the Hodges porch, had a final request: "P.S. Ask the preacher for a prayer for all George Company for we are about to move into bloody territory."

The three weeks to come would be the bloodiest of a three-year war for the U.S. Army. Needing every man it could muster, Eighth Army quickly shuttled the wounded back into the line. Hodges's friend Buddy Wenzel returned from a hospital in Japan. "I was scared. It didn't take much of a noise. Nothing seemed real," Wenzel said of the tense days of incoming artillery fire and stealthy North Korean probes in the night. Fox Company's garrulous Ralph Bernotas, his wrist wound mended, also returned to the unreal war on the Naktong. A few days later, on Hill 303 north of Waegwan, he was with three buddies when a mortar round hit. "I'm holding the can of beer we're passing around. Brumagen and Dean are dead, and me and Berryman are looking at each other. We didn't get a scratch," Bernotas recounted. "It's like, why them and not me and Berryman?"

The North Koreans were mounting a final, fierce push to take Taegu, and in a tangle of knobby and sharp-ridged hills 15 miles northwest of Taegu, men of the 7th Cavalry would die by the dozens in early September 1950.

Wading silently through waist-high waters, filing across submerged "bridges," the North Koreans had infiltrated in strength into the hills east of the Naktong. Detecting them, the 1st Cavalry Division attacked. The enemy counterattacked, looping around the Americans. Soon the area was a maze of ambushes and deadly dead-end valleys. "We have penetrated them and they have penetrated us," a troubled General Gay told reporters in the rear.

In heavy rains on September 6, the Garryowens' 2nd Battalion was ordered back from forward hill positions and fell into an enemy trap. An antitank round to the head killed executive officer Maj. Omar T. Hitchner, acting as battalion commander in the absence of a wounded Colonel Huff. Captain Chandler of H Company then took charge and led battalion remnants, without water, food and proper maps, low on ammunition and at times under enemy fire, through a zigzagging, miles-long trek to the safety of friendly lines. It took 40 hours. The isolated G Company, making its own hazardous withdrawal, had to carry out its wounded on makeshift litters of tree branches and ponchos.

The North Koreans pressed on, not just against Taegu, the Eighth Army headquarters city, but at other points around the perimeter. By September 11 they stood just seven miles north of Taegu. But in the heavy heat and downpours of September, the North Korean thrust ground to a halt, its strength too diluted in widespread offensives, its long supply lines too exposed for sustained attack. A fresh battalion of Garryowens, the 3rd, counterattacked on September 12 and took heavy casualties, but also took back Hill 314, the strongpoint on the North Korean line.

The North Koreans were spent, having lost tens of thousands of men since the June 25 invasion. The Eighth Army had been badly hurt, too. In ten weeks at war, it had lost 4,280 killed in action, 12,337 wounded and 2,508 missing or known captured. Ralph Bernotas was finding few old Tokyo buddies around him: By mid-

September, an unreinforced F Company numbered just forty-five men, one-third its strength when it landed in Korea.

July's parade-ground soldiers were now September's professional fighters. But they were men who avoided making new friends, not wanting to see them die, men learning both the best and worst about themselves and their fellow man. "I got old fast," said Wenzel. "Believe me, I was only nineteen but I got old fast." A devoted mother's letters still reached Art Hunter, but the machine gunner never wrote back. "I didn't know what to say. 'Hey, Mom, I'm being shot at today and they just missed me'?"

Then, on the fifteenth day of September, everything changed in Korea. In an end run long planned by Gen. Douglas MacArthur, Marine and Army units made an amphibious landing at Inchon, west of Seoul, far behind the North Korean lines. It was now the enemy's turn to retreat, and the Garryowens would help lead the charge out of the Pusan Perimeter.

ON SEPTEMBER 18, THE MEN OF G COMPANY, BY NOW WITH SOUTH Korean "augmentation" soldiers in their ranks, joined in an attack on Hill 300, north of Taegu, to punch a hole in the North Korean line and allow other 7th Cavalry troops to roll north. Enemy mortar and machine-gun fire drove the assault force back down the hill for the night.

The next morning, South Korean soldiers scouted the slope. "They came back and said there's a dead GI up there," Wenzel recalled. He and a medic scrambled back up, to a spot 100 yards up the 1,000-foot-high hill. "First thing I saw was a tree splintered real bad when a mortar round hit it," Wenzel said. Then he saw the soldier facedown in a ditch. His back had been gouged open by the giant splinters. Wenzel saw the blond hair and knew. "It was James."

The medic checked James Hodges's dogtag identification and retrieved his billfold, his wristwatch and his harmonica, beginning the process of getting the body into the hands of the division's graves registration unit. Wenzel rejoined G Company, the attack resumed, and in hours of furious combat the 2nd Battalion drove the enemy from Hill 300's commanding heights. The Eighth Army's push north, to link up with the Inchon beachhead troops, could now jump off up the road below Hill 300. The 7th Cavalry's war diary noted the heavy cost to take the hill: 28 Americans killed and 147 wounded. In the cold accounting of company morning reports, where casualties are registered by name, one name, strangely, was missing from the dead: Cpl. James L. Hodges, RA18304354.

Days later a package from Florida reached G Company. Disguised as "glassed fruit," it was a bottle of Canadian Club sent to James by a disapproving but loyal Juanita. In the comfort of a Korean mud hut, Wenzel and a few others shared the bounty, toasting the memory of the quiet Browning Automatic Rifleman.

A letter Juanita sent was returned to her. In it, she pleaded with her brother to write. "It has been about three weeks since I heard from you," she said. "I am so worried about you I don't know what to do." The war might be over soon, she wrote. "I do hope it is and you can come back home to see us all. You just don't know what a happy time that will be for all of us."

Besides "Return to Sender," the envelope sent back to Florida bore another stamp, from an adjutant general's office: "Verified Missing in Action."

Buddy decided to wait before writing pen pal Dorothy Hodges, wait for Army channels to notify the family of James's death. He didn't know that James Hodges, on paper, had not yet officially died in the "bloody territory" of Korea.

ON SEPTEMBER 20, GENERAL GAY TOOK THE 7TH CAVALRY AWAY from a miscast, cautious Col. Cecil Nist and gave the command to the aggressive Lt. Col. William A. Harris, a slightly built Texan who adorned his Jeep hood with a horse soldier's saddle and knotted a cavalryman's yellow scarf around his neck. "Wild Bill" Harris led the Garryowens north, leapfrogging on the road to Seoul against collapsing North Korean resistance.

Along the way, American soldiers found a war always offering fresh horrors. Rolling back into Taejon, where the South Koreans slaughtered 1,800 leftists before the July retreat, U.S. troops discovered mass graves of rightist political prisoners—and at least forty American soldiers—executed by the withdrawing communists. The Army history later put the number killed by the northerners at five thousand or more, but historians questioned whether that count combined the two groups of victims.

Across the recaptured territory, U.S. troops saw the South Koreans exacting revenge against real or imagined collaborators. Riding into one village, a 3rd Engineers company found that ROK army troops had just massacred inhabitants after discovering North Korean flags in huts. "We heard the machine-gun fire and saw them burying them in this big pit," recalled ex–engineer private Donald Lloyd. "There were women in that pit holding babies. I'd say one hundred people."

In the Seoul-Inchon area, thousands were slain—suspected rightists or leftists summarily executed by the departing communists or by the returning army and government of President Rhee, and other civilians caught by the unchecked firepower of the U.S.–South Korean invasion force driving from Inchon into Seoul.

Seoul was recaptured on September 26 after a painful, harrowing first two months of war for the Garryowen regiment, a war that had begun for them in July at a place called No Gun Ri. On September 29, the *New York Times* carried an obscure news note about a slaughter of South Korean civilians by U.S. troops: "One high-ranking United States officer condemned as 'panicky' the shooting of many civilians last July by one United States regiment." The little paragraph was buried deep inside a larger story. It did not say where the killings occurred or name the regiment, and it was not followed up.

If they weren't aware of No Gun Ri when it happened, high-ranking U.S. officers knew about it in general terms no later than mid-August 1950. In an internal communication dated August 2, North Korean officers reported the discovery of "barbaric" killings of civilians by American troops around Yongdong, including many found dead in a nearby tunnel. That document was captured by U.S. troops, translated by Army intelligence and distributed within the 1st Cavalry

Division command on August 17, and at Eighth Army headquarters and Tokyo's Far East Command by August 22. The declassified record gives no indication of any follow-up investigation.

SOMETIME, SOMEWHERE DURING THE PUSH NORTH—IT WAS STILL warm, he remembered, but he never knew the location—Art Hunter found his personal nightmare. George Company was sitting on a ridge; another rifle company was sweeping through a valley below. Hunter, on his machine gun, spotted an elderly couple in the valley bustling around their mud hut. He thought they might somehow be helping the enemy. A company officer was nearby. "Should I stop them?" Hunter asked, and then fired a hammering burst of .30-caliber bullets in their general direction. The Koreans froze, squatted for a moment, then began working again. He fired again, the tracers streaking past the old peasants. They stopped once more and resumed once more. "You want me to shoot them?" the machine gunner asked.

He waited for the officer's response. "Whatever you think," he said. Hunter took aim and opened fire. The man fell. The woman dashed here and there. Hunter fired again. "I just killed her, too."

The young soldier never did make out their faces; they were too far off. They were left lying there, an old man and an old woman. "I never found out if they were just innocent people I killed."

THE U.S. CENTRAL INTELLIGENCE AGENCY HAD COUNSELED THE White House against invading North Korea because of the "grave risk of general war." Its August 18, 1950, analysis also said that imposing the southern government on all Korea might prove impossible. "Syngman Rhee and his regime are unpopular among many if not a majority of non-Communist Koreans." In fact, the CIA said, any free election might bring the communists to power throughout Korea.

The election the White House worried about, however, was the midterm U.S. congressional election. Republicans were still assailing

Truman-Acheson "appeasement" in Asia, many in Washington concluded that the Chinese and Soviet communists would never intervene in Korea, and so the president decided to send American forces into North Korea to crush the communists.

The 1st Cavalry Division led the way to Pyongyang, the northern capital. "Wild Bill" Harris's Garryowens regiment scored a coup crossing the Yesong River and then fought on, with steady losses, against a stubborn enemy defending his homeland. The grim, soul-searing job of soldiering grew more grim by the day as Korean temperatures fell. The Garryowens had headed north with just one wool layer of uniform. Warmer clothing was reaching them only sporadically; the Army had been caught unprepared. When supplies did come in, the 1st Cavalry Division was outrunning them, so that in early November most of its winter clothing was still in Taegu, 300 miles away. Some men had already suffered frostbite to toes and fingers.

After Pyongyang fell on October 19, the 7th Cavalry Regiment passed through the capital to seize its major port, Chinnampo, in an urgent midnight assault. The Bible-reading Gil Huff, back in command, didn't know the enemy's strength, but he later said he found inspiration in Gideon's defeat of the Midianites. He had his 2nd Battalion turn on all headlights and radios and fill the night with noise, so the North Koreans would think "God's own army" was descending on them. The defenders, it turned out, had fled. Across the front, in fact, remnants of Kim Il Sung's army faded into the rugged wintry mountains to the north.

The capital had been seized and the enemy routed. The Garryowens thought their war was over, that they would soon be parading victoriously for MacArthur, in their yellow cavalry scarves, across Tokyo's Imperial Palace Plaza. In Chinnampo, they settled into the comfort of living under roofs and sleeping for more than two hours at a stretch. They had regular hot meals, and counted on shipping out for home by Christmas. Bob Hope flew to Pyongyang and entertained the troops.

General MacArthur had more ambitious plans, however, for the famous 7th Cavalry, the rest of the Eighth Army, and a new joint Army-Marine command called X Corps. He ordered them north to destroy the last of the North Korean forces and to drive to the brink of the Chinese border at the Yalu River. This contravened Washington's caution against provoking China's intervention by putting U.S. troops threateningly on its doorstep. MacArthur had insisted to the Joint Chiefs and Truman that the Chinese wouldn't dare take on his army, dubbed the "U.N. Command" because of the token addition of British, Greek, Turkish and other nations' units.

The Garryowens who moved north, colliding again with the North Koreans, were a hardened fighting force ever angrier at their fate in being caught in this war between Koreans, the war that wouldn't end. "We had a lot of hate," said Buddy Wenzel. Men tossed grenades into village huts not knowing whether they held snipers or sleeping families. "They fire on anything moving," G Company's Sgt. Bob Spiroff noted in a letter home. Said Tom Boyd, then a Browning Automatic Rifleman man with F Company: "In combat you either become an animal and live, or stay timid and die. I personally killed anything in front of me when we moved up."

But bullets couldn't defeat the winter. As November wore on, the frigid Siberian winds blew biting snow and freezing rain into their faces. Their vehicles bogged down in muddy ruts or slid off narrow, snow-slick roads. They couldn't get warm—no shelter, cold rain running into foxholes, too few layers of wool. Some wrapped newspaper around their midsections.

The enemy was often elusive, the combat fitful and small-scale. Deep in North Korea, more than 60 miles north of Pyongyang, the 7th Cavalry enjoyed a hot meal, from turkey to mince pie, on Thanksgiving, November 23. The regiment then retired about 10 miles south to a reserve bivouac, where the men assembled for a memorial ceremony overseen by General Gay himself. At parade rest in 15-degree cold, before the regimental colors, they heard the chaplain recite the psalm that soldiers have always heard, about the "valley of death," with its reminder that "surely goodness and mercy shall follow me all the days of my life." Then the Garryowens gathered up their grenades and guns and headed back into the line, to a rendezvous with the might of China, to a frozen place where goodness and mercy dared not follow.

ON THE NIGHT OF NOVEMBER 29, 1950, SGT. SNUFFY GRAY WALKED the G Company perimeter. It was frigid, just zero degrees. The Garryowens were dug in north of a town called Sinchang-ni, 40 miles northeast of Pyongyang in the heart of North Korea. Moonlight gleamed off a landscape coated with heavy snow.

"Somebody hollered at me, 'Hey, look, Snuff! That goddamned road is turning black!' " Gray recalled. "The road was white, but sure enough it was turning black. Chinese were marching down the road in columns and they had no idea we were there."

A Chinese army of approximately 300,000 men had poured largely undetected into the mountains of fir and spruce that run down North Korea's spine. For four days its advance divisions had been pounding at Eighth Army and ROK army units in western and central North Korea. The 7th Cavalry Regiment had taken up position on a road running along Eighth Army's right flank, at a point where the mountains meet the coastal plain, to help relieve pressure on the nearby 2nd Infantry Division.

This collision of armies set new tides of refugees in motion, northern Koreans this time. Earlier this day, November 29, in the morning darkness, retreating South Korean troops crossed through a 7th Cavalry roadblock, followed by thick columns of refugees. The Americans heard that enemy troops had infiltrated the civilians. When the E Company commander, First Lt. John E. Sheehan, stepped forward to inspect one group of men, they pulled out weapons and fired. Sheehan was killed, some of his men were wounded, and the Garryowens opened fire on the white-clad throng. "They were mixed in with them," recalled Joseph Burton, a recoilless rifleman in the 1st Battalion's D Company. "We had to open up on them—women, children, old people. It was terrible." The regimental war diary took no note of the civilian casualties.

It was some 20 hours later that the white road intersecting the 7th Cavalry's 2nd and 1st Battalions darkened with Chinese troops. Exchanges of fire exploded into a chaotic nighttime battle, the Garryowens' first with the Chinese. The attackers' vanguard drove the center of the 7th Cavalry line back, reaching the 2nd Battalion command post in a building on the edge of Sinchang-ni, where machine gunners finally cut them down. The regiment remained hard-pressed by masses of Chinese troops, blowing bugles, sounding whistles. Dozens of American wounded soon jammed the aid station, a small village house, where U.S. Army doctors did their best to save lives by flashlight.

Second Battalion commander Huff took up a forward position with his Jeep and called in barrage after barrage of artillery fire on coordinates where he thought Chinese would be maneuvering. The shelling went on for hours, into the morning. "Whiskey Red" Huff was unsteady. "He was stone drunk, leaning up against his Jeep calling in the coordinates," Gray recalled. "But he was a better soldier drunk than other people were sober."

The wall of artillery and the raking machine-gun fire from line companies stopped the waves of Chinese attacks. The next day the 7th Cavalry counted 350 Chinese dead. Hundreds more bodies were strewn outside the regiment's perimeters. Thirty-eight Americans were killed, and many more were wounded or missing. Huff, the man who hated war, had shown again how to fight one. But across the warfront, from the ROK army troops beside the Yellow Sea to U.S. Marines at the Changjin Reservoir in the far east, fighting spirits wavered before the formidable new enemy, an army of great numbers and brave attacks. MacArthur's command began a general withdrawal.

The 7th Cavalry Regiment joined in this vast winter retreat unprecedented in U.S. military history—a "retrograde movement," the planners called it; "the Big Bugout" to the men. Demoralized soldiers, blank faces behind frozen beards, trudged down the bruising roads, or clambered onto overloaded tanks or trucks that sometimes broke down in the cold or keeled over into roadside ditches. The hellish cold and wind left men with frozen feet and fingertips, noses and ears. Some 1,500 "weather casualties" were reported across the front over nine days of the pullback in December, including 300 men who lay wounded in the snow and ice for hours or days.

Once more, Eighth Army "scorched the earth" on its retreat,

burning houses in the broad swath of its path, destroying livestock and food, wrecking machinery. "We burned everything," said F Company's Ralph Bernotas. "Food—whatever the hell—they left nothing. It was just like the Civil War, the same as the Russians and Germans in the Ukraine." Korean peasants and townspeople, faced with freezing and starvation in the northern winter, stacked what they could on their A-frame backpacks and flooded south.

Retreating back through Pyongyang, the Americans left the city in conflagration. The engineers set U.S. supply depots ablaze; up to 30,000 gallons of gasoline were ignited, and ammunition dumps blown. They dynamited a warehouse full of fruitcake, whiskey and other rations for the "victorious" army's Christmas feast. Quartermasters gave away supplies to retreating units. Buddy Wenzel, riding through the North Korean capital, picked up a case of fruit cocktail, every GI's favorite, and clung to it, atop a tank, through a 100-mile journey south. Korea's oldest city, Pyongyang burned to the ground beneath flames towering into the winter sky. The U.S. Air Force later destroyed what was left.

The Eighth Army pulled back 120 miles in ten days, and the 7th Cavalry stopped at Nakpon-ni, just north of Seoul. The Chinese had made little contact with the withdrawing divisions, but they were clearly massing for a push south.

Back in the United States, popular support for the war collapsed. A Gallup survey that had shown 66 percent backing when the 7th Cavalry landed in July indicated only 39 percent of Americans now supported U.S. involvement in Korea. On December 15, a somber President Truman told the nation in a radio address that it faced a threat of general war with aggressive communism, and must rely on a vast, permanent military establishment. "Our homes, our nation, all the things we believe in, are in great danger," he said. America was "in deadly peril," declared Sen. Millard Tydings of Maryland, a Democrat.

The Garryowens, at least, were in peril, on a ragged defense line stretching eastward from Seoul. Hearing snatches of holiday songs by Bing Crosby or the Andrews Sisters on radios sent up from the rear, veteran fighters longed more than ever for relief and for home. It was a bleak Christmas for a battered American army.

Buddy Wenzel finally wrote to Dorothy Hodges, to tell her how sorry he was about James's death. Not long after, his captain summoned Wenzel to the company command tent; the distraught Hodges family had written to the Army for an explanation.

Asked how he knew James Hodges had been killed, Wenzel recounted the September 18 events to the captain. The surprised officer told him his friend had somehow been listed as missing in action, and the family so informed. Buddy now signed an affidavit attesting to the death, and the family at least could rest assured about James's fate. The remains of the Florida sharecropper's son still lay somewhere unknown in the turmoil of the war, misplaced or misidentified.

Another soldier's death got more notice. Three days before Christmas 1950, Lt. Gen. Walton H. Walker, Eighth Army commander, was killed in a road accident near Seoul. Lt. Gen. Matthew B. Ridgway, a renowned paratroop commander in World War II, flew in from Washington to take over. In one of his first acts, Ridgway decreed a halt to scorched earth tactics, no more "destruction for destruction's sake." But the mass killings and the destruction went on, particularly from the air.

IN JANUARY 1951, SOME 90 MILES SOUTHEAST OF SEOUL, AN OBSERVER aircraft circled over a cave, and then four planes streaked in and dropped incendiary bombs, suffocating or burning to death about 300 refugees sheltering there. That bombing was one of dozens of such U.S. air attacks on refugee columns and concentrations in South Korea in 1950–1951, reported by survivors decades later. Most of the attacks came long after the Fifth Air Force's operations chief, Col. Turner C. Rogers, recommended to the generals in late July 1950 that the practice be halted. Let the Army shoot them if they're afraid of them, Rogers had said.

American journalists saw lines of bullet-riddled refugee bodies along roadsides in South Korea, but little more than hints of what was happening ever got to American newspaper readers. Military censorship was now stricter, even threatening courts-martial for reporters who "bring our forces into disrepute." Those who were there bore witness, however. "The most horrifying part of this last advance has been the hundreds of refugees killed by our strafing," Associated Press correspondent Stan Swinton wrote to his parents in a January 30, 1951, letter among his posthumous papers. "The children weren't hit; they just tumbled off the mothers' back and froze to death by the roadside. . . . Do not the enemies we make among the civilian population counterbalance and more than counterbalance the damage we do to the Reds?"

"DON'T LET A BUNCH OF CHINESE LAUNDRYMEN STOP YOU," MAC-Arthur's right hand, Maj. Gen. Edward Almond, told a subordinate at the start of the Chinese offensive in November 1950. By late that winter, the Chinese had stopped the Americans. They and their North Korean allies had MacArthur's forces locked in a debilitating seesaw war over Korea's midsection, a war in which the 7th Cavalry and other U.S. and South Korean regiments climbed and fought and died for the next ridge, or peak, or barren dome, only to abandon it the next day, or be driven from it with more men wasted.

On January 21, 1951, Gen. Ridgway issued a "Letter to the Men of the Eighth Army," invoking God and "Western civilization" and the fear of "Godless" communism, to try to explain why they were fighting. He also invoked the pitiful Korean refugee, saying the war would determine "whether the flight of fear-driven people we have witnessed here shall be checked, or shall at some future time, however distant, engulf our own loved ones in all its misery and despair."

For the Garryowens and other GIs, the loftiest goal was staying alive, and the life of combat, of flashes and deadly thunder in the night, of screams from the wounded, became life itself. "Hey, Joe! We're coming!" the enemy would shout in the blackness. Then came the chilling blare of tinny bugles and brass gongs, and finally the "Chinks," rushing up the slopes into the American guns.

War's sheer inhumanity was now routine. In the 2nd Battalion, with a courtly lieutenant colonel named John Callaway as new commander, and the tough survivor Mel Chandler, a major now, as executive officer, the men were taking few prisoners, battalion veterans said.

The grisly ironies of war also became routine. One day the clerks found themselves assigning dead men to 2nd Battalion companies. An enemy shell had hit a truckload of replacements, killing every green private before he could be processed, but the Army paperwork went on.

Through it all, these cold-eyed young men couldn't shake their own humanity. Art Hunter remembered "seeing little kids laying in ditches, starving. We'd be on trucks moving through. Nobody stopping. Kids laying in ditches with mud all over them and dirt. Nothing but bones. It was tough . . . tough." The medics reported the psychiatric casualty rate climbed sharply again among Army troops in the early weeks of the "Chinese war."

"LET'S RUN DOWN THAT DAMNED GOOK KID!" WHITE GIS IN A JEEP had spotted Suey Lee Wong walking back to Fox Company from a field hospital. The wounded rifleman, who didn't have his weapon with him, sometimes felt he also didn't have a place in a white man's army. He jumped out of the swerving Jeep's way.

A Seattle-area immigrant, son of a real "Chinese laundryman," the small, tough, intelligent corporal joined the Garryowens in January 1951. "No one would even talk to me. I was the only Oriental in the platoon," he recalled. He soon felt he was "fighting two wars"—against the enemy out there, and against bigots around him, men like the platoon mate who ranted at him, "I don't know what we're doing over here to help you gooks!"

Corporal Wong, born in China, fought a third war, too, over his own feelings about killing young men who looked like him while he was striving to be "American." During one assault, he scaled a ledge and quickly killed two Chinese at the top. Then he shot a third who reared up. "His guts were on the ground. He was in agony, writhing in pain, and so I then put two or three more rounds in him," he said. Their deaths weighed on him. "Maybe in a couple of weeks," he reflected, "a mother in a village would get a notification that they'd lost the son to farm. In a Chinese village, it's tragic. Who would grow the rice? Who would work the fields and harvest the crops? Who would look after the family and keep the name going?

"That day I felt remorse," he said.

Many white comrades, in a war with people of another color, felt little remorse, Wong learned. "The GI attitude was basically, 'They're just a bunch of gooks. Shoot them.'" In fact, the replacement corporal heard from old hands about the Garryowens' shooting of a "bunch of gooks" months before down south, under a railroad trestle somewhere. It was one bloody event among many, but one that somehow stayed with them.

BOLTS SNAPPING, BANDOLIERS SLAPPING OVER BACKS, WATER splashing into canteens—the overture to combat could be heard around G Company in the morning fog. It was April 10, 1951, and the 7th Cavalry, with "George" on the point, had drawn a high-profile assignment: Capture the towering, 826-foot-wide Hwachon Dam. The Chinese had begun to open its gates, and the U.S. command feared they planned to flood American positions on the Pakchon River, just above the 38th Parallel.

George and Fox Companies attacked up a rugged half-mile-wide tongue of land, with the Hwachon Reservoir on their right, ending at the dam, and a loop of the meandering river on their left. They soon ran into strong resistance, mortar and machine-gun fire that pinned them down.

On high ground behind G Company's forward elements, Buddy Wenzel lay with an M-1 fitted with a telescopic sight. He was a sniper now, his job to pick off troublesome Chinese. "I enjoyed it. I had the edge." Trapped GIs were running back under fire, and Wenzel rose to shout at them. A machine-gun round ripped through his right hand—his gun hand, his writing hand. As he was evacuated, a friend told him, "You're the last one." The G Company boys who had landed at Pohang nine months earlier were now mostly dead or maimed or broken men.

The attack was failing and men were dying. Two of the 2nd Battalion's five company commanders were killed. Beginning at 3:45 the next morning, April 11, Army Rangers paddled quietly across the dark, mile-wide reservoir to try a flanking attack. They were mauled on shore and were ferried back. Frustrated commanders next ordered F Company to send men over the lake in boats. Ralph Bernotas, three times wounded in Korea, soon to rotate to the States, had always felt like a survivor, but "that was the only day that I sort of gave up," he said. "I said, there's no way we're going to get out of this. We're sitting ducks, in broad daylight, on the water." Men, feeling their time had come, entrusted personal items to friends or officers.

Then word came from the rear: Break off the attack. The threat of flooding appeared less than feared. "It was a miracle," Bernotas said. How many friends had died? Brumagen and Dean, "Pop" Boehm and Cole, how many others? But Ralph would live.

Marines moved in and the regiment headed to Eighth Army reserve. A historian would later describe the Hwachon operation as "an insignificant gesture." Few knew that in the midst of it, Colonel Callaway, 2nd Battalion commander, was seen off alone, weeping.

THE DAY OF RALPH BERNOTAS'S MIRACLE WAS THE DAY PRESIDENT Truman relieved Douglas MacArthur of command in the Far East. The general had agitated one too many times for a global war against communism. The 7th Cavalry fought on, and replacement Garryowens died, until the unit returned to Japan in December 1951. It won a unit citation from the South Korean government "for outstanding and heroic performance of duty on the field of battle." In all, Custer's regiment suffered 1,080 men killed or missing in Korea.

Losses to the people of Korea during this time proved incalculable. A classified report to Truman said almost 400,000 homes had been destroyed in South Korea alone in the war's first year. The number of Korean civilians killed, including those killed by the U.S. military, was unknown. But the killing went on into 1951.

In the 7th Cavalry itself, during the pullback from North Korea in December 1950, the regimental staff ordered troops to use mortar and artillery fire against refugees trying to head south through their lines, the declassified record shows. The highest command in Korea, Eighth Army, sent similar instructions across the warfront—one declassified document dated it to December 1950, another to January 1951—telling corps commanders, "You have complete authority in your zone to stop all civilian traffic in any direction. Responsibility to place fire on them to include bombing rests with you."

Not every top officer accepted such tactics. A memo from the intelligence staff to the operations staff at Far East headquarters in Tokyo in December 1950 said indiscriminate killing of refugees was "extremely prejudicial to the UN cause, which is largely founded on the humanitarian principle of protecting Koreans from Communist aggression."

In April 1951, however, still further instructions went down from Eighth Army to shoot refugees trying to cross front lines, and one regimental intelligence officer objected. The 38th Infantry's Capt. Rizalito Abanto reported to his commander that the directive was difficult to carry out, because of "the hesitancy on the part of the younger soldiers to fire directly upon groups of old men, women and children." He recommended that refugees be let through the lines. The record gives no indication his words were heeded. In fact, three years later, after the armistice, a U.S. Army War College study on lessons learned in Korea on handling refugees stated, "Strafing fire from low-flying aircraft is very effective in clearing a road."

Surviving Garryowens began rotating home in the spring of 1951. At the time, researchers in the United States were growing more interested in the impact of combat on men's minds. At the annual meeting of the American Psychiatric Association in Cincinnati, a research team reporting new findings said the wartime killing of defenseless civilians, in particular, triggers "traumatic war neurosis." It engenders guilt, they reported, great and long-lasting.

7

July 30, 1950
No Gun Ri, South Korea

Many hours after it ended, after the last cries echoed off the concrete walls, the elder brother stood outside the mouth of the tunnel. "Koo-hak!" he shouted through the darkness and rain. "Koo-hak!"

Chung Koo-hun had crawled away on his naked belly that first night of the killings. He crept up a slope and hid among the scrub pine. Over the next two days, he circled home to Chu Gok Ri, a village now in ruins. Then the guilt-stricken seventeen-year-old warily made his way back to the No Gun Ri bridge, staying out of sight of strafing American warplanes. The American troops had pulled back the day before, and Koo-hun heard from survivors that his eight-year-old brother was near dead when they last saw him in the underpass.

A single North Korean soldier, a nervous teenager, stood guard at the trestle. Koo-hun could make out the heaps of white. They were his neighbors, bodies stiff and swollen in the summer night.

"Koo-hak!" he shouted. Inside, the boy heard but could not

answer. A bullet had sheared off his nose and torn his mouth. He was weak. His throat had gone dry. He tried to speak, but had no voice.

The elder brother drew a breath and jumped over the wall of dead blocking the way. Now he stood in the black shadows beneath the bridge. He stumbled over bodies spread on the underpass floor. "Koo-hak!" The boy heard him come closer, but still he could not speak. "Koo-hak."

Suddenly, a hand shot out of the darkness and locked onto Koo-hun's pant leg. His heart stopped. He reached down. He felt the shirt, the same coarse shirt he had worn as a child. He pulled him up, lifted him onto his shoulders, and found his way back out into the night, carrying a maimed little boy, the last survivor of the bridge at No Gun Ri.

"COMRADES, YOU ARE LIBERATED NOW." THE HANDFUL WHO SUR-vived remembered North Korean soldiers, on the afternoon of July 29, stepping among the bodies under the trestle to find those still stirring. They told them to wait until dark before leaving because American planes were strafing the roads.

The soldiers found "indescribably gruesome scenes," a North Korean journalist accompanying them reported. "Shrubs and weeds in the area and a creek running through the tunnels were drenched in blood, and the area was covered with two or three layers of bodies. About 400 bodies of old and young people and children covered the scene so that it was difficult to walk around without stepping on corpses," Chun Wook wrote in an article published August 19, 1950, in *Cho Sun In Min Bo,* a communist newspaper in Seoul.

The half-blinded "Golden Girl," Hae-sook, and little brother Yang Hae-chan had shielded their wounded mother for three days. Now the mother, her legs riddled with shrapnel, told Hae-chan to lead his sister home. "Don't worry about me. Hurry and go!" she told them. The boy and girl began a painfully slow overnight trek, the small ten-year-old leading the tall sister whose face was raw and burned, and who could see only when she peeled back a closed right eyelid with her hand. They didn't know what lay ahead, but Hae-chan told Hae-sook he would take care of her.

Close to dawn, the weakened children and other refugees encountered North Korean soldiers along the road. They gave them rice and meat to eat. Brother and sister slowly walked on, hiding whenever they heard planes. Finally they saw the pear tree, entered their *matang* and, to their shock, heard their mother's voice calling to them. Their father had gone to the trestle and carried her home on his back A-frame. He had escaped from the Americans during the chaos of the first air attack on the refugees. Now their mother would live, too. But the children's older and younger brothers, their grandmother, an uncle and two aunts, two cousins, a cousin's wife and her baby boy—all lay dead at No Gun Ri.

As some survivors staggered home, under the eyes of the North Koreans, others were headed south, following the tide of the American retreat.

Park Sun-yong, her life spared after losing her two children, had been taken by Jeep on a stretcher to a U.S. Army field hospital in Kimchon, 18 miles southeast of No Gun Ri. She remembered little but the sight of an American military doctor standing over her there, checking her wounds, and then the sounds of roaring engines as the 1st Cavalry Division headquarters began to pull back from Kimchon. She had "a horrible dream of death" there, she remembered. She was confused, lost. Why did they kill her children? Where was her husband, Eun-yong?

That day, July 28, on the main road through that same small city, an intense young man in a barley-straw hat was searching the faces of the thinning column of refugees from the north, looking for his wife, hoping that somehow Sun-yong would appear. Chung Eun-yong had been in Kimchon for three days. It was there that he heard the frightening tale of No Gun Ri from his nephew Koo-shik. But the ex-policeman knew he must head south or risk capture by the North Koreans. As the woman he had come to treasure lay in a hospital bed nearby, fading in and out of consciousness, Eun-yong boarded a train overflowing with people—"The last train south!" they announced—and it slowly pulled away from Kimchon station, as his eyes still searched the platform crowd.

It was not the last train. That evening another was loaded with patients from the Army field hospital. Park Sun-yong's journey from No Gun Ri would stretch into weeks. Within days, U.S. forces would set the city of Kimchon ablaze, as they had Chu Gok Ri and scores of other South Korean villages.

A CHUBBY BOY WITH A LITTLE GIRL ON HIS BACK WALKED DOWN the southbound road, two small figures lost in a white river of humanity. Park Chang-rok was the thirteen-year-old who had watched from the foxhole as Americans machine-gunned the villagers at No Gun Ri. He assumed his parents were dead. His duty now, he knew, lay in saving his four-year-old sister, but this resourceful country boy couldn't know what that would mean in this summer of war.

A U.S. Army officer had taken them away from No Gun Ri and driven them up to Autumn Wind Pass, about 10 miles east. There he dropped them off, and gestured for the boy to walk south. "I still feel grateful toward him," Chang-rok said. As they trudged down from the pass, "there were tremendous thuds of artillery in the hills. I walked on carefully with my sister on my back. I was afraid and tired." The girl, Chang-soo, was wide-eyed and silent.

They spent the first night sleeping in a pile of barley straw in the front yard of a roadside house. The next morning, barefoot, in short pants, they rejoined the files of refugees moving south. Chang-rok spotted a police officer. "I was so happy to see a Korean policeman and I rushed to him just to talk and tell him what happened at No Gun Ri," he recalled. "But he shooed me away."

Ten miles beyond Autumn Wind Pass, at Kimchon, Chang-rok found some young men from his village, Im Ke Ri. Helpless and afraid, the boy tried to join them, but they shook off the two children. "They began running," he said. "I chased them with my sister on my back, pleading and shouting to them to take us with them."

He couldn't catch up. "I collapsed. . . . I cried on the road," and again they were swept along in the refugee flow. "I survived on food that I begged from people."

Dry July's dust was turning to mud in drizzle and rain. Finally, 15 miles farther along, at Yakmok, the weary boy heard people saying that no refugees were being allowed across the Waegwan bridge, up ahead, where U.S. troops—Maj. Gen. Hobart R. Gay's 1st Cavalry Division—were crossing the Naktong River. A train sitting at Yakmok station would be the last to cross the river, he heard, but refugees were barred. At the station, American military police fired shots into the air to hold back the crowds of desperate civilians.

"I knew this was my last chance, and I thought hard about how to get on the train with my sister," Chang-rok said. The boy gathered up rice straw from around the station, wove it into rope and made a harness to carry his little sister, freeing his blistered hands. He then hid behind some trackside trees to await his chance.

"One of the MPs went away from the train and I rushed to a boxcar," he said. "The door was open and I saw South Korean soldiers inside. I begged for our lives. I said all we wanted was to get across the river, not any farther. The soldiers threatened me. They told me to go to my father. I told them what happened at No Gun Ri, about how American soldiers killed the villagers. I told them my parents were killed by American planes at No Gun Ri."

The soldiers took pity. "They lifted me and my sister up, like a piece of baggage, and put us in a corner with a blanket over us." The whistle sounded, the car jerked, the last train rolled out to cross the slow, muddy Naktong. On the far shore, a hard road still awaited the boy Chang-rok and his little sister.

OTHER SURVIVORS FROM NO GUN RI FAMILIES, NOT AS CLEVER OR lucky, were stranded on the river's west bank.

The two Kim brothers from Chu Gok Ri—Bok-jong, who talked the Americans out of shooting the two dozen "suspects" in the ditch on July 25, and Bok-hee, who escaped from under the trestle—had found each other by chance on the road south, and they headed down the west bank of the Naktong to cross the bridge at Tuksong-dong. Just after dawn on Thursday, August 3, the two young men were approaching the bridge, which lay around a hillside, when they heard a thunderous explosion. The 14th Engineers had just destroyed the span.

"People rushed back toward us," Bok-jong said, "and they said a lot of people were killed in the explosion." After the initial shock, refugees turned back toward the river, spreading down the shore, looking for places to cross. "We were desperate. To us, safety was just across the river," Bok-jong said. "Word spread that North Korean communists were killing everybody behind us."

Finding what looked like shallow places, refugees began wading out with bags on their heads, but many underestimated the Naktong. "When several people began crossing, others followed like a swarm of bees," Bok-jong said. "Some people held the tails of their cows. A woman held her baby on her head and when the river swallowed her, she just lost the baby or abandoned the baby. Some people completely disappeared under the water. Many, I mean many, people drowned." Said his brother, "It was total chaos."

Before long another deadly threat appeared over Tuksong-dong, American planes strafing refugees trying to cross the river, witnesses recalled. The determined Kim brothers eventually managed to swim to the east side.

TWENTY-FIVE MILES UPRIVER AT WAEGWAN, AS THE HOURS DRAGGED by that August 3, the press of the Eighth Army's deadline weighed on General Gay. One of those among a stream of civilians crossing the Waegwan road bridge early that evening was a sixteen-year-old boy from the city of Kimchon named Lee Duk-soo. He could see his father a few paces ahead, his A-frame packed with baggage. People had simply pushed past a flimsy barbed-wire barricade at the bridge's western end, Duk-soo remembered.

Suddenly, "the bridge shook and I was knocked off my feet. I had never heard such explosions." His father was simply gone, Duk-soo said, apparently blown off the roadway. "I thought the whole bridge would be blown up, and I instinctively jumped off this very high bridge, with my bag on my back, instead of running back to the riverbank. . . . In the water, I heard people moaning around me. I cried for my father, but I couldn't find him." The boy waded back to the west bank. He never crossed the Naktong; he never found his father.

Another teenaged boy, Kim Jin-sok, waiting on the west bank a mile downriver, heard the terrible explosions and saw the bright flashes as a section of the bridge was brought down that evening. The next day, the fifteen-year-old from nearby Yakmok, with his father and his twelve-year-old brother, joined three hundred other refugees fording the Naktong.

The murky water came to Jin-sok's neck. He held the family cow's tail, and he and his father grasped his younger brother's hands to keep him afloat. Then, when they were two-thirds of the way across, Jin-sok said, American soldiers on the east bank began firing at them, groups of people almost immobilized in chest-high water.

"My younger brother let go of our hands," he said. "I saw that he was shot in the chest. His head dipped underwater. He was just swept away." His father also was hit, but he just stood there in the water, still carrying a tall load of quilts and bags on his back frame.

All around, the slow current turned red with blood, Jin-sok said. "People and their baggage floated slowly downstream like bundles of rice straw in flood water." The frantic Koreans didn't know why they were being shot. Some tried to turn back. Some pressed on toward the nearer shore.

Jin-sok said he and about a hundred others made it to the east side, and there the soldiers stopped shooting "when they saw I was nothing but a half-naked kid." After pleading with the GIs, the boy waded back out and brought his father in from the river. He was gravely wounded in the abdomen. The boy sprinted to a nearby village for help but found it abandoned. Returning to the riverbank, he tried to comfort his father, who soon died in Jin-sok's lap. Unable to dig a grave, the boy simply covered the body with quilts and bags, while American soldiers watched, and then left for the south. Months later he managed to return and gather his father's bones for burial at home.

Seven weeks into the Korean War, South Korean civilians were finding that the killing of noncombatants had become a routine tactic in U.S. Army front-line units and of the U.S. Air Force to eliminate any possibility that disguised enemy soldiers or southern guerrillas would penetrate U.S. lines. But contradictions were rife, and fatal for innocent Korean families. Two days after Jin-sok's father and brother and other refugees were killed around Waegwan, General Gay allowed thousands of similar refugees to cross the river to safety. Three days after that, one of Gay's colonels issued his flat order to "shoot all refugees coming across river."

The deadly inconsistencies were well known to the people of one Yongdong County hamlet. American troops had ordered them to leave their homes and head south. By the time they reached the Naktong, the bridges had been blown, and they tried wading across. But now the Americans considered them targets. One woman, Cho Koon-ja, eighteen at the time, said U.S. soldiers opened fire on her group as they tried to cross north of Waegwan. "Bullets popped and sizzled into the water. It was such a barrage," she said. "The surface was covered with dead people and injured people and cows and bags floating down."

Terrified, Koon-ja turned around and began a long journey back to the hamlet, No Gun Ri, where she and her neighbors were about to discover the horrors that had unfolded in their absence.

THE PIGTAILED PARK HEE-SOOK, THE IM KE RI GIRL WHO SAW HER sister, mother, father and baby niece die at No Gun Ri, had turned back earlier from the Naktong. She had heard what many were hearing along the refugee road: American GIs were allowing only young women to cross the river's bridges. "People were also saying everywhere that GIs did bad things to young women," Hee-sook said.

Soldiers of every nationality undoubtedly raped Korean women during the war. The precise extent of the crimes would never be known, but at times South Korean officials were driven to complain to U.S. commanders about the attacks. Under a U.S.–South Korean agreement hurriedly reached July 12, only the U.S. military had criminal jurisdiction over U.S. forces in Korea. The reports rippling through the refugee columns, however well grounded or exaggerated, made many women more fearful of the big, fatigue-clad foreigners. Hee-sook, whose mother hid her in an urn when the Americans came to her village, had gone as far as Kimchon when she turned back toward Im Ke Ri.

This devastated sixteen-year-old was a shocking sight along the road. She was still coated with caked blood from hiding beneath the bodies at No Gun Ri. Her clothes were stiff with it, her hair matted and sticky with it. She was so weak from hunger and her bare feet so battered that she could hardly walk. "I was a living ghost," she said. Other refugees "clicked their tongues and wondered what happened to me. Some cringed at me."

She had companions, a woman and two daughters who also had escaped from the trestle killings. They grew desperately hungry and then fell violently ill when they devoured some green pumpkins. They collapsed and lingered in an abandoned house for a time. Finally they separated, but the woman told Hee-sook that No Gun Ri was not far off.

The dazed girl stumbled on. "When I walked, I felt like I was floating." Somehow she reached the trestle. From a distance she saw the ground covered with white clothing. "When I got closer," she said, "the hair on the back of my neck stood up."

Park Hee-sook had come upon a "scene from hell": flies thick on corpses; dead babies atop dead mothers; faces bloated to twice their normal size; white maggots "as big as fingers" squirming in bodies; water pooled around them turned to grayish yellow muck; the dead's bulging, staring white eyes.

Family members, neighbors, playmates who had surrounded this girl's young life were now "a junkyard of mangled human bodies." Her first instinct drew Hee-sook in among the heaped and strewn remains to search for the bodies that were hers. She couldn't find her mother, but recognized her father by his cotton vest. She took his money, stained now with water and rot. She broke off a pine branch and left it to mark his remains.

She looked further but still couldn't find her mother, nor her dead sister on the tracks. Exhausted, disoriented, sinking deeper into despair, she began moving haltingly down the road toward Yong-dong, the road she last walked when her family was ordered south by the Americans. Two men were coming the other way. They were a cousin of her father, and her own cousin and good friend Lee Duk-hwan. Hee-sook broke down as they approached.

"I flailed my arms wildly and sobbed, trying to explain what happened," she said. "But Duk-hwan kept stepping backward to try to keep a distance from me. He mumbled that he heard I had died. He seemed to think I was a ghost. He gawked at me and then said, 'Is that really you, Hee-sook? Why do you have all that blood on you?' He picked up a stick and lifted the sticky hair off my face, to get a good look. He was afraid to touch me. And then he said, 'Ah, you really are Hee-sook.' "

They took her back to Im Ke Ri, where they talked over the grim business of bodies and burials. Hee-sook found the village man who oversaw most funerals. "I told him I didn't want my father to become food for ravens. The man said, 'I remember your father. He was very kind to me and a good son to his mother, too. Let's go and I will see what I can do.' "

With a stretcher made of rice-straw mats, the four of them set out for No Gun Ri. They hid in the bush when American planes appeared. They reached the trestle and entered the tunnel. They began to push the father's body onto the stretcher. But half the body had been resting swollen in water. It snapped in two, the upper half rolling onto the straw mats.

"It seemed that the bones and flesh moved separately," Hee-sook said. "The others were scared and stepped back." The girl grew frantic. "I cried, and I virtually scooped up the remains of my father—like mucus—with the cup of my bare hands. That was how we collected my father's remains and brought them back home."

As they carried the dead man's disintegrating body homeward, they again and again ducked out of sight from prowling American planes. The relatives finally suggested they temporarily bury her father where they were hiding at the moment, at a hamlet not far from Im Ke Ri. She dug the shallow hole with her own hands, and there he was laid, and Hee-sook went home, a girl alone.

Such final scenes, of great love and devotion amid the gruesomeness, were played out in family after family in Chu Gok Ri and Im Ke Ri. The heat and humidity, the rain and the insects were all rapidly breaking down the bodies, forcing villagers to confront unspeakable sights and difficulties in doing their duty to the dead. One man's family knew him only because he had stitched his name on his hat. One nine-year-old girl returned to the scene and saw her dead mother's pregnant belly burst open, the fetus liquefying on the ground. Two boys and their mother found their father because she tied a strip of green cloth to his ankle when she left the tunnel. "My mother carried him on her back, and my brother and I each held a leg," son Hwang Sam-ryang said. "We all cried and carried the body up the hill to bury it temporarily." Months later, after the war passed them by, villagers returned to the trestle area, dug up shallow graves, and bore bones back for a proper interment among the hillside burial mounds of their little valley.

Many bodies—unrecognizable, of strangers, of families that were largely obliterated—went unclaimed, and were dealt with by the villagers of nearby No Gun Ri. When they returned home, those villagers first found that the Americans had burned most of No Gun Ri's thatched-roof huts. Then they discovered bodies blocking the pathway through the trestle. They pushed these unclaimed bodies to the side in the underpass and threw dirt on them, and there they remained through the winter. In the spring, villagers said, the men of No Gun Ri, consuming considerable *malkgulri,* rice wine, to fortify themselves for the unpleasant task, buried those remains in two places outside the tunnels. Some villagers remembered bodies placed in a line of trenches the Americans had dug. Some said other bodies were buried on a trackside slope.

In a land of elaborate funerals, where the spirits of the dead seem ever-present, where holidays honor the ancestral departed and meals are symbolically shared with them, these crude farewells for so many of No Gun Ri's victims scarred the souls of those they left behind. Villagers would always say that these spirits were not at rest, that they would wander at No Gun Ri until the *han*—the injustice—was resolved. Until then the restless souls would linger in a kind of Buddhist limbo called Ku-chun—Nine Springs—a place for those who die unjust deaths.

OBLIGATIONS TO THE DEAD MAY HAVE KEPT THE BOY KOO-HAK among the living. After carrying his little brother, the last survivor, from the tunnel the night of July 30, Koo-hun rested a few hours with the boy in an abandoned hut, and then set out through the darkness for Chu Gok Ri, passing North Korean soldiers who were on the move. The spindly eight-year-old drifted in and out of consciousness on his brother's shoulders. By the time Koo-hun walked up the valley toward Im Ke Ri, to hide in the mine out of sight of U.S. planes, the sun had risen above the eastern ridges.

The boy moaned for water. Koo-hun put him down and went to the nearby stream, cupping some water in his hands. Coming back, he looked at the boy's face in the morning light for the first time. "I dropped the water and froze in place," Koo-hun recalled. "My brother's face was gone. It was black with dried-up blood and flesh. I ran away, quite a ways. Then I stopped. My heart raced and my mind raced. What should I do? He was not the brother I used to play with. He had a monster's face. . . . But Koo-hak still was my little brother."

Koo-hun went back, picked up the boy again and walked on. Their father soon came down the path toward them. The despondent man looked at his two sons. One, he saw, was dead. "When I put him on the ground and looked at him, he did seem to be dead," Koo-hun said. The father said Koo-hak should be quickly buried on the hill, but the elder brother protested. "I told him the boy died such a tragic death and we should let him spend a night at home before his burial. I insisted."

In Korea, to die away from home is to risk an unsettled afterlife, eternity as a roaming soul. The high school student Koo-hun, who had wanted to learn so much about the modern world, still felt the pull of age-old beliefs.

Back at their house, one of those in Chu Gok Ri that had been spared burning, he placed his brother's limp body in one room, to "die at home," and he went to sleep in another. The next morning, the father shook the elder brother awake. The boy was alive.

"He said we had a big problem," Koo-hun recalled. "I said, 'Why is it a problem?' He said Koo-hak was not going to live like a normal person and that was a big problem. I told him that even if that was a problem, it was a problem for me, not for him, because I was going to take care of my little brother."

Koo-hun learned that North Korean army doctors were working at the old Salvation Army hospital, one of the few buildings still standing in Yongdong. The tall, strong teenager put Koo-hak on his back and walked to town, three miles away. Homes still smoldered in Yongdong, and bodies were scattered along the streets. Bombed and burned buildings held still more dead, many of them South Korean civilians killed by the continuing American air attacks. At the hospital, Koo-hun found the courtyard filled with wounded, moaning in pain, both soldiers and civilians.

He could barely squeeze through hallways packed with broken, bloody bodies. He put Koo-hak down in front of a North Korean clad in a white doctor's smock, and asked for medicine. The soldier scowled. He didn't have enough medicine for the troops, let alone civilians, he said. Koo-hun's desperation made him unafraid. "You are a so-called people's army and you refuse to treat a villager! What kind of people's army is that?" he asked loudly. The impressed soldier relented, giving Koo-hun some powder to make a medicinal paste for the wound.

The boy's injury was severe. Parts of his nose, his lip, his cheek, his gum were gone. Through the summer it did not heal. Pus ran from it and it smelled badly, making Koo-hak something of a village outcast. He wore a mask to hide the grotesque hole in his face. He remained weak, too, and his brother had to carry him for months. Koo-hun found two civilian doctors doing relief work in Yongdong, and he lifted his brother onto his back and walked there every day for a month to have the wound checked and antiseptic applied. It would be months before Koo-hak could walk, and years before the young man who lost half a face, but found an unbreakable brotherly bond, could face the world.

VILLAGERS' HEARTS POUNDED WHEN THEY HEARD THE FIGHTERS and other warplanes shrieking in from the east and south in those days of August and September. American pilots attacked anything that moved. When he carried Koo-hak on his back every day to the doctors, "we almost got killed several times because of the American planes," Koo-hun said. Villagers took to hiding in the hills during the day and returning to their homes after dark, when the planes stopped flying.

The rice cycle still governed their lives. They tried to weed and cultivate in the late-night gloom, as the autumn harvest approached. But families had been decimated, survivors were often too disabled or weak to work the paddies and North Korean soldiers would sometimes keep them from the fields, drafting villagers for labor gangs to repair bombed stretches of railroad overnight, or to transfer boxes of ammunition from place to place on their A-frames. In the end, however, the two villages were blessed: It was a healthy crop that year, one that "grew on its own."

The North Koreans occupied the Yongdong area for barely two months in mid-1950, but their political takeover was swift and well planned. Later, in decades of repression that followed in South Korea, it became a crime to speak well of the North Korean occupiers of 1950. But that short-lived regime was popular, at least at the outset, among some ordinary Koreans, from Chu Gok Ri to Seoul.

Although tens of thousands fled Seoul in late June, more stayed behind, some donning red arm bands to welcome the invaders from the "Red" north to the southern capital. American intelligence reports later said most of Seoul's student population actively worked with the northerners. Many Koreans with strong nationalist sentiments, bent on making their country whole again and expelling the foreigners, supported the northern cause, whatever its ideology. Many Koreans were simply disgusted with the corrupt, autocratic

Rhee years. That opposition deepened with the bloodbath of executions carried out by the retreating government through the summer, when military police and other agents shot thousands of leftist political prisoners and dumped their bodies in mass graves outside Taejon and Taegu and elsewhere in the south.

As the northern army rolled over most of South Korea, leftist activists from north and south restored local "people's committees" as provisional governing bodies, the committees that had been outlawed by the U.S. military government in South Korea in 1945–1946. Beginning in late July 1950, the new regime conducted elections for permanent committees, a vote designed to favor candidates of the communist Korean Workers Party. Popularly elected village committees, largely of young and poor peasants, then chose representatives to township committees, which in turn elected county committees. The communists promised things many in Korea's vast lower class had never imagined: an end to unemployment, an eight-hour workday, improved medical care and schools, equality for women. The new rulers quickly confiscated the property of the *yangban* landed elite and of Rhee government officials, and announced an elaborate land reform. Many peasants were simply told they now owned the small plots they had been renting.

The North Koreans were not a heavy-handed presence in Chu Gok Ri, villagers said. A small armored unit settled in for a time, its two or three tanks hidden beneath the village's big persimmon trees. Villagers said the northern soldiers treated local women respectfully. Nine village youths were drafted into the People's Army. Three eventually fled and returned home, and six were never seen again. New allegiances were declared and old ones hidden, but years later the villagers generally chose not to relive those days. Chung Koo-hun recalled that the young Chu Gok Ri woman whose rape he witnessed at the hands of the Americans became active in the pro-communist Women's Alliance. Other villagers said one Rhee government official in their midst avoided persecution by transforming himself into a school janitor who taught pupils songs in praise of North Korean leader Kim Il Sung.

Those who were children then invariably remembered the music sessions. Up at Im Ke Ri, local leftists gathered people in a tobacco shed in the evenings and led them in political song. "If some people did not join, the young leftists found them and slapped their faces, humiliating them in public," Yang Hae-chan said. His sister Hae-sook recalled one lyric in particular: "General Kim Il Sung. Ah! Ah! Our General Kim Il Sung. His name will shine forever!"

While children glorified him across more than 90 percent of the land, Kim himself had his eyes on the one corner of Korea where they did not yet sing his praises. "The Korean people are determined to fight until all the American invaders are expelled," Kim told a French journalist as the U.S. Army withdrew into its Naktong River defense perimeter.

ONCE ACROSS THE NAKTONG, STOPPING IN WAEGWAN, THIRTEEN-year-old Park Chang-rok dropped down from the boxcar with his sister, as he promised the soldiers he would. Taegu, the big town, lay 12 miles to the southeast, over the Shindong Pass. With four-year-old Chang-soo on his back once more, Chang-rok trudged through the thick dust of the road over the pass. Finally reaching teeming Taegu, he didn't like what he saw. He walked straight through.

"I knew that it would be harder to beg for food in a city," Chang-rok recalled. "In the countryside, houses at least left their doors open and you could enter and get a chance to beg. But in a city, people locked their doors."

Walking on several miles, he found what he was looking for, a village free of refugees called Wooksoo, and an empty village shrine. "We begged food from villagers and ate it in the shrine and slept there. It was spacious and it was all for just the two of us."

Then other refugees began arriving. The Park children were shunted into a corner of the shrine, and eventually the floor was filled and they moved outside, to eat and sleep in a field, or to huddle under the eaves when it rained, hugging each other as they slept. From inside, they heard parents softly singing lullabies to children. "On those nights, I cried a lot. My sister cried, too."

Soon the other refugees ran out of supplies and began begging, competing with Chang-rok for food. Seven or eight would stand in line before each village house. Each might get just a spoonful of boiled barley before moving on to the next house. The boy was lucky to collect five spoonfuls a day, and his little sister would get most of that.

"She ate like a baby bird. She opened her mouth whenever she saw food. I was starving."

Village grandmothers, seeing the boy growing thinner, took pity on the motherless children, sometimes giving Chang-rok rice balls or yellowed rice scraped from the bottom of a cooking jar. Some even told the boy he should give his sister away, or otherwise starve. They weren't serious, but Chang-soo heard and she never strayed more than arm's reach from her big brother.

Finally, Chang-rok made up his mind: He would go to the township office for help. With his sister on his back, the boy found the building and strode in, asking to see the head of the township. "An official slammed his fist down on my head and threatened to beat me more if I didn't go away. But I was desperate. I locked onto his leg and pleaded. I made quite a scene. I yelled and begged for help. I talked about how I became a war orphan at No Gun Ri and had to flee with my baby sister."

Hearing the commotion, the *myon-yang,* or township chief, came out of his office, took the children back inside and listened to Chang-rok's story. The *myon-yang* gave the spirited boy a government ration ticket, a guarantee of food. Chang-rok returned to Wooksoo, his sister on his back, his ration ticket in his pocket, the only refugee in all the village to possess such a prize.

THE TRAIN FROM KIMCHON, WITH PEOPLE CLINGING TO ITS ROOF-tops, steamed into Taegu's chaotic main station. Repeated announcements ordered refugees to continue southward; they were barred from the overcrowded city. Chung Eun-yong paid no heed. The stern-faced young man slipped through the station crowd, into the sweltering streets and straight to Taegu prison, where Kwan-yong, his elder brother the prison guard, had found shelter. It was July 28, four days since Eun-yong had left Im Ke Ri.

The ex–police lieutenant was a smart and determined man, but in the face of war's upheavals he felt increasingly helpless. Somewhere, back where he came from, his young wife and two small children were in danger. His brother was just as distraught, having left his wife and four children behind. Their cousins the Kims, the two young men who had swum across the Naktong, soon found the Chungs at their Taegu refuge. Kim Bok-jong's first words were a blow to the heart. "Our whole village was wiped out by Yankee bastards!" he told them.

The Kims, in rags, sunburned, dust-covered, sputtered with curses for the Americans. But Kim Bok-hee reassured Eun-yong, as nephew Koo-shik had done previously, that Sun-yong and the children were all right when he saw them under the trestle.

Days dragged by without news. Then, on August 17, a long-distance call came for Chung Kwan-yong at the prison. When the grim-faced brother returned, he told Eun-yong that his wife, Sun-yong, had called from a military hospital in Pusan. Eun-yong asked for more details, and his brother fell silent. Go to Pusan as quickly as possible, he told him.

Eun-yong set out by foot the next morning for Pusan, 70 miles to the southeast. The Kim brothers joined him. They found they were accompanied by tens of thousands. Seven artillery shells fired by advancing North Korean troops had landed in Taegu before dawn, and by midmorning the provincial government was distributing handbills advising the population to evacuate the city. Learning that President Rhee had left the day before, people panicked. Taegu's population of 300,000 had swollen to 700,000 with refugees, and much of the city now packed up what they could and poured out on the southbound road, in the now-familiar scenes of young and old, oxcarts and the occasional automobile, boxes and bundles atop heads. Eun-yong and the Kim brothers were caught up in the southbound sea of white. By midday, after reconsideration within the government, police loudspeakers began urging people to return home. In the heat of the afternoon, the frenzy slackened and many turned around.

The midsummer sun finally drove the three young men from the road as well. They took to traveling only in the morning and evening, and began following the winding route of the Naktong River toward Pusan. Refugees still filled the roads, the shade of every tree seeming to hold one or two exhausted people. Villages along the way ran low on food to help their displaced countrymen. Eun-yong and the Kim brothers, eating poorly, grew weaker and walked with sticks.

Reaching the town of Namsung, Bok-jong spotted an army recruiting table at the railroad station and decided on the spot to join up. He asked Eun-yong to take care of younger brother Bok-hee.

The two trekked onward, begging food where they could, sleeping in the rain. They reached the outskirts of Pusan, only to find people heading north, saying new refugees were being turned back from the jam-packed city. Eun-yong found a policeman who listened sympathetically to his story and helped them enter town.

The old port city was seething with the flood of homeless from the north, tens of thousands crowding every possible shelter. "Homes" made of packing cases blanketed the hillsides. Filthy, barefoot children roamed the streets, begging, selling fruit. Refugees trying to peddle their possessions or services crowded the city's Kukje Market, in streets shaded by white canvas. Telephone poles were plastered with scribbled notes—people trying to find lost parents or children, brothers or sisters. Bicycles, rickshaws, oxcarts, U.S. Army Jeeps crawled through the throngs.

Chung, more than a week after Sun-yong's call, finally reached the hospital, but she was no longer there. She had been released and had gone to a refugee center on the harbor island of Young-do.

Sun-yong's three weeks in the makeshift hospital was a time when her injuries began to heal, but she grew sicker at heart. A kindly older woman helped clean her up and bought her new clothes. The woman's husband, like many civilian patients in the hospital, was being treated for wounds suffered in a U.S. strafing attack. With the aid of penicillin, Sun-yong's own wounds, in her right arm and torso, were mending. The woman's son, a telephone worker, arranged for Sun-yong's call to her brother-in-law in Taegu.

In the evenings, after meals, civilian and soldier patients alike would join in singing songs of loss, of faraway hometowns. Sun-yong, day in and day out, would kneel atop her cot, praying for Koo-pil and Koo-hee. "I cried a lot, day and night. I could not stop it," she said. "My mind kept returning to my dead children."

Eun-yong hurried across the bridge to Young-do and the refugee shelter, an old school. Children swarmed, playing, over the dusty grounds. Their parents cooked over open fires in cans discarded by the U.S. military. Eun-yong's eyes searched for Koo-pil and Koo-hee among the ragged youngsters. Then he spotted a woman with a bandaged arm doing laundry at the school well. It was Sun-yong. He ran to her and they embraced. She collapsed in tears, her face buried in his chest, her back heaving with sobs. He asked again and again about the children, but she couldn't answer.

"At that moment, I realized what happened," Chung Eun-yong remembered. "And I knew that I was never going to have another happy day in my life."

The twenty-seven-year-old husband, guilt building in him, joined his grieving wife in the bare, empty existence of refugees, a life of waiting for life to begin again. At night, among snoring men and filthy baggage, the young couple would startle awake, reaching out in their sleep for the children who were no longer there. Sun-yong told her husband of a strange vision preying on her mind. Over and over she would see Koo-pil's blistered, bloody little foot, that morning on the road to No Gun Ri, and the boy's tear-stained face. "I think I'll go crazy," she told him.

Eun-yong ran out of money, and the law student walked Pusan's noisy, jostling streets looking for work. He found it with the Americans, unloading U.S. military supplies at a Pusan wharf, joining hungry teachers, journalists and others desperate for any employment. It was hard, unpleasant work, under GIs who yelled orders at the "gook" laborers and sometimes whacked laggards in the buttocks with a stick. "I felt my blood rising when I saw that," Eun-yong said.

On his third day on the job, he heard a soldier holler "God-damn!" and saw him drag out a worker who had been eating stolen sugar behind a stack of boxes. The American took the Korean into an office, had him kneel down and then poured sugar into the man's mouth. When the humiliated worker struggled, other GIs kicked him in the rear. After that day, a disgusted Eun-yong never returned to the wharf.

Church workers came regularly to the Young-do camp and gave Sun-yong food and other items. One day, sixteen-year-old Kim Bok-hee left the center to look for work and never returned; he had been seized by police and impressed into army service. As August turned to September, Eun-yong would sometimes climb a hill over the harbor and stare out at the calm aquamarine of the sea. In his mind Eun-yong would see his children and imagine their terror at No Gun Ri. If he could just know where they were buried, that would be something. "The sorrow and the sense of guilt was staggering," Eun-yong remembered. "I would wonder to myself whether I would ever overcome this sorrow. Sometimes I thought my heart would knot up and knot up until it exploded." It was during those days in Pusan that Sun-yong persuaded her husband to go to a Christian church with her. Together they prayed.

THE PADDIES AROUND CHU GOK RI TURNED A RICH GOLDEN YELLOW as September wore on. Despite the dry spells, the well-timed rains gave the hungry villagers a strong rice crop, even with too few hands doing too little tending. But the peasants were worried, since the new regime was methodically checking the fields. They feared all their crops would be confiscated.

The communists enlisted an educated helping hand in Chu Gok Ri. Chung Koo-il, the twenty-three-year-old college student who pleaded futilely for mercy with the GIs at No Gun Ri, had escaped from the trestle with cousin Koo-hun that first night. His mother, his schoolteacher sister Koo-ok, another sister, and her small son had all died.

"Of course, my brother had anti-American sentiments because of what happened at No Gun Ri," said Koo-il's younger brother, Koo-hong. "But I don't think my brother became a communist. He was a troubled man and didn't know what to do. He was angry but he didn't quite want to become communist."

The family of fishmonger Chung Hee-yong, the village patriot of 1919, had the only tile-roof home in Chu Gok Ri, a house that quickly caught the invader's eye. North Korean officers commandeered it as a headquarters, confiscated family possessions and consigned the father, his surviving eldest daughter and the two brothers to a single room. But Koo-hong said the soldiers were "not too bad." They sometimes gave villagers rice and even meat.

Like other villagers, the Chungs hid in the hills during the day, when American warplanes roamed the skies. The strong, tall sons had an added motive: to avoid the local Korean Workers Party cadets who drafted villagers for a "People's Righteous Army."

As the rice harvest approached, the local party committee finally summoned Chung Koo-il, the village's star scholar, to Yongdong. They wanted him to work on rice "donations." He began going from village to village collecting data about each farmer's production to report back to party officials. Koo-il did this for three weeks leading up to Chusok, the harvest moon holiday. Shortly after dawn that day, September 26, 1950, the grieving family performed a hurried ancestral ceremony at home, with a meager food offering of steamed barley. Koo-il then left, dressed in his usual white shirt and black pants. He said he had to survey the crop at Shimwon, over the mountains a few miles to the north.

That afternoon the Americans returned to Yongdong County, and his family never saw Chung Koo-il again. The rebuilt 24th Infantry Division, breaking out from the Pusan Perimeter, had pushed up the main road through Kimchon, to Hwanggan and now Yongdong. The 1st Cavalry Division this time followed a route to the east. Demoralized North Korean units, trapped by the Inchon landing force to their rear, scattered into the countryside.

Koo-il's family, fearing he was killed by advancing American troops, searched the route to Shimwon but found no trace. Villagers then speculated that the young student had joined the northerners, and may even have made his way to North Korea. A village legend took root. Over time Chung Koo-il, once the promise of Chu Gok Ri, would be remembered as "the American-made leftist."

THE TREE BRANCHES IN IM KE RI DIPPED UNDER THE WEIGHT OF apples and ripe red persimmons. Wildflowers tinted the hillsides with pink and white. The cry of the wild goose fleeing Siberia's chill would soon announce the height of autumn, the season in Korea when "the sky is high and horses are fat." But the autumn of 1950 in the valley was most of all a season of tears and fearful home-comings.

One day in early October, a boy with a little girl on his back strode up the road. Park Chang-rok had seen soldiers moving north and knew the tide had turned. The grandmothers of Wooksoo cried when their favorite refugee told them he was going home. With an empty U.S. Army can dangling from his neck and oversized shoes on his feet, the thirteen-year-old walked all the way from Wooksoo village, more than 60 miles, wading across the Naktong in water up to his chin, his sister on his shoulders. Finally he reached No Gun Ri and his grandparents' house. They saw the children from a distance, the boy's unshorn hair now brushing his shoulders.

"They were so happy that they forgot to put on their shoes before rushing out to cry over us," Chang-rok said. Then came the news: His two-year-old brother and paternal grandmother had been killed at No Gun Ri, but his mother and father survived the carnage. His father later searched the tunnels and tracks for the bodies of the two missing children but finally gave up, thinking they must have been blown to pieces.

From the grandparents' home, brother and sister pressed on to Im Ke Ri, where their shocked parents burst into grateful tears at the sight of them. The news spread down the valley. "Some people came to see me from Chu Gok Ri," he said. "I was a village hero." The dutiful son had come home, many weeks and miles after first dashing for the small culvert with a wide-eyed girl on his back.

ALTHOUGH ACCEPTING A RIDE FROM A U.S. ARMY TRUCK DRIVER frightened Park Sun-yong, her husband insisted they climb aboard. Eun-yong and the childless young mother were hitchhiking back home after two months in the south, joined by his brother Kwan-yong. They walked part of the way, fording the Naktong River at a shallows where people had placed stepping-stones. They saw the ruin and butchery of the war in the blackened hulls of villages, in bodies along the road. At one village they saw people pulling decaying soldiers' bodies from a hut, North Koreans who had been packed wounded into a room during the retreat, only to die there.

A final Jeep ride with a South Korean soldier left them at the doorstep of Chu Gok Ri. It was almost dark, the evening of October 2, but they could see the Chung family home had burned down when the Americans "scorched" the village. Family survivors were crowded into a single room of a relative's house. There, amid the choking tears of reunion, the mournful accounting was made: Kwan-yong's wife, Min Young-ok, had died in the tunnel; her baby, their only son, died of a head wound after his grandmother brought him home; one of their three daughters died of her wounds soon after. Now the prison guard was a widower with two girls to raise, children forever changed by the terror they had witnessed.

AS THE AUTUMN NIGHTS LENGTHENED AND THE AIR GREW CHILL, survivors struggled to reestablish village life. The snow came early that year, dusting the mountains by late October. Although the war had moved north, even into North Korea, its dangers were never far away. The leapfrogging American offensive northward had bypassed thousands of North Korean soldiers. These stragglers, often armed, sometimes riding horses, often wounded and on stretchers, would pass through the villages in the night, trying to make their way north, as residents huddled behind closed doors. Sometimes they would stop and ask for food.

One cold winter's night in Im Ke Ri, a female soldier came to the door of the hut of Park Hee-sook, the orphaned teenager. She told the pigtailed girl how she hoped to find her way back home to North Korea. "I fed her well, and she stayed in my home for a few days," Hee-sook said. "Because I was living alone, I welcomed strangers." Villagers remembered women soldiers asking for help in arranging marriages for them locally, so they could settle in the south and drop out of the terrible war.

The daytime belonged to the Americans, troops who would appear along the road headed north. At the sight of them, village children, survivors of No Gun Ri, would hide in terror.

During the two-month North Korean occupation, rumors spread through the valley that the communists had drawn up blacklists of local people to be executed as political enemies. By the time the North Koreans fled, no one had been killed in Chu Gok Ri or Im Ke Ri. Other places, the villagers learned, were not so fortunate.

Chung Eun-yong returned to Taejon, a city now in ruins, and heard from an aunt a tale of North Korean atrocity. Before retreating from the city, she said, the northerners took their rightist prisoners out of their detention places and did to them what South Korean military police did to the leftists in July. They took them to a nearby valley, forced them to dig a long ditch, lined them up on its edge, and then shot each prisoner in the head, to tumble into the mass grave. Returning to his job at Taejon prison, Eun-yong's brother was told the prison's well had been filled to the brim with the bodies of executed detainees, most of them policemen, soldiers, government officials and their relatives, all shot or beaten to death by departing North Koreans. These mass killings were the ones discovered by advancing American troops in the Taejon area in late September.

Witnesses across the occupied territory attested to "people's court" spectacles at which handfuls of alleged enemies of the people were denounced before an assembly of frightened neighbors and then bludgeoned to death or otherwise executed. Especially in Seoul, the sudden North Korean military setbacks inspired hasty killings of political enemies by young leftists. Returning briefly to the capital in November, Eun-yong learned that a professor at his college had been murdered by one of his own students, a communist. Some southerners were simply transported north and into oblivion.

The brutality alienated many in the south who had tolerated the leftist takeover, but many southerners were outraged anew by the bloodbath that followed as the Rhee regime reasserted power over South Korea and eliminated alleged communist collaborators. Village feuds, clan grudges, business jealousies produced baseless allegations of collaboration, and countless people with little link to leftist politics were summarily executed by southern authorities.

When Eun-yong visited his Taejon aunt, she was distraught because her son was being interrogated and beaten in the police station for having served in the Workers Party during the North Korean occupation, even though he had been forced to become a party member, she said. Another son had been drafted into a North Korean art troupe and disappeared with the northerners.

Back in Chu Gok Ri, the vanished Chung Koo-il's "rich" family, targets of North Korean harassment over the summer, now became victims of the Rhee rightists. The family's home was a command post once more, this time for South Korean police guarding the rail line against guerrilla attack. The railroad police repeatedly abused them, beating the father, Chung Hee-yong, and his surviving daughter, Tae-gu, with rifle butts and wooden bars from field cots, demanding to know where the "collaborator" Koo-il was. For Hee-yong, battered nationalist hero of 1919, only the identity of the batterers had changed, from Japanese to Korean.

A DIFFERENT KIND OF WAR, GUERRILLA WAR, DRAGGED ON IN THE south for many months. As in 1949, people heard the crackle of gunfire in the night as police combed the Yongdong hills for armed leftists. As late as 1952, guerrillas descended on Yongdong and attacked and burned the county administrative building. Stranded

North Korean soldiers joined forces with southern guerrillas, especially in the rugged Chiri Mountains of the far south. The Rhee government crushed them with scorched-earth campaigns, burning mountain villages suspected of supporting the leftists. Hundreds, perhaps thousands of villagers were killed, including women and children. These killings went largely unreported.

Politics in the south, behind the front lines of war, deteriorated into a bald power struggle between the seventy-six-year-old Syngman Rhee and his opponents in the National Assembly. The assembly elected the president and was prepared to bring Rhee's corrupt rule to an end in 1952. But his strong-arm methods prevailed. On May 24, 1952, he had dozens of assembly members arrested for "communist connections" and then put the body under virtual house arrest, ringed by right-wing militants, to coerce a unanimous vote amending the constitution in favor of popular election of the president. Rhee subsequently claimed 86 percent of the popular vote later in 1952.

The North Korean occupation bequeathed one legacy to the countryside: The Rhee government did not try to undo the reassignment of land to tenant farmers. A U.S.-inspired land reform, interrupted at the war's outset, was resumed and it accommodated what the North Koreans had begun.

But the wantonness of the war had left the rice-and-barley heartland devastated. Thousands of southerners' homes had been destroyed by American soldiers and by American jets' 100-gallon napalm bombs. Then, just weeks later, civilians were allowed back to live among the charred shells. A classified report to President Truman said half the livestock in South Korea, mostly used to work the fields, had been destroyed, along with 70 percent of South Korea's industrial capacity.

By late 1951, when the 7th Cavalry Regiment left Korea, the war had stalemated. It stretched on, with mounting human losses, until the armistice of July 27, 1953. By then, battle-related deaths included more than 33,000 Americans and an estimated 200,000 or more South Korean soldiers. The South Korean government put the number of North Korean and Chinese soldiers killed at 479,000.

On this peninsula whose people had not waged their own war for centuries, the civilian death toll was enormous, but never conclusively calculated. A South Korean history estimated 244,000 South Korean civilian deaths. In 1974, however, the Seoul government reported 990,968 civilian "losses" during the war. Reviewing the uncertain numbers, American historian Allan R. Millett wrote, "U.N. officials think 900,000 deaths not unreasonable" among southern civilians. The huge noncombatant toll in North Korea remained undocumented outside the country. The American air war against the north was catastrophic, climaxing with the bombing of giant irrigation dams, triggering calamitous floods that swept away villages, rice crops and thousands of lives through drowning and starvation.

"We attacked every type of target. We did some major damage out there," the Air Force's Maj. Gen. Emmett O'Donnell Jr. told U.S. Senate committees in 1951. "I would say the entire, almost the entire Korean Peninsula is just a terrible mess. Everything is destroyed." Gen. Curtis E. LeMay, the U.S. bombing expert, came away from the three-year war with this impression: "We burned down every town in North Korea, and South Korea, too."

Even a little schoolhouse: The new wooden building where the children of Chu Gok Ri and Im Ke Ri were taught was burned down. No Gun Ri's youngest survivors, many scarred and maimed, sat on straw mats under the trees, in the open air, and tried to begin anew. An indomitable boy named Park Chang-rok scored first in his class.

FOR THE PEOPLE OF THE VALLEY, THE DAMAGE WAS NOT ALL VI-sible, the wounds not all of the flesh. Chun Choon-ja, the girl who wanted to see big towns, had been taken to the far south by helpful adults after being saved at No Gun Ri and was cared for by an older couple in a town south of Taegu until finally her grandmother traced her, with information from travelers, and brought the ten-year-old home. But at home all had changed. The Chu Gok Ri house was badly damaged, the family of nine was now just four, and her father, who fled from the trestle on the second day, was a broken man.

"He used to hold me on his lap and weep all day," Choon-ja remembered. "People said he went back to the tunnel and went through the decaying bodies over and over looking for me." He didn't work the fields; he was sick, complaining of choking and difficulty in breathing. The grandmother prayed for him, before an offering table of food and fruit. Then she called in a shaman, a *mutang*.

Your son is possessed by the spirit of his wife, the woman told her. Choon-ja's mother had lived a hard life and died an unjust death at No Gun Ri, the *mutang* said, and her spirit now will not rest in the afterlife.

Choon-ja came to believe that what possessed her father was guilt, that he was overwhelmed at having survived when his wife and father, his brother and sister-in-law, and his new baby son did not. What Choon-ja didn't know was that the baby, her parents' "Great Success," had died at the hands of his own father, silenced in the shallow water of the trestle.

For some in Chu Gok Ri and Im Ke Ri, death's timeless rituals provided some consolation. The seventeen-year-old student Chung Koo-hun found his mother's body at the trestle and temporarily buried her nearby. Then, in the winter, he exhumed her remains and laid her in state at their home. The family prepared food, as is traditional, and placed it before the deceased, and then they gave her a proper burial on the valley's slopes. The Suh family buried an empty set of clothes in place of the grandfather whose remains they never found. For months, such processions wended up the village path, led by the funeral bell, the bell whose knell, one midsummer's day, had told of the Americans' arrival.

Some could not be consoled. Cho Nam-il's wife, the young woman who gave birth on the tunnel floor and who abandoned her infant there, was seen in later days running aimlessly up and down the crooked village lanes, wandering through the fields barefoot, floundering in the stream, laughing hysterically, her mind seemingly gone. The family took to locking her up in a room. They bought herbal medicine. Slowly the frenzy subsided.

In her lonely hut, sixteen-year-old Park Hee-sook "waited" for her mother, the woman lost among the heaps of dead. "It was as if my mother would open the door and step in any minute." And at night Hee-sook would kneel before a scrap of paper stuck to a mud wall, a funeral tribute to her father, scrawled out by his cousin. "I cried all night, day in and day out. I could not believe my father died." Years later, a man who had been an Im Ke Ri watchman told her he remembered passing the dimly lit house on winter nights and hearing the girl weep. "It was such a sad wail, the man said."

IN DECEMBER 1950, CHUNG EUN-YONG REJOINED THE POLICE AT THE provincial headquarters in Taejon, in part to avoid conscription into the army. He and Sun-yong moved in with his brother and the two surviving nieces. The young husband resumed his studies part-time and completed his college course just before the war ended in 1953.

Sun-yong drifted through the months, disturbed, sleepless. Her full face paled and thinned, showing her cheekbones. In January 1951, Eun-yong suggested she spend some weeks with her parents at Shimchon. She improved in her home village. She found a devout Christian deaconess there who prayed with her for five straight days, after which Sun-yong felt her faith restored. She knew she would meet her children again, in the kingdom of God. But Koo-pil and Koo-hee never let go of her; their faces appeared before her; their spirits tugged at her unconscious.

For the father who left his family to the mercy of American soldiers, no prayer could lift the weight. Eun-yong would always hear his boy's cry that last morning to take him along. Now Koo-pil was just a face in a photograph. The picture from his first birthday celebration, buried in a leather box with other keepsakes, had somehow survived the fire that consumed the Chung home. The Americans had taken his son's life and left the boy in a lost grave. All he had was a photograph, its edges singed by heat, and a burning sense of guilt, and duty.

8

The old soldiers took up positions, video cameras loaded and ready. The younger men, in boots and blue, sidled their mounts into formation. A bagpipe's sour "Garryowen" floated over the parade ground. The 7th U.S. Cavalry, Custer's regiment, had come back to the Black Hills, this time as a saddled-up cadre of actors in antique uniforms, and a gray-haired corps of war veterans in sunglasses and soft-soled shoes.

Four decades after they fought for their lives at the apple orchard, forty-three years after falling tragically short at the Hwachon Dam, Snuffy Gray and a handful of other 7th Cavalrymen from Korea had come to the Sioux Indian heartland on this day in 1994 for a symbolic gathering, a *Wolakota,* a reconciliation of warriors from another conflict, another century.

These veterans of 1950 had largely found each other in the 1980s at reunions of the 7th U.S. Cavalry Association. The South Dakota excursion, and its ceremonial joining of flags and offering of friendship, was a combined vacation and lesson in nineteenth-century history, a detour from the usual circuit of casinos and convention hotels. Some veterans donned the old Stetson hat of the Indian fighters. "They're very proud of their heritage, very proud of their background, and very proud of the fact they're combat veterans and combat soldiers," the burly sixty-eight-year-old Gray, the day's booming-voiced master of ceremonies, told an audience of 250 ex-soldiers, Sioux and others assembled at Fort Meade, site of an old 7th Cavalry outpost.

For the natives of this forgotten frontier, history was not a dress-up day. It lived in their hearts, and to many the "Bluecoats" had not been warriors but agents of plunder and slaughter. As the choreographed program of feathered Indian staffs and regimental flags unfolded, one old Sioux's heart turned back to that melancholy past.

"I sat back here and observed the cavalry, mounted horses, and I wondered what my people felt when the 7th Cavalry came into the Greasy Grass and the Rosebud," Simon Looking Elk, a Presbyterian minister and Lakota Sioux, told the gathering before leading them in prayer. "My great-grandfather and great-grandmother and grandfather and grandmother were there. Then I sat back here and thought a little bit more about how my other ancestors, the Big Foot Riders, felt when the Cavalry were there."

At the Greasy Grass and Rosebud Rivers in 1876, the cavalrymen attacked the Sioux to destroy their independence and take their lands. Lt. Col. George A. Custer and 264 of his men were killed at the Little Bighorn battle, but the Indians finally were scattered. Fourteen years later, a Sioux band led by Big Foot was massacred by the 7th Cavalry at a stream called Wounded Knee. Up to 370 men, women and children were killed, many by the Garryowens' new automatic cannons.

The ceremony on this gusty, bright morning, 118 years to the day after Custer's "Last Stand," was the idea of the South Dakota state government, long sensitive to relations between Native and other Americans. The governor himself tried to set the tone. "It's important to remember what happened here and at sites like Wounded Knee," Walter D. Miller told the parade-ground assembly. "From those events we have built the foundation for reconciliation."

The veterans showed goodwill, too. "We respect to this day the Native Americans and the reasons they fought against the 7th Cavalry, trying to preserve their land, their villages," the 7th Cavalry group's president, Korea veteran Edward L. Daily, told a local newspaper.

But the federal government did not take part in the *Wolakota*, the U.S. Army having withdrawn representation at the last minute, and among the Sioux the attendance was low and opposition strong. "It is not a peace ceremony that is needed between the Sioux Nation and the 7th Cavalry," the newspaper *Indian Country Today* editorialized. "It is a proclamation written and signed by the president of the United States apologizing to the Lakota/Dakota/Nakota people for the attempted genocide against them."

As long ago as 1912, the Big Foot Survivors Association petitioned the U.S. Congress, without success, for compensation for the deaths of their loved ones at Wounded Knee. In 1990, the Congress finally expressed official "deep regret" for what it recognized as a "massacre." But the Sioux rejected that resolution, demanding a formal apology and compensation.

Lt. Gen. Nelson A. Miles, who commanded the region at the time of Wounded Knee, described the killings years later as "cruel and unjustifiable." Chief Big Foot's followers were headed for the safety of a reservation at a time of renewed unrest among Native groups in the Dakotas. They were under 7th Cavalry escort when, according to the most reliable accounts, soldiers began disarming the men, a shot was heard and the troopers opened fire in a frenzy of killing. A soldier later recounted that "women with babes in their arms were brought down as far as two miles from the Wounded Knee Crossing." It was late December. The Indian refugees' bodies were left to freeze on the ground, and there their restless spirits still abide, Indians believe.

Now, in 1994, the Rev. Looking Elk asked the Fort Meade gathering to pray with him for peace, "to ask God or the Great Spirit to touch the hearts of many so that our words will not go by like the wind blowing."

A 7TH CAVALRY REGIMENTAL HISTORY, *OF GARRYOWEN IN GLORY*, published in 1960, said the wars against the "savage Indians" were part of an "inevitable struggle between the aborigines and an advancing civilization."

The author of the lavish, 462-page history was Lt. Col. Melbourne C. Chandler, the hard-driving officer who had ended his Korea tour as commander of the regiment's 2nd Battalion and who had begun it as the inexperienced captain leading H Company when the refugees were killed at No Gun Ri.

Throughout the rest of his Army career, mostly in Germany and at the Pentagon, Chandler remained proudest of his affiliation with the famous 7th Cavalry. His work on the book, which was richly illustrated, meticulously compiled, became an obsession. Behind its gold-embossed cover of crossed sabers, he dedicated it to all 7th Cavalrymen for their "noble accomplishments." He wrote glowingly of the Garryowen esprit de corps: "It is more than likely that if a unit distinguished itself on the western frontier, it did so again in the island campaigns of the Pacific and again in Korea, the latest exploits having a definite connection with the successes of the past." The book devoted ninety-three pages to the regiment's operations in Korea, but nowhere did it hint at the killing of the refugees at No Gun Ri.

After his return from Korea, Mel Chandler, the Tokyo dance-floor charmer, began drinking heavily, relatives said. When he did discuss the war, "he referred to it as a pretty tough time," recalled his uncle, the Rev. E. T. Cooprider.

As early as 1953, Army doctors were prescribing antidepressants for the crew-cut thirty-two-year-old major. He was hospitalized after he finally published his book, complaining of chest pains. Doctors found no sign of a heart attack, but noted he had been unable to sleep well and was under considerable stress.

The colonel was a likable man, Cooprider said. "He'd make some people believe they were the only people in the world when they were with him. He had that type of personality." But he changed after the war, and the book was part of the problem, the uncle said. "It became quite a burden on him financially." Chandler paid for the publication himself, borrowing money in hopes of recouping it from sales. The debts would weigh on him for years.

As a self-publisher, the colonel could choose his own publication date. He made it June 25, 1960—Custer Day, but also the tenth anniversary of the start of the Korean War. For Mel Chandler, as for many of his men, it had been a hard ten years.

IN THE EARLY EVENING OF SEPTEMBER 2, 1953, IN A SECOND-FLOOR apartment in Alexandria, Virginia, a young soldier drank four beers and then exploded in fury, punching his wife, then his mother-in-law, throwing furniture out a bedroom window, finally grabbing the older woman's baby and running screaming into the street, swinging the child in the air. It took five policemen to wrestle the maddened man to the ground. He was hustled off to the Army hospital at nearby Fort Belvoir, strapped to a gurney and sedated.

"KOREA WAR HERO GOES BERSERK IN ALEXANDRIA HOME," read the headline at the top of page 5 in the Washington Daily News.

Art Hunter had come home to Virginia from Korea more than two years earlier with a record of bravery and a mind in turmoil. The 7th Cavalryman who had cut down dozens of North Korean attackers at the Naktong apple orchard became a machine-gun instructor at a Stateside post. But he fell into repeated trouble with the Army, going absent for long periods without leave.

In January 1954, four months after the violent episode in Alexandria, the Army discharged Private Hunter as "undesirable," a category ineligible for the usual veterans' benefits. His mother, Ruby, later wrote to a U.S. senator hoping to get her son's honorable service recognized. It was a plea from a woman bewildered at what war had wrought.

"He had been through so much, he should have been hospitalized," she wrote. "His nerves were shot, to say the least. He was always a hardworking boy. He got in no trouble before he went into the Army."

But the woman who managed to get a battered birthday cake to her boy in his foxhole was no match for the Washington bureaucracy. Art Hunter, wracked by sleeplessness, terrifying nightmares from the war, flashbacks, faces in the dark, had only just entered his "living hell."

THE AMERICA THAT MEL CHANDLER, ART HUNTER AND OTHER GARRY-owens came home to in 1951 was a land changing rapidly. Americans could now direct-dial their own telephone calls across the continent. Televisions, costly novelties when they went to basic training, were now in 16 million homes. The wealthy didn't have to exert themselves behind the wheel anymore: Luxury cars had power steering. Returning GIs learned the latest celebrities in the land were named Mickey Mantle and Marilyn Monroe. America was changing in more fundamental ways as well: In May 1951, courts ruled unconstitutional the segregation of blacks from whites in the restaurants of Washington, D.C., the nation's capital.

That month another drama played out elsewhere in Washington, as Gen. Douglas MacArthur, fired as Far East commander in the midst of the Korean War, testified before a U.S. Senate panel about his showdown with President Truman. MacArthur again advocated full-scale war against China, but Gen. Omar Bradley, Joint Chiefs chairman, told the senators that would be "the wrong war, at the wrong place, at the wrong time, with the wrong enemy."

It was also in May, in Seattle, that Ralph Bernotas and three Fox Company buddies stepped off a troopship from the Far East and decided to reacquaint themselves with their homeland at the ground level. Bernotas paid $400 for a well-worn 1940 Plymouth, and the four soldiers drove up the Columbia River Valley, over the Great Divide and down across the heartland, winding their way home.

From combat soldier to domesticated citizen, the lives of these young infantrymen were about to change radically, but each carried with him unseen baggage, shards of memory of Korea's horrors, the kinship and grief of combat. Bernotas, a "soldier's soldier," good buddy to many, felt the burden especially, his thoughts turning back incessantly to Brumagen and other dead friends, men like Dick Cole, a squad leader who was wounded during an F Company attack in the Naktong and died, lying in shock on the ground, when medics were slow reaching him.

Driving east, Bernotas made up his mind. Before his final leg home to Girardville, after dropping his friends off, he would detour to Erie, Pennsylvania, to visit Dick Cole's parents. He could tell them how bravely their boy died. He even picked up a red geranium in Ohio for Mrs. Cole. Then, at the last minute, he didn't turn off. "I chickened out. I didn't go to see her. It was just too emotional. I just didn't know how I could look at them."

He drove on into the rumpled valleys of coal country, and at the end of the road found a fire truck with lights flashing. Girardville's mayor had arranged a "parade" to welcome Sergeant Bernotas home. He presented Ralph with a new wallet and good-luck pennies. Led by the fire engine, the soldier and his parents rode in a borrowed red convertible up the main street as neighbors waved. It was Mother's Day. For the poor miner's son who left at age seventeen and returned at nineteen as the town war hero, it was a memorable moment.

"Then we made a turn at the bank, and then we went home," Bernotas said. "And I think I stayed drunk the whole month." That wasn't difficult in Girardville, a town of 5,000 that supported 33 bars in 1951.

Bernotas served out his few remaining months in the Army and then settled back into the family's frame house on North 2nd Street, where "Pop" sat upright in bed, slowly dying of black lung. Empty months followed, of looking for work where there was little, of living off Army savings his father had faithfully kept for him, and of drinking. Ralph asked the same mayor for a job and was rebuffed. And again and again his mind turned back to Korea, to what he had seen, to the faces of lost friends, to an unanswerable question. "I was constantly puzzled why I made it home and so many guys didn't."

One starry night not long after his discharge, Bernotas was out driving, from Frackville to Ashland to Girardville and back again in circles, until finally he took aim and smashed his automobile into a bridge abutment. The car was wrecked, but Bernotas suffered only minor injuries.

"I don't know why," he said, looking back. "I just hit the bridge in Ashland on purpose. Just to join my buddies. . . . I wanted to join my buddies."

ON THE PLATFORM OF THE PLANT CITY RAILROAD STATION, AMONG the canneries and orange groves of central Florida, a solemn-faced farmer stood in wait for the train bringing his boy home, in a flag-draped coffin, more than two years after his lonely death on the slopes of Korea's Hill 300. Waiting there with Cauley Hodges, James's father, was Buddy Wenzel.

Wenzel had needed months of healing and rehabilitation for his serious hand wound after returning to the States in the spring of 1951. His homecoming had been joyous and tearful. When his two older brothers first arrived at his Army hospital in Massachusetts, they lifted him up and carried him over to a surprise visitor—Dot, "Green Eyes," the girlfriend who had waited almost three years for him.

Back home in New Jersey, out of uniform for good, Wenzel saw her often. But Buddy had changed. The quiet boy who had cared for two little sisters, who had earnestly written hundreds of letters to pen pals, was now an angry, explosive man. "The least little thing set me off," the ex-sniper said. "She got scared of me." Their relationship fell apart.

Buddy was living with his mother, who also grew frightened. He seemed to hallucinate and couldn't sleep. If he did sleep, nightmares would leave him in a cold sweat, shaking. He began seeing visions of people, the same people over and over, Koreans, especially a little girl and boy. He knew who they were; they had been in his gunsights at No Gun Ri.

Dorothy Hodges, one of his original pen pals, had gotten married, but soon another of the Hodges girls was writing from Florida. Decar—"De"—was a sweet-faced, blond fifteen-year-old with a single overriding ambition in life. "When I was young I used to pray that all I wanted, when I get married, is a good husband," she said. Buddy was seven years older than De, but his snub-nosed looks gave him a boyish attraction.

James's death, as he himself had foretold in a letter to sister Juanita, left the family "sitting purty." The $10,000 death benefit freed them from sharecropping, allowing Cauley Hodges to buy a ten-acre farm in Plant City, where he began growing strawberries and bell peppers. But the farmer's spirit had been wounded by the loss of his runaway son, and in the end the father, too, would prove a war casualty.

When the Army notified Cauley and Eula Mae Hodges in 1952 that it had finally found their boy's remains among Korea's unidentified dead, the father called up James's friend Wenzel, and paid his way down to be with them for the funeral. From the train, beneath a glaring Florida sun, the coffin was borne to the Turkey Creek Baptist Church for the service, and then to the dusty, weedy graveyard out back for a rifle salute and interment. Father, mother and grandmother posed grimly for a photograph at the grave. Buddy Wenzel stood by their side.

Wenzel returned to New Jersey, but a conviction grew in Cauley Hodges's mind that he needed his dead son's friend closer by. He invited Buddy to come work on the farm and live with them. Having no special plans of his own, Wenzel accepted. He sensed he would be filling a role, "kind of taking the place of James, I think," he later explained.

He slept in a spare room in a garage, drew $13 a week plus meals and worked hard in the fields for the demanding Hodges. He also grew closer, over the months, to the pretty teenager De. Finally the couple asked for her parents' signed permission to wed—a legal necessity for a seventeen-year-old.

On June 20, 1955, Decar Hodges and twenty-four-year-old

Leonard B. Wenzel were married at the Turkey Creek church. "I didn't know what I was getting into when I got married," she said later. "I was so young." First a daughter was born and then a son, a boy they named Leonard James.

Over at the churchyard, a government-issued marker was placed over James's grave. With bland abbreviation, the chiseled gray stone identified his rank and unit. It gave his dates. As for why James Hodges died, it read simply, "Korea." The secretary of the Army had ruled that the "police action" in that far-off land would not be known as the "Korean War."

"THE KOREAN WAR IS A BASTARD WAR RECOGNIZED BY NO ONE. WE lost so many good old soldiers. We lost too many good people. The average citizen had no conception what Korea was," Snuffy Gray said of the uncaring reception many found on their return from Korea. Ralph Bernotas's welcome-home parade was a rare exception. "Nobody knew. Nobody gave a damn," remembered Gray, a leader of the 7th Cavalry veterans. "When I was home on leave I never wore my uniform. It just wasn't the thing to do."

They had fought a war unique in U.S. history, the first that Americans had not felt they won. By mid-1951, Gallup polls already showed only 35 percent of Americans viewed the war favorably. Veterans felt slighted in many ways: Supplementary pay, "combat pay" for Korea, was not approved until 1952; their GI Bill educational benefits, when finally adopted, were less generous than those for World War II veterans; and some veterans from that "good war" tried to exclude Korea returnees from their organizations. As the war neared its end in 1953, the *Army Times* editorialized that Korea "is the most 'forgotten war,' and the men who fight it are lonesome symbols of a nation too busy or too economy-minded to say thanks in a proper manner." When it ended in an unsatisfying negotiated stalemate, the American fighting man seemed partly to blame.

Many who fought it wanted to forget it, but couldn't. Gray, who made the Army a career, remembered crossing paths with Korea buddies at U.S. and European posts in the 1950s and learning that for them, too, the damage was deep—unbearable nightmares, flash-backs, some with severe drinking problems. "They'd say, 'Did you hear about so-and-so? Boy, is he screwed up.' "

The Korean War's impact ran deep at another end of the scale as well, as a pivotal event in modern history. It established the capitalist-communist Cold War as a military standoff, one that would define the second half of the twentieth century. American military spending quadrupled to $50 billion between 1950 and 1952, and the United States began building a huge, global military network of almost three million men and women, its manpower needs met by a permanent military draft. The fears of communism aroused by Korea led to the rearming of Germany and Japan under U.S. auspices, and the strengthening of the North Atlantic Treaty Organization's military structure.

Korea also planted a seed that would grow, a generation on, into a debacle. Buried in President Truman's announcement of U.S. inter-vention in the Korean conflict, on June 27, 1950, was the news that Washington would also step up its military involvement in another corner of Asia, aiding the French fighting to retain colonial control in distant Vietnam.

Underpinning all, Korea became Exhibit No. 1 in the case to prove that a centrally directed communist bloc was bent on military domination of the world. For domestic communist hunters like Wis-consin's Sen. Joseph McCarthy, it was a useful political platform. "Without the war, the senator probably could not have sustained his crusade of gossip, scandal, and innuendo," diplomatic historian Lisle A. Rose later wrote. "The war suddenly made the Red menace an immediate instead of an abstract reality."

The "menace" drove American politics to extremes. Congress authorized wartime concentration camps—never established—to incarcerate known communists. Those accused of leftist sympathies were blacklisted from jobs in the film industry and elsewhere. One category of Korea veteran became a special target of the communist hunters. Because some American prisoners of war, under pressure, cooperated with their Chinese or North Korean captors—by signing statements denouncing the U.S. war role, for example—word spread that all POWs were being brainwashed by the communists. When they finally were freed, they all fell under vague suspicions of betrayal, were isolated, and underwent lengthy debriefings. The shadow did not lift for years.

More than one-third of the over 7,000 American prisoners died in North Korean or Chinese camps from disease, starvation or brutality; others were coldly "executed" at the point of capture. The U.S. military planned trials for enemy captives accused of such war crimes, but the negotiated armistice prevented such Nuremberg-like prosecutions.

The U.S. Far East Command defined "war crimes" only as acts committed by the enemy. Col. Howard Levie, the Army lawyer who oversaw war crimes investigations from MacArthur's headquarters in 1950, acknowledged years later that U.S. commanders in Korea and other wars worked with blinders on. "I think we've done very badly on trying our own people on war crimes," Levie said. He said American brutalities were relatively rare in Europe during World War II, but became more common in Korea, "because American soldiers considered Orientals to be 'gooks,' that's why. They considered them to be lesser beings."

The blinders stayed on as American histories of the war began to appear in print. The official Army history of the conflict's critical first months, *South to the Naktong, North to the Yalu,* was published in 1960 after years of preparation. Nothing in the densely detailed book pointed to the refugee killings at No Gun Ri. It made no mention of the explicit orders in the 1st Cavalry Division and 25th Infantry Division at the time of No Gun Ri, in July 1950, to shoot refugees and civilians in the war zone. It did not note that the Air Force was strafing refugee columns at the Army's request.

The book did, however, report for the first time—ten years after the fact—that hundreds of South Korean refugees were killed when Maj. Gen. Hobart R. Gay ordered the Naktong River bridge at Waegwan blown up on August 3, 1950. That information came from Gay's own correspondence with the author, Army historian Lt. Col. Roy E. Appleman. But Appleman did not address the moral and legal implications, or military correctness, of Gay's decision, although 218 pages earlier the book noted that South Korean authorities court-martialed and executed a Korean officer found responsible for similar deaths in blowing the Han River bridge in June 1950. In 1960 America, Gay's revelation, deep inside an 813-page Army publication, was little noticed. The deaths of many other refugees on the Naktong bridge at Tuksong-dong, also on August 3, were not reported at all in the history.

Army sensitivity on the subject surfaced in 1952, when the Pentagon withdrew official endorsement from RKO's *One Minute to Zero,* a Korean War movie in which an Army colonel played by actor Robert Mitchum orders artillery fire on a column of refugees. "This sequence could be utilized for anti-American propaganda," a Pentagon official said in an internal document. Although shown in commercial theaters, the film was banned from U.S. military bases.

If American historians tended to look away from indications that U.S. troops shot prisoners and indiscriminately killed civilians in Korea, the reality could still sometimes be found in print, as in war veteran Thomas Anderson's 1956 novel about Korea, *Your Own Beloved Sons,* in which an American soldier protagonist "executes" two prisoners and then reflects. "Two goddamn gooks, he thought disconsolately. What's two goddamn gooks?"

THE "GOOKS" WERE SOON BACK IN THE U.S. MILITARY VOCABULARY, this time not in Korean white but in the traditional black of Vietnamese peasants. Snuffy Gray, George Preece and other old 7th Cavalrymen were among the combat veterans of 1950–1951 sent to this new Vietnamese frontier.

In the aftermath of Korea, President Dwight D. Eisenhower kept American troops out of Indochina, not wanting the United States enmeshed in another Asian land war. But by the mid-1960s, the U.S. leadership thought it could accomplish in Vietnam at least what it did in Korea: keep the country divided and half of it friendly. Just as in 1950, the generals of 1965 were confident that once the communist enemy saw the "first team," the U.S. Army, they would collapse.

But the American forces that poured into South Vietnam had little idea of who the enemy was or how to find him. They patrolled an unfriendly countryside of booby traps and snipers. They heard variations on stories about children and old women killing GIs with grenades. They soon viewed all "gooks" as potential enemies, all villagers as communist supporters. "Scorched earth" returned; in South Vietnam's heavily contested Quang Ngai Province, the majority of the province's hundreds of villages were destroyed by U.S. ground and air bombardment in 1965–1967.

On the morning of March 16, 1968, the 20th Infantry Regiment's C Company was lifted in by helicopter to attack a hamlet in Quang Ngai's "Indian Country." The relatively inexperienced troops were told they would find a Viet Cong unit in the hamlet, but instead they found defenseless civilians. Over four hours, the Americans slaughtered and burned, killing hundreds, mostly women and children, many of them babies, in what would become known as the My Lai massacre.

Some men refused to fire. Some men would later claim, falsely, that they were fired on. An Army helicopter pilot, Warrant Officer Hugh Thompson, who saved some Vietnamese in the midst of the bloodbath, later reported the slaughter to superior officers. Word went up to commanding generals, but it was covered up.

A year later, a soldier informant's letters to members of Congress finally led to a quiet Pentagon investigation, and that led to exposure of the massacre by journalist Seymour Hersh. Over time, twenty-five enlisted men and officers faced military charges related to My Lai, but only one was convicted at court-martial—First Lt. William L. Calley Jr., who in the end served only three years under house arrest. No solid evidence was produced linking higher U.S. commands with the indiscriminate killings of Vietnamese noncombatants, in contrast to what the declassified record later showed about the Korean warfront of 1950–1951, when high-ranking officers ordered civilians shot.

Army investigators said Charlie Company killed at least 175 people and possibly more than 400. But the figure of 504 dead, based on South and North Vietnamese sources, eventually was accepted by the world. The Americans suffered one casualty, a soldier who shot himself in the foot.

"We weren't in My Lai to kill human beings, really. We were there to kill ideology," Calley later wrote. "I looked at communism as a Southerner looks at a Negro, supposedly. It's evil. It's bad."

Calley's various statements seemed to exemplify two "mechanisms" that former West Point psychologist Dave Grossman has identified as facilitating killing in war: racial differences and "intense belief in moral superiority." The danger in such attitudes "is, of course, that every nation seems to think that God is on its side," Lt. Col. Grossman wrote in his book *On Killing*.

Army Secretary Stanley Resor, faced with a blot on the military's image and growing opposition to the war, declared that My Lai stood "alone in infamy." The U.S. press reached back to the Indian Wars to find parallels. "In the search for precedents, nothing can be found from World War I or World War II or the Korea conflict," the *Washington Post* reported.

But veterans of Korea knew better. "We had concealed from the American people the true nature of war," Col. Harry G. Summers wrote about Vietnam—the same Summers who went to Korea as a young corporal with a "hollow" division, and who witnessed months of horrors there.

ON MARCH 17, 1970, THE DAY THE MY LAI INVESTIGATORY COMMISsion announced its chilling findings, Mel Chandler lay comatose in an Oklahoma hospital, dying from the effects of his alcoholism.

Chandler left behind admirers, but the retired colonel left behind no known clues to who ultimately may have ordered the refugee killings at No Gun Ri. He apparently never spoke to relatives about the civilian slaughter. "Really, something bothered him," stepdaughter Patricia Dutton said. "I would think it was the Korean War that made it so hard. . . . The drinking got very bad."

Chandler retired in 1963 after a final, one-year tour of duty in South Korea, at U.S. Army headquarters. He didn't move on to another career. "He just never could get back out into civilian life," said his uncle, the Reverend Cooprider.

Cooprider officiated at his nephew's wedding to his second wife, Maybelle Blackwell, in Oklahoma City in 1965. Things soon deteriorated. Maybelle filed for divorce in November 1969, asking the court to immediately order Chandler out of the house because he "drinks excessively and is subject to fits of rage."

By 1968, Mel Chandler's liver had developed cirrhosis, but he continued drinking. He spent his final weeks in a hepatic coma at Tinker Air Force Base hospital in Oklahoma City and died on March 22, 1970. They buried him, with military honors, in a lonely cemetery on the plain, up the road from tiny Mildred, his boyhood home in the old Osage Indian country of east Kansas. He was forty-nine years old. It was the war, Patricia Dutton believed. "People come back, and they just don't seem to adjust."

Chandler's grand chronicle of the 7th Cavalry Regiment, "etched in the glittering pages of American history," was his legacy. "Mel Chandler lived for the 7th Cavalry Regiment," recalled Snuffy Gray. Sadly, when he died, the newspaper got it wrong, its obituary mistakenly assigning the proud Garryowen to the "7th Infantry Division."

PEOPLE HAD LONG KNOWN THAT MANY MEN DIDN'T "ADJUST" AFTER war, that many were afflicted by strange mental and physical maladies—"shell shock" and "combat fatigue," it came to be called. But the root causes were not understood. In a report to the American Psychiatric Association in 1951, researchers said troubled combat veterans shared symptoms of intense anxiety, nightmares, sudden rages. One "hitherto unnoted factor" was guilt, particularly over the killing of civilians or defenseless enemy soldiers, they wrote. But ignorance persisted: An article in the military's *Combat Forces Journal* in 1954, on the psychological impact of combat, stated flatly, "It takes five to 12 days for a soldier to recover from combat strains." It wondered whether a pill might be developed to immunize soldiers against "mental crack-up."

Many men back from Korea were left floundering. Joe Ipock, one of the engineer privates who witnessed the blowing up of refugees on the Tuksong-dong bridge, said the bridge and other experiences left him a "nervous wreck," plagued by nightmares, nausea and other problems. "And they had no rehabilitation for us guys. . . . We come back and we started drinking. That's how we dealt with it."

Delos Flint spent only two days at the warfront, being evacuated with wounds in the early chaos at No Gun Ri, where he was trapped for a time with refugees in the small culvert. But the terror never left him. "After I came back home I used to go walking at night and I wouldn't know where I was," he said. "I was staying with my brother and I woke up one night and I had my nephew by the throat. I nearly killed him."

When soldiers began returning from Vietnam with rage, paranoia and severe drug-abuse and alcohol problems, Veterans Administration psychiatrists puzzled over it. In Connecticut, Dr. Robert A. Rosenheck remembered trying to understand them in the diagnostic lexicon of the day—a psychoanalytical approach stressing such factors as childhood influences and innate drives. "I did not think of it as war trauma. . . . There was no training, no words to say this was related to war."

The mounting evidence enabled the American Psychiatric Association in 1980 to define it as post-traumatic stress disorder (PTSD), an affliction whose cause was not some inborn neurosis, but outside the individual—in a veteran's case, a traumatic wartime event. Research would eventually show that such events actually change the brain chemistry. "It is a hidden cost of war," Rosenheck said.

The professionals found three symptom clusters: "intrusive recollections," such as sudden psychotic flashbacks and traumatic nightmares; avoidance or "numbing," the withdrawal of an individual from intimate or broader social contacts; and the rage and edginess known as hyperarousal.

In 1990, a congressionally mandated survey of Vietnam veterans concluded that some 500,000 were suffering currently from full-blown PTSD, and a similar number had experienced it in the past.

Korean War veterans were never studied so comprehensively. But a limited 1982 study found that the Korea generation seemed as affected as the Vietnam veterans. The researchers found this striking for veterans of a "traditional war," apparently believing Korea to have been more like "traditional" World War II than like the televised horrors of Vietnam.

Researchers continued to find evidence of something nontraditional about Korea. A 1987 survey by the VA found that 35 percent of PTSD patients who had fought in Korea had attempted suicide during their lives, quadruple the rate found among PTSD patients from World War II; and the Korean veterans were much more likely than those slightly older men to have lost jobs multiple times and to have been incarcerated at some point in their lives.

Inside families, PTSD had powerful repercussions: alcoholism and drug addiction; unemployment; failed marriages; failure as a parent, because the veteran showed either "numbed" disregard or rage to children in need of discipline.

Afflicted veterans found help in medication—for sleep disorders, for suppressing nightmares and explosive moods—and in group or one-on-one therapy sessions, in which they could recognize the wartime roots of their problems and work with therapists to control their behavior. By the year 2000, VA hospitals were serving more than 50,000 patients a year in special PTSD programs. But that was a fraction of those who needed help, since more than two million older Americans were combat veterans and, "with respect to mental health, it is likely that combat exposure is particularly 'toxic,' " as VA specialists wrote in a 1994 study. Doctors found war-related symptoms first appearing even fifty years after combat, possibly triggered by such events as retirement or the death of a spouse.

In a way, thousands of American war veterans were diagnosing and treating themselves, by attending annual reunions where they found old friends who understood them. To psychologists, they were men rebuilding "social connectedness." To Shakespeare, they were a "band of brothers" forever joined by war.

"OUR REUNIONS GO A LONG WAY TO HELP PUT OUR GHOSTS TO bed," Snuffy Gray wrote in a 7th Cavalry Association newsletter. "They offer an opportunity for us to get together, discuss the way things happened and provide a better understanding in our minds of why and how things happened."

Veterans of "the forgotten war" were slow in getting together. The Korean War Veterans Association was not formed until 1985. Retirement from careers, the easing back of life, may have produced both the need to meet again—to put some "ghosts to bed"—and the opportunity.

Many Garryowens from Korea had seemingly adjusted well, furthering their educations, successfully raising families, making good livings. They had become civil and aerospace engineers who worked on the Alaska pipeline and the International Space Station; the owner of a small trucking fleet; a mapmaker; a banker; a sales executive; a school principal. One officer even became a priest. Dozens stayed in the Army, one lieutenant of 1950 rising to the rank of major general.

But few could truly put Korea "behind them." They had daily reminders, not just in framed displays of their Purple Hearts, Bronze Stars and other decorations on walls at home, but in the aches of old wounds, the ugly shadows of shrapnel in X rays, the steel plates in their bodies, the wintertime tingle from their frostbite. For some it was much worse—lifetime paralysis, missing limbs. And, even for the "well adjusted," invisible wounds lingered.

Year after year, hundreds of men and their wives checked into hotels in Las Vegas or Omaha, St. Louis or Philadelphia for the gatherings of the 7th Cavalry group's Korean War Veterans Chapter. They would take bus tours of local sights and meet for dinner to hear historians or active-duty "Cav" officers speak. But for many old soldiers the highlight was the quiet time in the hospitality room, sitting with each other, handing around scrapbooks and old snapshots, remembering names and faces. Association activist Ed

Daily drew from recollections and contacts gathered at the reunions in compiling two books about the 7th Cavalry's 16 months in Korea.

The pull of the annual gatherings was powerful. In 1998, in St. Louis, an eighty-two-year-old Gil Huff appeared with his daughter, forty-eight years after the frigid night when "Whiskey Red" helped stop the Chinese and save his 2nd Battalion at Sinchang-ni. The frail, forgetful Huff, who would die a year after the reunion, was blind in one eye, the result of head wounds suffered in his final action in Korea.

That partial blindness kept him from rising above colonel, even though he had emerged from two wars a seasoned combat officer with rows of battle ribbons. At age thirty-nine, however, this soldier who gave up a Japanese beauty for the sake of his career finally did marry. Stationed in Turkey, Huff wrote a sentimental "Mother's Day" letter home to Greenville, South Carolina, a letter Mrs. Huff proudly passed on to the local newspaper. Reading it there, and charmed, a young widow named Nina Hicks began corresponding with the bachelor colonel. In 1955, they were wed.

The colonel retired in 1957 to a new home they built in pretty little Abbeville, South Carolina. He dabbled in real estate and reared a daughter he doted on, Susan, to whom he told cautionary tales of war. "He always said soldiers as well as civilians were the pawns of war," Susan Huff Rush said after her father's death.

The 7th Cavalrymen in their hospitality rooms would recollect the heat and numbing cold of Korea, the Chinese bugles, the good life in Tokyo, the buddies long dead, but they would also remember "the people who suffered the most," as they often described the refugees. In late-night snatches of conversation, in half-finished sentences, men pondered the "why's and how's" of those first days in Korea, and wondered who ordered the killings at No Gun Ri.

Fox Company veteran Don Down recalled that at the St. Louis reunion he and a buddy, having a late coffee, were served by a South Korea–born waitress who told them American soldiers were highly respected in her homeland. "I said, 'Why?' She said, 'For what you did for our country.' It kind of choked me up," Down said. "I told her, 'Yes, but you don't realize how much your people suffered.' "

While some veterans stayed in touch regularly, others, like Norm Tinkler, lived alone with their memories. Back in Cloud County, Kansas, after Korea, the ex–machine gunner at least saw his prayer fulfilled: The four children he had with his wife were all daughters, no sons to send to war. In their century-old farmhouse, as the decades passed and Tinkler farmed, delivered milk, ran a bulldozer and finally retired, he never shook his feelings of guilt over No Gun Ri.

"You got to pay for your deeds sooner or later," he said. "That old boy upstairs is going to do the judging on it. And so if you've done wrong, you don't stand too good a chance of getting up there." The old soldier paused. "I ain't figuring on making it, 'cause of the Korean War and things that I had to do. That I done. I don't know if I had to do it or not, but I done it."

SPECIALISTS DEFINE ATROCITY IN WAR AS ABUSIVE VIOLENCE, ESPE-cially the indiscriminate killing of noncombatants. "Committing an atrocity is the single most toxic pathogenic experience leading to PTSD," said psychologist Alan Fontana, who with Rosenheck has conducted intensive studies from the West Haven, Connecticut, VA hospital. "All the studies show it," said Rosenheck, ". . . those who killed civilians experience more severe symptoms."

One VA survey of PTSD patients found that the proportion of atrocity participants leaped fivefold, to 21 percent, from World War II to Korea, and then grew again by roughly half, to 33 percent, among Vietnam veterans. Among the Korea veterans, an additional 23 percent reported witnessing atrocities.

Korean combat veterans felt that fellow Americans had little idea of their war's savagery. In the 1980s, University of Chicago historian Bruce Cumings sought to educate readers to the reality. His two-volume work on the origins and early days of the Korean War included a section, "American Atrocities," focusing on the unlimited air war and sketchy accounts of killings by ground troops. "This

Korean War, I think, was a far dirtier war than the Vietnam War," Cumings said later. "I've always believed that the Korean War could not stand the light of day."

The cover of Cumings's volume I reproduced a little-known painting, of huddled women and children about to be slaughtered by soldiers with raised rifles. Pablo Picasso called his 1951 work *Massacre in Korea*—an image conceived by a great Spanish artist in distant France, but one that could have been drawn from the mind's gallery of any young American retreating from No Gun Ri.

ON A DECEMBER MORNING IN 1994, RALPH BERNOTAS, NOW SIXTY-three, awoke in Ward 6 West at the VA hospital in Wilkes-Barre, Pennsylvania, grabbed his notebook and began sketching. He was drawing a picture of a nightmare for his psychiatrist. In ballpoint pen, he quickly sketched in railroad tracks, a tunnel and a flurry of lines curving up and out, with human figures trapped in them, flung upward. After four decades, the "fountain," the image of shells exploding among the refugees at No Gun Ri, still clung to an old soldier's subconscious.

The ex-rifleman also put down some thoughts for the day: "I hurt for the whole world that has so much of man's inhumanity to man. What to do? What to do? Pray young of world can live in peace and harmony."

Bernotas had been sketching and painting since his Korea days, when he was hospitalized repeatedly for wounds. His farmhouse home outside Girardville was filled with his vivid art, including stark scenes remembered of friends being killed in the war.

Since the cross-country trip home in 1951, the ex-sergeant's life had been deeply troubled. He was twice divorced, and became largely estranged from his six children. He was a barroom brawler in his twenties and drank heavily well into his sixties. After the war, this "good buddy" had grown withdrawn, incommunicative. "I had a chip on my shoulder." He made a living with small coal mines, as a machinist, and for about twenty years as a transient boilermaker.

Around 1980, the residual pain from his wounds—leg, hand and lower back—began to sharpen with advancing age, and that, apparently, turned his inner mind back to the war. "I couldn't sleep at night, and if I did it was only nightmares and turmoil." He sought help at the VA hospital, beginning two decades of mental and physical care that included drug regimes and long inpatient stays. He came to credit it with restoring some peace to his life.

But reminders of Korea were everywhere. In 1995, his beloved farmhouse burned down, with his best paintings, his medals. As he grieved, he thought again of a village that Fox Company burned in South Korea, where GIs had to carry out an elder who refused to leave. "I used to sit over at the farm at my fireplace, and I'd think, boy, in our country nothing like that could happen—somebody come in here and tell me to move out, they're going to burn my house. We have a country where that can't happen."

For all the inner turmoil, the scrappy miner's son still had a knack for making friends, like the aged World War I veteran he amused in Ward 6 West. "Sang 'The Yanks Are Coming' for Mr. Corr, 99 years old doughboy, yesterday," Ralph's notebook read. "He had tears."

BUDDY WENZEL, TOKYO PEN PAL, COULD NO LONGER WRITE. THE strong right hand, the one with the old wound, had finally given out. But De was still by his side after forty-five years. It hadn't been easy. "Some of the wives did stick with their husbands. My wife did, although we did have our problems," Wenzel said.

A few years into the marriage, Wenzel's drinking grew heavy and stayed that way. This quiet man could turn rough and frightening. He worked eighteen years at the Florida fertilizer plant from which he retired, but before that he had gone through some thirty other jobs, from loading boxcars to casting concrete. Tragedy followed the family. In 1973, old Cauley Hodges, having lost the farm he gained when he lost his son, took a gun and killed himself. Hardest of all for Buddy and De, their tall, handsome Leonard Jr. died of cancer at age forty-one, after years of drug abuse and alienation from his father.

De walked out on Buddy a half-dozen times. But every time "I'd take him back, because I felt sorry for him, and I loved him, and I knew there were two people in him, a good person and a bad person," she said. "I didn't understand the bad person, where he was coming from." Wenzel never talked about the war.

The nightmares never stopped. "He'd start hollering so loud," De Wenzel said, and then he'd moan, sadly sometimes, or terrified. She'd touch him in his sleep, "and his skin would be so cold with chill bumps." Finally, in 1995, his hand growing increasingly crippled, Wenzel went to the Tampa VA hospital and mentioned his sleeping problems to a physician, who promptly sent him to the PTSD clinic. When De met with the psychiatrist, she recalled, "I started crying. I said, 'I'm glad he's getting help. We both need it.' "

Therapy and medications did help ease Wenzel's sleeping and began to lift his depressions. "If it wasn't for the doctors and medication, I couldn't have made it," he said. "I was going to commit suicide two or three times."

But De still sometimes found Buddy in their roomy Florida backyard sitting alone and weeping, his mind reeling back to 1950. In nightmares, in alcoholic hallucinations, the little girl and boy who pursued him from No Gun Ri were still with him. "Don't you see her?" he shouted at De. "Don't you hear her?" A long-dead girl stood there, in an old soldier's mind, trying to speak. Somewhere he heard crying.

Buddy Wenzel knew he was not alone. "The Korean War, the ones that went through the worst part of it, it took the heart and soul out of them and it ruined a lot of their lives, and they still suffer today, just like I do," he said.

"When I think about that Korean War—those people never did anything to us. It's nothing like the Second World War with the Japanese and Germans, because they gave us a reason to have a war. You didn't mind giving your life in that war. The Korean War—I didn't know those people. They never did anything to me."

ART HUNTER SAW THEM THOUSANDS OF TIMES OVER A HALF-
century—"intrusive memories" reaching out for an accounting,
across an ocean, across time. They stood in the darkness, he said,
faces hovering over his bed, the old man and old woman he
machine-gunned in a forgotten valley in South Korea. Awakened in
a cold sweat by this subconscious stirring, in his solitary cottage in
the foothills of Virginia's Blue Ridge, Hunter would rise, pull his
hunting rifle from a bedroom corner, and go sit on his front porch,
sometimes for hours, in a comforting ritual, smoking, remembering,
as though on alert once again in Korea. "I don't know what I'm
looking for, but . . ."

Other memories rose up, too, nightmares or waking flashbacks
of dying buddies, of the terror of shellfire. But it was the accusing
faces of the old Koreans, above all, that "made my life a living hell,"
Hunter said. "That's the worst, to me, that's the worst part of the
battle, knowing I killed two civilian people that may or may not
have done anything."

After years of trying, Hunter in 1966 got the "undesirable"
dropped from his Army discharge. That same year he and his wife,
a high school sweetheart, parted ways. He reared their four children,
working as a plumber until the late 1970s, when he retired on a
disability pension with an injured back. In the late 1980s, he finally
began receiving VA treatment for his post-traumatic stress disorder.
It included lengthy hospital stays. Several small plastic bottles of
psychotropic drugs took their place on the kitchen counter of the
hilltop cottage. "My wounds don't show on the outside. Mine are
on the inside," Hunter said. "I wish this leg or arm was gone so
you'd know."

Inside, too, he harbored great bitterness toward the government.
It was not until thirty-eight years after he went "berserk" in Alexandria, and thirty-seven after an episode in which he served jail time
for assaulting a neighbor, that the government recognized him as
war-disabled. In 1991, with the help of a veterans' advocate, he won

his case before the U.S. Board of Veterans Appeals and was declared entitled to 100 percent disability pay because of PTSD.

In a more symbolic battle with the bureaucracy, Hunter's victory was emptier. His discharge papers said he was awarded a coveted Silver Star for that day on the Naktong, when his single-handed valor "saved G Company," as his comrades always said. But he didn't get the medal for more than forty years, until he prodded the Army. Then it arrived in his mailbox unaccompanied by any commendation or certificate. "They sent me nothing, why I got it or anything," he said. Disgusted, he gave the medal away, and his Purple Heart, too.

Husky and bearded at sixty-nine, the ex–machine gunner looked back on his long-ago war. "Korea, I think, was a waste."

SUEY LEE WONG'S CHANCE FOR A SILVER STAR DIED IN THE U.S. Senate.

In 1989, after 7th Cavalrymen began renewing friendships and reviewing the Korea days at reunions, Wong's old commanders corrected an oversight and wrote commendations for his bravery in an operation in June 1951, when he killed four Chinese. A Senate bill was introduced to allow such late filings for awards, and Wong was cited as a deserving example. But the bill never reached the floor for a vote.

The tough little corporal, the Chinese-American who had been slurred as the "gook kid" by fellow soldiers, came home to Seattle in 1951 disturbed, unable to sleep, shaken by his combat experience. "There'd be a party and I'd want to go, to meet a girl, and I was so afraid to go. . . . How does an animal fit back in society?" Decades later, the Veterans Affairs Department could have been describing Wong or Hunter when it noted in a primer on PTSD, "Often it is precisely these exemplary soldiers who are the most psychologically disturbed by war because they are able to endure so much of it with such courage."

Despite the handicaps, Wong built a career as an engineer with

Boeing, Rockwell International and other aerospace companies. Then in the 1990s, like so many Korean veterans, he sought the help of VA mental health specialists and came to understand the roots of his anger and restlessness, and to learn methods of control. Suey Lee Wong, at sixty-four, also finally found a "girl," a partner, a former nun he met through a singles club in 1991. But just two years after they were married, Eva was diagnosed with terminal cancer. In her final days, Snuffy Gray flew across the country to be with them. Suey Lee would still have his band of brothers.

"We lost our friends, our youth," Wong said of Korea. The old Fox Company point man was torn by many feelings about the Army, about the Chinese he killed, about what he heard of No Gun Ri. "I'd think about this racial bullshit. Why did I get this treatment? . . . We feel, a lot of us, like victims, of circumstances, of the war, of the fighting."

But, he said, "I also feel proud of the fact that I participated and served with honor and responsibility."

"I LOVE A PIANO! . . . I LOVE A PIANO! . . . I LOVE TO HEAR SOMEbody play . . ."

On the evening of July 27, 1995, the entertainer Liza Minnelli, in trademark bright red, was delighting a "Korea night" audience at the White House with one of her mother's songs from *Easter Parade,* the same Judy Garland film the troops missed out on long ago in Tokyo, before their "couple of weeks" in Korea.

President and Mrs. Clinton had invited South Korean President Kim Young-sam and his wife to dinner along with 180 other guests. Earlier that day, the nation had dedicated the Korean War Veterans Memorial in Washington, on the forty-second anniversary of the Korean armistice. The staff had brought out the green-on-ivory Truman china to add a touch of early 1950s to the East Room tables. The dignitaries—diplomats and senators, political donors and bemedaled generals in dress blue—dined on lamb and morels, and finished with a taste of Korea, ginseng tea truffles. The thunder and lightning outside meant the evening gala scheduled for the war veterans themselves, outdoors on the Mall, was rained out. But the thousands of ex-soldiers and wives fended for themselves, in hotel bars and hospitality rooms, in restaurants around town, sharing memories with old friends.

Across the Potomac, the Garryowens had settled into a suburban Virginia hotel for their annual reunion, a year after the 7th Cavalrymen's excursion to the old Indian frontier in South Dakota. Art Hunter and Suey Lee Wong were there, along with Snuffy Gray, Colonel Callaway and dozens of other 7th Cavalrymen from the Korea days. Earlier that Thursday, when the memorial was dedicated, the tropical heat and humidity of the Washington afternoon had kept many at the hotel, watching the ceremony on a giant-screen TV.

Finally the nation was giving them, giving their war, a measure of recognition. Many said they felt obliged to be there to represent buddies who never made it home. At the center of the new monument, on 2.2 acres on the Mall, nineteen larger-than-life soldiers in ponchos, cast in steel, trudged wearily toward an objective. Old GIs nodded approvingly at the authenticity of the details.

In his dedication address that afternoon, President Clinton saluted the 1.5 million men and women who served in the Korean theater from 1950 to 1953. "They set a standard of courage that may be equaled, but will never be surpassed in the annals of American combat," he said to applause from thousands. "You put the Free World on the road to victory in the Cold War. . . . You kept the flame burning so that others all across the world could share it."

The new monument, across the Reflecting Pool from the Vietnam Veterans Memorial, bore this dedication statement: *Our Nation Honors Her Sons and Daughters Who Answered the Call to Defend a Country They Did Not Know and a People They Had Never Met.*

"They are good people. It's a good country," Clinton said of the South Koreans. This theme of the righteous crusade was struck again by the president that evening at the East Room dinner, in the Executive Mansion whose occupants first sent the 7th Cavalry west against the Sioux, and then eventually farther west to the Philippines, to Korea, to Vietnam. Clinton toasted the cause of 1950. "Righteousness overcomes all obstacles," he declared.

The glittering, music-filled evening capped a day of celebrating heroism and sacrifice, of reaffirming friendship. But on that day in 1995, sitting unread in one of the U.S. bureaucracy's millions of file drawers, a document addressed to "His Excellency Bill Clinton" told a different story from 1950. It was a petition written by some of those "good people," a group of South Korean villagers, and it told of the "killing of innocent noncombatants by your country's soldiers" at a place called No Gun Ri. They asked for an investigation, an apology, compensation.

The veterans marched that Saturday, some in wheelchairs, some with canes, parading proudly up the capital's Constitution Avenue to the sound of bagpipes and brass. The polished helmets and even ranks of Tokyo 1950 had given way to ragged lines of men in "Korean War Vet" baseball caps, wearing faded battle ribbons, their shoulders sagging with the weight of the years and the memories, and with the weight of the ghosts, American and Korean, who had never left them.

9

Her hair was ashen now and short, her body arthritic and halting. The ribbon of red and yellow silk had disappeared a lifetime ago. But the face, below the sad eyes, still bore the proud cheekbones of the pigtailed girl.

"My mother comes to me more often these days," Park Hee-sook said. She wept gently. Her daughter-in-law held her hand. "I think I'm seeing things, and that means I've lived enough, that I don't have many days left."

When alone at her son's home in Pusan, she said, she would suddenly see her long-dead mother at the trestle, a small figure in the tunnel, face covered with dust and streaked with sweat, rocking her dead daughter's child on her back. "I can hear my mother calling the baby's name over and over, trying to soothe her, to stop her from crying."

Even in daytime, Hee-sook would see the heaps of dead before her. She would feel her father's disintegrating flesh, sticky in her hands, and wonder whether her mother became food for birds. Her chin would shake uncontrollably at times. "I'm alive but I'm already seeing scenes from hell. It just doesn't go away." Under a neurologist's care, she was taking nine pills each night to help her sleep and fight off the visions.

"Often I just want to grab Americans by the throat. . . . I want to ask them why they killed my family," said Hee-sook, now in her mid-sixties. Old soldiers shouldn't go to prison, she said, "but they should repent. Some say war is war and it's dirty. But still, what's wrong is wrong."

In that lonely time long ago, living alone in her dead parents' mud-walled house, the orphaned girl struggled to bring in the family harvests of tobacco and rice. In January 1951, she entrusted her father's land to his cousin, whom she called "Uncle," and was married off through the intercession of Im Ke Ri villagers to a man from the nearby village of Yangkang. He was a good man, with whom she had a son and daughter, but he died young, at forty-nine.

The older woman's mind turned back to the day when she journeyed to meet her in-laws for the first time, a poor seventeen-year-old bride with a single set of clothing. It was the day after her wedding, and in the wooden sedan chair she wept the whole way. "Finally my uncle stopped the sedan and warned me he wouldn't go with me if I kept crying. . . . I couldn't have been sadder. My heart was crushed." On the eve of a new life, Park Hee-sook could think of nothing but No Gun Ri.

BY THE TIME THE AMERICANS, CHINESE AND KOREANS STOPPED fighting in the summer of 1953, most of South Korea was a wasteland of burned villages, bombed-out towns and cities, roadsides littered with the rusted hulks of trucks and tanks, bridges down, rail lines severed, factories and schools flattened. The fishing fleet in this maritime country had been wrecked. More than five million people relied on outside relief; half of those were homeless. Along with food, thousands of tons of used clothing and shoes were shipped in.

The war had created some 100,000 orphans and 100,000 widows. Many others never knew what happened to their husbands or wives, and many languished for years, not remarrying, in the fading hope of finding them. Hundreds of thousands, especially those from North Korea, never saw their loved ones again.

American aid, some $1 billion between 1954 and 1960, helped in the country's slow resurrection, rebuilding railroads and power stations, roads and bridges and schools. Tens of thousands of U.S. troops remained in South Korea after the armistice. Supplying their needs—from basic commodities to service workers to bar girls— became a major economic activity. Black-market trading in goods smuggled off U.S. bases swelled into a vast underground economy.

President Syngman Rhee's government grew still more autocratic. In 1954, it forced another election bill through the National Assembly, this time allowing Rhee to run for as many presidential terms as he desired. In 1956, he was elected to a third term. The dictatorial leader took to executing his political opponents as alleged collaborators with North Korea.

The regime grew still more corrupt as well. A few business families colluding with Rhee became rich in the "white industry," cornering the market in surplus U.S. sugar, flour and cotton sent to South Korea. The government controlled the banks and funneled loans to its favorites. The economy stagnated; in 1960, South Korea's per-capita income still remained near the bottom worldwide.

In this bleak landscape, small things loomed large. For the surviving villagers of Chu Gok Ri and Im Ke Ri, the arrival of movies— silent films in a tent amid the ruins of Yongdong—was a milestone of the early postwar period. Silence descended elsewhere as well those evenings, over all the towns and villages, as a nightly curfew took effect at 10 P.M. in the continuing campaign by government forces against communist guerrillas who clung to the highlands of South Korea. The last two guerrilla leaders surrendered in 1955, but stragglers in the Chiri Mountains clashed with police as late as 1963.

The insurgencies, the mass political executions, the indiscriminate killings of the war itself—all the bloodshed since the late 1940s led

South Koreans in the 1950s to describe their nation, a land of mass graves, as a land full of *han,* of hearts crying out against injustices done to the dead.

No Gun Ri villagers remembered local farmers in the 1960s tilling a hillside beside the trestle and turning up many bones. They were thrown away, some said; others said they were sold to lepers, who believed bone had healing power.

The trestle was a forbidding presence to its neighbors. "It was a frightening place for village women like me," recalled Lee Won-hee, an elderly No Gun Ri resident. "When it rained, we could see ghost flames flickering in the tunnel."

Hon bul, or ghost flames, were a deeply rooted notion in Korean lore. They may have been caused when phosphorous from bones, kicked up by wind, flickered in the moonlight. Others believe they were a hallucination caused by malnutrition. Whatever the reality, the "flames" in the hills and valleys of the south became associated, in the postwar days, with the restless dead of Korea.

CHUNG EUN-YONG, A POLICEMAN AGAIN, WAS UNHAPPY WITH HIS job. The police had little respect among the people, and the wages were so poor that Sun-yong's parents sometimes had to send them rice for their larder. But in 1954 Eun-yong managed to build a modest house in Taejon for his growing family. Sun-yong had borne him a new daughter, Koo-sook, in 1952, and then a son, Koo-do, in 1955.

The young couple could finally smile; their lives had begun again. But they could not escape the pain of the past. While others welcomed the warm breath of spring and its blossoms, Sun-yong dreaded each turn of the seasons. "Summer was no longer the same," she said. "When the summer came, the memory revived," with its wrenching images, of Koo-pil's bloody foot, of his thin hair stirred by the breeze as he lay dead.

The guilt grew inside Eun-yong year by year. "I was a cowardly father. . . . I left my family to the killers. . . . I was ashamed to be alive." He thought about what might have been. "I stopped and rested in that tunnel on my way south! How could I know what would happen there in a couple of days?" Sun-yong did not blame her husband. "He might well have died, too," she said. "It's only God's grace that saved him. Five in my family died."

Eun-yong took to frequenting a Presbyterian church in Taejon in search of spiritual support. But within the peacefulness of its walls, amid the words of Christian forgiveness, *han* still burned inside him. It found its release, with the rest of South Korea, in 1960.

President Rhee's tactics had grown increasingly heavy-handed, climaxing with widespread vote-rigging suspected in his election to a fourth term in 1960. Students took to the streets in huge protests, first in Taegu and Masan down south, and then, in April, in Seoul. Rhee declared martial law and troops opened fire on pro-democracy crowds, killing 180 and injuring 6,000 across the country. But the upheaval finally drove him from power on April 26, 1960. The eighty-five-year-old strongman, disgraced in his homeland, retreated to a U.S. exile in Hawaii.

His downfall led to a brief "spring" of political liberalization in South Korea, when labor unions, led by leftists, could finally form, as the Koreans say, "like bamboo shoots after rain"; when young activists began challenging the U.S. dominance of the country; when the National Assembly blocked a new U.S. economic aid treaty because of the control it gave Washington over South Korean politics and economics. After seven years of relentless postwar tension with the Pyongyang communists, students in the south called openly for reunification of the two Koreas.

For the first time, too, the silenced, fearful families of leftists executed by the Rhee regime—before, during and after the war— called for an investigation of the summary killings. The National Assembly opened an inquiry.

In this atmosphere of new beginnings, Eun-yong spotted a newspaper article in the fall of 1960 saying a U.S. government office in Seoul was accepting claims for compensation related to U.S. actions in the Korean War. Eun-yong contacted several survivors from Chu

Gok Ri and together they sent a letter to the Americans asking for an investigation of the No Gun Ri killings and compensation. The U.S. office replied by letter that they had missed a filing deadline.

Eun-yong wrote again, saying ordinary Koreans had been unaware of the claims process, and asking that their appeal be referred to Washington for reconsideration of the deadline. "This was an extremely atrocious incident for the victims and their families," he wrote, ". . . a violation of the laws of war because it was a killing of unarmed civilians." The letter asked: How could American soldiers have killed old people, children and women over three days when GIs, in fact, had approached the tunnel and could see they were not enemy troops?

Seventeen years as a policeman, on and off, seemed to entitle him to respect from the authorities, Eun-yong thought. But he never received a further response from U.S. officials, he said, and then the "spring" ended. Park Chung-hee, a major general who had graduated from the Japanese military academy, led a coup in May 1961 that threw out the civilian government and ushered in a generation of even greater right-wing repression and enforced silence. It would prove impossible to press the case of No Gun Ri.

"We couldn't say publicly that the Americans committed such things during the war," Eun-yong said. "The United States was such a powerful country. Speaking against the Americans was tantamount to calling yourself a communist."

Chung Koo-hun, the tall, quiet student from Chu Gok Ri, a twenty-seven-year-old schoolteacher in 1960, was one of those signing his name to the original claim. After the coup, he received anonymous telephone calls threatening his life. "The message was clear," he said. Like the others, he now would have to deal in private with the anguish of No Gun Ri, an anguish that tore at him every time he looked into his little brother's mutilated face.

THE BOY WITH THE MASK AND THE TALL YOUNG MAN HAD WAITED in line together for days outside the Swedish Hospital in Pusan. It was March 31, 1956. Chung Koo-hun had heard that Swedish doctors in the port city were helping people badly hurt in the war. He brought fourteen-year-old Koo-hak the 100 miles from home, only to find sick and lame and disfigured Koreans thronging the hospital entrance, hoping for admission.

The boy's wounds had been slow to heal, and he hadn't regained his strength after the ordeal of the tunnels. He could be seen around Chu Gok Ri with cotton balls stuffed in the giant tear across the right side of his face. He often wore a mask. The naturally lively boy played with other children, but grew quieter, more withdrawn as time passed. In school, he stopped learning.

Outside the Pusan hospital, people simply waited, day and night, cooking, eating, sleeping in line. There was no shelter. But the line barely budged, and Koo-hun finally became desperate. He had to get home or lose his year-old job as a teacher in the Yongdong primary school.

Seeing a European woman in a white doctor's gown, he rushed over to her with the boy with the hidden face. "I lied. I told her my brother's terrible injury was inflicted by the bad North Korean communists, because I thought she'd get upset if I accused the Americans of doing this. I said I was a schoolteacher, I had no money and I had to get back to work.

"She lifted the mask on my brother's face and took a look."

The Swedish specialists kept Koo-hak for six months, operating on him several times, transplanting flesh from his hips, thighs and upper arms to the right side of his face. They put some substance and skin back, but it was still a partial face. Koo-hak remembered happy days at the seaside hospital, where he found he could be useful and appreciated. "I ran around the hospital, running errands for patients who couldn't move very well," he recalled. He ate well and was dressed in "relief clothing," made from flour sacks.

Once back in Chu Gok Ri, however, the teenager resumed a peasant's hard life in the Chung household, scaling mountains in search of firewood, climbing nearby slopes to pull weeds for mulch, carrying rice to the market—a life spent with an A-frame on his back, work that would have been hard even for a stronger boy. "All the time I was thinking, thinking," Koo-hak said. How could a young man with a grotesque face make his way in the world?

For all the body's weakness, the will grew stronger with age. One day, at about age twenty, he went to Koo-hun, told him he wanted to become a postman, and asked for his help. The elder brother's response was brutal. "I probably thought I had to force him to face reality," Koo-hun remembered. "I said, 'Don't overestimate your-self. . . . A crippled man like you can't become a government official. With a face like yours, no one can pass as a normal man.'" The younger brother cried; the older brother regretted his harshness and couldn't sleep that night.

Three days later, Koo-hak returned, in despair. He reminded his brother he was too weak to become a farmer, but had no idea what to do with his life. This time Koo-hun did. Their father's fish shop had burned when U.S. planes destroyed Yongdong in 1950. The family had rebuilt it, but the old man languished in a depression after No Gun Ri, and the business with him. The schoolteacher now suggested that his little brother become a fish peddler, travel-ing to outlying villages with crates of salted pollack and mackerel and squid.

A peddler would need a bicycle, however, and a bicycle was an expensive luxury in an impoverished Korea. The brother who once carried a "dead" boy back from the grave knew he had no choice. He gave Koo-hak his own.

BEYOND THE SONANGDANG ROCK, BENEATH THE FRESH THATCH OF rebuilt roofs, Chu Gok Ri was a village of desolate souls in the 1950s, none more desolate than Chun Soon-pyo, father of little Choon-ja. The man the *mutang* declared to be "possessed" by his dead wife's spirit became a *mutang* himself, not an unusual trans-formation in a land still attuned to age-old spiritism.

Believers felt that the unhappy spirit of Choon-ja's mother, killed at No Gun Ri, was the father's link to the nether world. He worked with a female *mutang,* the pair dancing, waving bamboo stalks, beating drums all night as they performed their *gut* ritual for villagers in the area. His "cures" of illnesses eventually earned this troubled man a living. He remarried and Choon-ja's stepmother bore him six children.

As the eldest child in the house, the young teenager Choon-ja carried much of the workload, along with her grandmother. "We worked like men," she recalled. Choon-ja collected firewood from the mountains, tended tobacco fields, sorted and dried leaves after the summer harvest. Even after going to seamstress school, she had to work full-time at home.

Choon-ja had wanted to go on to middle school, something she believed her mother would have liked. But her father and stepmother refused. Unable to play with other children or go to class, Choon-ja grew lonelier and sadder. But she had a secret. "I envied my friends so badly that I made a beautiful school uniform for myself—I had the skills—complete with a white collar. I kept that uniform in my closet, and I tried it on when I was alone. Sometimes I even wore it outside when my stepmother was away at the market."

She also found comfort at the rebuilt Salvation Army church, a thatch-and-mud hall where congregants sat on straw mats for the song-filled evening services. Her parents didn't like Choon-ja's flirtation with Christianity, but she stubbornly had her way. "I could sing and meet friends there and trade gossip." On Christmas Eve, she remembered, they would go around the village singing carols. She even dreamed of becoming a nun.

The girl saved by fate from the carnage at No Gun Ri had found escapes from reality and memory. But she believed one fantasy was real—her grandmother's story of how Tae-sung perished in the tunnel, starving without his mother's milk. Choon-ja still did not know the truth of who killed her beloved baby brother.

ON BUDDHA'S BIRTHDAY, A SPRING HOLIDAY, TWO YEARS AFTER NO Gun Ri, a group of Im Ke Ri girls was climbing a mountain path, beneath pink clouds of cherry blossoms, to picnic high above the valley. A few village youths, meanwhile, were coming downhill. One spotted the tall girl in the group and shouted out, to the other boys' laughter, "Here comes a one-eyed monster!"

Yang Hae-sook, fifteen at the time, recalled the pain of the moment. "I wanted to die on the spot. If there was a rat's hole, I would have crawled in. Ever since I've been ashamed of myself."

The Yangs couldn't afford an artificial eye for their "Golden Girl" until she turned seventeen, when she was fitted with a plastic eyeball at a Taegu hospital. She was married three years later, in 1957. Marrying off such a handicapped daughter was a daunting task, but the Yangs found a poor family satisfied to have a son connected with a respectable, if humble, *yangban* clan. Ultimately the couple had four children, but it proved a hellish match for young Hae-sook.

Her husband was drunk every night and took to beating her, she said. He ridiculed and reviled her for her missing eye. He forced her from their bedroom; at times she had to sleep at neighbors' homes. He threatened to gouge out her good eye, and attacked her once with a scythe. "For four years, I secretly took rice to the Buddhist temple and prayed for a happy marriage with my husband."

Her family heard the rumors, and one day in 1958 her brother Hae-chan, a teenaged student, came to her house and accosted her husband. "Hae-chan and I made a pledge at No Gun Ri," Hae-sook said. "That day we vowed to look after each other for the rest of our lives." She remembered what he told her husband: "Why didn't you make an issue of my sister's eye in the first place? Didn't we discuss it before the marriage?" He handed his brother-in-law a blank piece of paper. "Write down that you want a divorce. I'm going to live with my sister for the rest of my life." As village elders listened, the husband meekly promised to treat Hae-sook better. But the marriage remained full of resentment and hate.

Hae-sook didn't want a divorce, feeling it would disgrace her family. To escape, she traveled as a peddler in the 1960s and early 1970s, selling matches or ginseng a county or two away, often taking her newest baby along, finding shelter in the homes of kindly strangers. She remembered the nightmares from those lonely days— of a plane firing into the tunnel, or a cow consumed in flames. She kept a knife by her pillow, not to guard against her husband but as a defense—a Korean superstition—against the midnight demons of No Gun Ri.

THEY WOULD TALK ABOUT IT ON ANCESTORS' DAYS, WHEN FAMILIES gathered in quiet reunions to honor their dead. But the survivors were publicly silent—not just the witnesses of No Gun Ri, but those who survived other U.S. strafings of refugee columns, the Rhee regime's mass executions or other injustices of the early 1950s.

In Park Chung-hee's police state, even talk among friends could be dangerous. Three times in the 1960s and 1970s, Yang Hae-chan was warned by the police to stop talking about No Gun Ri after he brought it up in unguarded moments among neighbors, usually after drinks, he said. If he hadn't been prominent locally, he believed, he would have been jailed.

Yang Hae-chan, the small, tenacious "loyal son," eventually became one of the best-known men in Yongdong County, a leader in agricultural development, a pioneer in replacing paddy land with a more lucrative crop, grapes. An admirer of the authoritarian President Park, Hae-chan was an activist in the "New Village" movement, the general's program for improving rural life in South Korea. It was Hae-chan who in 1983 finally got the road paved between Im Ke Ri and Chu Gok Ri.

The Park regime encouraged industrialization and exports, setting the stage for a South Korean "miracle" of 8 percent–plus economic growth annually in the 1960s and 1970s. But growth was accompanied by widespread corruption, the concentration of power in a few business conglomerates and suppression of organized labor. Independent unions were discouraged and strikes banned.

Anti-communism more and more resembled a state religion. Thousands of political activists disappeared, hundreds of newspapers and periodicals were shut down. Red-lettered signs appeared in villages declaring, LET'S ACHIEVE REUNIFICATION BY ELIMINATING COMMUNISTS. The National Security Law promised seven years in prison for expressing support for "anti-state groups."

Tens of thousands were stigmatized and put under surveillance. Chung Koo-hong, brother of the vanished "American-made leftist" Koo-il, was an example. Despite his college degree and good test scores, his superiors made clear that political suspicions at high levels kept the Chu Gok Ri native from advancing in his career with the railroad. The bosses were told to report on his activities. "When I moved into a new house, police detectives came to check on why I moved into their area." And all his life Koo-hong would wonder whether his brother might be alive in North Korea.

The Americans were officially South Korea's "saviors"; public criticism of the U.S. military was taboo. The United States became known as "Mee-Kook"—"Beautiful Country." Park Chung-hee sent 45,000 South Korean troops to help the Americans fight the war in Vietnam in exchange for increased U.S. military and economic aid. Korea benefited, too, from the U.S. demand for war supplies.

The Park years ended in October 1979, when the general was assassinated by his own intelligence chief. A civilian administration took shape, promising popular elections, but soon other army generals stepped in and took command in Seoul. Then, in May 1980, the junta's troops crushed a pro-democracy uprising in the southern city of Kwangju, killing hundreds of people. Many young Koreans blamed the United States, since the South Korean military still remained nominally under U.S. command. Protests against the U.S. presence sputtered on through the 1980s.

In 1986, a student activist tried a new tactic in the campaign, sending anti-American letters to 20,000 high school students. He was thrown in jail. Among the allegations in his notorious circular: that American soldiers massacred South Korean civilians during the 1950–1953 war.

THE GRAYING, STERN-FACED GENTLEMAN, SMALL AND SLIM IN A well-worn business suit, shuttled among libraries in Taejon, called on historians in Seoul, packed his files with photocopies of pages from military histories, old newspapers, archival documents. A scholar recalled Chung Eun-yong the researcher of the early 1990s.

"He was looking for anything, just anything. He was collecting data like a magpie," said Yang Young-jo of the Korea Institute for Military History. The amateur investigator devoured everything in Korean, and then went on to Japanese, and even found U.S. Army material his son could read for him. Through it all, he had a special focus: American military operations in Yongdong County in July 1950.

Chung Eun-yong, the promising young man of Chu Gok Ri, had lived a "life of rags," he would later say. He left the police force in 1960 to study for the national examination for a judgeship. He kept failing the notoriously difficult exam by narrow margins, ran low on money and had to look for work. A friend got him a job with the National Anti-Communist Coalition, but Eun-yong left after a few years, disgusted with the corruption of the government organization. As his Japanese bosses on the railroad found out long before, his quick mind and temper, and rigid ideas of right and wrong, made him a poor fit in some organizations.

Eun-yong joined with a partner in operating a small bottle-making plant in Taejon, but that failed in the early 1970s. After that, he took on odd jobs, sometimes helping friends with small construction companies, until retiring in the mid-1980s. Through it all, he said, "No Gun Ri never escaped my mind one single day."

Sun-yong bore three sons and a daughter in the years after No Gun Ri, but for her, too, time in many ways stood still in July 1950. "She would get up at night and shake me, and ask if I heard something like the dead boy's voice," Eun-yong said. "She would wake up in the dead of night in a sweat, and screaming."

His wife put on weight and developed serious arthritis over the years. Whenever it rained, her wounds from No Gun Ri would ache. The children grew up knowing their parents were haunted by black memories. "At night, I heard Mother having nightmares, shouting the names of my dead brother and sister," said Koo-do, their eldest son. Once she was found praying, crying, on the snow-covered roof.

As Eun-yong traveled the Seoul-Taejon trains, sketched out maps of troop movements in July 1950, meticulously organized his volumes of material, his sons began to worry that his obsession with

No Gun Ri would ruin his health. But the stubborn father paid them no heed. He was making progress. Poring over the histories and maps, he had come to a conclusion: His two children must have been killed by a unit of the 1st Cavalry Division.

THE FISH PEDDLER'S FACE MAY HAVE HELPED HIS BUSINESS. KOREAN housewives, by custom, would not talk freely with strangers, but no husband would be jealous of Chung Koo-hak. Village women found it easy to deal with the young man who came around on the bicycle, with the full crate of fish and half a face.

Elder brother Koo-hun next talked their father into turning over his indebted dried-fish business to Koo-hak. The younger brother worked long hours to make it profitable. Late at night, he read books, educating himself. But Koo-hun knew his brother needed the helping hand and stability of a wife. The Chung family searched for a match, but even physically handicapped women recoiled from the offer. Finally they found a poor family with an eligible daughter in the next-door village of Ha Ga Ri. Persuasive emissaries overcame resistance, and twenty-year-old Chang Soon-yi was wed to twenty-six-year-old Chung Koo-hak in 1968. Her disapproving friends may have had second thoughts when they saw her travel off to a spa for something called a "honeymoon." The young man had money.

"I was determined to become rich," Koo-hak said. Soon-yi became the support underpinning that driving ambition, as well as the mother of two daughters and a son. The couple worked from before dawn to after dark, Koo-hak resting only on two holidays a year. By the 1980s, the store on Old Market Alley grew into the biggest fish business in Yongdong, a rebuilt town of quiet streets and colorful shops. Koo-hak became active in the community, with Soon-yi's encouragement, joining the local soccer club and Rotary Club. An energetic, helpful member, he won friends and eventually was elected Rotary chairman. Arts festivals and other Yongdong events benefited from the fishmonger's sponsorship and money.

Despite the success, Koo-hun still worried about his little brother, still called to check on his well-being. "When I see Koo-hak's face today, my heart aches," said the retired school vice principal, erect and vigorous in his late sixties. Koo-hak could never overcome the shame of his disfigurement, his dread of the eyes of others. "I never took my children to school because I was afraid their friends would see my face, embarrassing my children," he said.

He also never overcame his shock at what happened at that trestle long ago. "Even if it's war, you can't just order your soldiers to shoot women and children," he said. "The Americans may not have thought we were human beings, because we were living in such destitute places, like animals."

Koo-hak, like other survivors, said he believed South Koreans finally climbed out of that destitution thanks, in part, to sacrifices made by young American soldiers during the war. "But the fact they fought to save us shouldn't stop us from telling the truth about what really happened at No Gun Ri. It was a mass killing of innocent civilians of an allied country."

At times the brothers wondered what could have been. In Chung Koo-hak's spacious, modern apartment in Yongdong, one vision of that life hung over the sofa, in vivid oils, a portrait that showed the successful businessman in his red Rotary blazer, in a dignified stance, with a face that is handsome, smiling and whole.

ON A SPRING DAY IN THE EARLY 1970S, YANG HAE-SOOK WALKED along the Pusan beach with her shoes in her hand. One cannot enter the afterlife with shoes on.

The half-blind "Golden Girl," now a mother of four, had decided to drown herself in the waters of the Korea Strait. "I was tired of my life. It was too much." She had come to Pusan to peddle ginseng, and was staying at the home of an old woman she knew. She left her money and possessions there, and went to Kamchon Beach to throw herself into the sea. But she found too many people there, and so she waited for darkness. In the evening, the fishermen came home, and children ran down to the shore to welcome their fathers. Hae-sook's mind turned back home. "I thought of my children, and my only eye blurred with tears," she said. "I slowly changed my mind. I decided to live, and to work hard, to feed my children and give them a better life than I had." She went back to the old woman's. They cried together.

Hard work—selling small things, working in other people's fields—helped one forget, she found. As with Chung Koo-hak, her embarrassment over her artificial eye denied her some of life's pleasures. She didn't attend her children's graduations. When it came time to arrange her elder daughter's marriage, she sent her sister-in-law in her place. But Hae-sook devoted herself to her children. Her husband had refused to enroll the elder daughter in high school; instead she was sent to work in a sweatshop in Seoul. Hae-sook, whose own father kept her out of school, took an overnight train and hunted the daughter down in the metropolis, brought her home and put her in school. "She was always at the top of her class," she said.

Her husband died in 1996. "He left me nothing." Four years later, sixty-two-year-old Yang Hae-sook, who taught herself to write, put down some reflections.

"I've lived my life in tears," she wrote. "Since the No Gun Ri incident, I've never been able to hold up my face with pride. . . . Who can I talk to about these feelings of mine?" Keeping her *han* to herself, she wrote, had been "a huge cold stone on my heart." Relatively few Koreans, even in the 1990s, received professional help for such mental disorders as post-traumatic stress. One doctor advised Hae-sook to sing to herself when the inner darkness descended. She sang constantly.

"SOMETIMES LIVING THROUGH ONE DAY WAS LIKE LIVING THROUGH 1,000 years," Chun Choon-ja said. "But, looking back, I realize a person's life is like the morning mist. It comes and goes so quickly."

Choon-ja, motherless child, lived many long days in her life. When she was married, at twenty-two, her stepmother filled her bridal quilts with dried weeds, and the humiliated Choon-ja had to secretly pilfer the traditional cotton filling from her in-laws' bedding. When her drunken husband, years later, discovered she was going to a Christian church, he flung her Bible into the fireplace. When he later quit his government job and ran for political office, he threw away most of their money on a losing election campaign.

But Choon-ja's longest day was March 3, 1983, when she got a telephone call telling her that her son, one of four children, had died in an industrial accident. "It was like the earth caving in under my feet."

She took in her son's one-year-old boy—"the same age as my dead brother when he died"—to rear at her home in Pusan. She had separated and then reunited with her husband, and had worked over the years in a factory, as a noodle vendor and at other jobs, losing touch with her old Chu Gok Ri neighbors. It wasn't until that grandson was in high school and she renewed contacts with her home village that Choon-ja finally learned the truth about her brother Tae-sung's death a half-century earlier. An unthinking villager, a No Gun Ri survivor, described to her the madhouse scene in which her father drowned the screaming baby beneath the trestle.

"It felt like a knife in my heart," she said. Tae-sung had not perished of starvation; her father had killed his own "Great Success," amid the terror of the American gunfire. The old man was dead now, but she finally understood his troubled mind. Her own was still more troubled. "I can't go to sleep very well," Choon-ja said. "The baby comes back to me at night . . . The souls of the dead won't rest until the full truth is known."

IN A SUNNY UPSTAIRS APARTMENT IN A CROWDED TAEJON NEIGH-borhood, above a garden of roses, persimmon and fig, Chung Eun-yong read and reread the books and documents, collated and compared the data, considered and reconsidered what he had learned from villagers, and then began to write.

"In the beginning, it was purely personal. I wrote about No Gun Ri to soothe myself," he said of those days in the early 1990s. "When I talked about it, few people seemed interested, and they said it was useless to talk about such things. It involves the Americans, they reminded me."

But beyond the narrow little garden of the aging couple, South Korea was changing. Through the mid-1980s, in scenes televised worldwide, pro-democracy and anti-American protests rocked Seoul and other cities, and hundreds were arrested. Over time the public pressure—and the U.S. shift toward democratic reform in the Philippines and elsewhere in east Asia—led the military regime to open up South Korean politics.

Above the 38th Parallel, communist North Korea remained a rigidly one-party, authoritarian state through the decades, even after Kim Il Sung died in 1994, after forty-eight years in power, and his son, Kim Jong Il, took charge. Economists believed that into the 1970s the northerners, under a Soviet-style centrally planned economy, were on average better off than South Koreans. But the weaknesses of Stalinist economics, with its often wasteful "megaprojects" and lack of individual incentives, eventually stultified North Korean growth. By the 1990s, food shortages were leaving millions of North Korean children malnourished; many died.

The South Korean economy, meanwhile, rapidly expanded. A country whose number three export item in the early 1960s was wigs made of human hair developed into a global export power, selling automobiles and computer chips in the United States and elsewhere. It also progressed politically. In 1987, under growing public pressure, the military leadership agreed to a popular presidential election under a new constitution that also guaranteed such rights as freedom of the press. Former general Roh Tae-woo, succeeding his military partner Chun Doo-hwan, won the election of December 16, 1987, because the opposition vote was divided between two major civilian candidates. But the ex-general, as president, did not try to stall the momentum toward full democracy, and in 1992 one of those opposition candidates, Kim Young-sam, was elected as the first civilian president in decades.

In Taejon, a man nearing seventy saw a window reopening after thirty-two years, a chance again to demand a public accounting for the deaths of his two children and of many others. By now Eunyong's eldest surviving son was at his side. "I often wanted to tell my father to forget about No Gun Ri," said Chung Koo-do, who inherited the unsmiling intensity of the ex-policeman from Chu Gok Ri. "But as I grew older and had my own family, my own children, I could understand my father. I knew nobody else would do it for us."

Eun-yong's writing had taken shape as a book, about his memories of the war with No Gun Ri at the center. When Koo-do, who worked for the public electric utility, came home in the evenings, he would sometimes pick up the handwritten pages. He said tears often welled up as he read. "I began helping my father with his manuscript, converting his old-fashioned style into today's language." Sometimes father and son would work until three or four in the morning.

Friends and relatives warned Koo-do that delving into the past might jeopardize his job with the power company. Most South Koreans simply viewed such subjects as untouchable. "I couldn't find any scholar studying these incidents," Eun-yong said, "and I felt that our people were cowardly when it comes to speaking out about the Americans."

The election of Kim Young-sam was the signal Eun-yong needed to take his manuscript to publishers. One house after another, about ten in all, turned him down, telling him it was too controversial; it would be the first book ever published in South Korea accusing U.S. troops of such civilian killings. A pastor's wife who was a novelist recommended some trimming and encouraged Eun-yong, but still he could find no one willing to issue the book. Finally, a friend of Koo-do's led them to an obscure young publisher who agreed to publish it, but who labeled it a "novel based on a true story."

Do You Know Our Agony? was published in April 1994. "I'm over seventy now," Eun-yong said in the foreword. "I began writing this book because if I don't publicize this incident to the world, I believe it will be buried in history forever. . . . We want to remain friends with the United States. We wish the United States will take conscientious and sincere steps on the No Gun Ri incident to ease the pain in our hearts."

After a few thousand copies were printed—many were bought by Eun-yong himself—the book went out of print. But it won some attention. Thanks to Koo-do's acquaintanceship with a reporter for

South Korea's Yonhap news agency, a review of *Do You Know Our Agony?* ran on that news wire. Other Korean journalists then called, and several newspaper and magazine articles followed. The articles, in turn, brought other No Gun Ri survivors to Chung Eun-yong. For Chun Choon-ja, in Pusan, it was encouraging to see what happened at No Gun Ri in print. "One of the greatest heartaches in my life was that I couldn't talk about it and what it did to me."

Eun-yong began hearing new accounts, through others' eyes, of what happened in July 1950. "I realized that the scope of the No Gun Ri incident was much greater than I had thought. . . . We needed to get organized and send petitions and ask for a formal investigation."

The ex-policeman formed a five-man survivors committee that included Yang Hae-chan, who had been elected to the Yongdong County Council, and Chung Koo-hun, the educator. In early July 1994, they drafted their first petition to "His Excellency Bill Clinton," a letter that told of "the killing of innocent noncombatants by your country's soldiers," and asked the U.S. president to "understand our pain and take measures, such as an apology and compensation, to console both the dead and the survivors."

Another committee member was Chu Gok Ri farmer Chung Koo-ho, the boy who was saved by his dying mother, the peasant woman praying to Buddha, in the tunnel at No Gun Ri. He had once sought to escape his haunting memories by retreating to a solitary mountain to raise silkworms. This convert to Christianity spent fifteen years there. He said he read the Bible thirty times.

"It was like David and Goliath," Koo-ho said of the appeal to the U.S. leadership. "Not many people would understand how overwhelmed we felt when poor rural people from a small country had to stand up against the world's most powerful country."

On July 5, 1994, Koo-ho, Eun-yong and the three other committee members traveled to Seoul to present their petition at the U.S. Embassy. A few hundred yards from the fortresslike building on broad, busy Sejong Boulevard, Korean plainclothes policemen intercepted the men and told them they could get no closer without an appointment. As the five debated what to do, they were approached by journalists they had alerted to their petition. The newsmen raised their cameras, the policemen retreated and the five petitioners were allowed into the embassy. There a woman came to the doorstep, took the document and walked away, without a word to the villagers.

They felt humiliated. "She didn't even ask us to sit down or have a drink," said Eun-yong. "On our way back home, we didn't talk," Yang Hae-chan recalled. "We were helpless, but I'm sure each of us was angry at what we saw as the arrogance of the big country, America."

They received no response, but grew still more determined to press their case. Over the next three years, the survivors said, they sent three more petitions to President Clinton, and nine to other American and South Korean leaders. Only one drew a reply, a letter addressed to President Kim that the South Korean Defense Ministry passed on to the U.S. military command in Seoul.

The local commander of the U.S. Armed Forces Claims Service, the office charged with handling compensation cases, responded to that petition. "It appears that the incident giving rise to your claims arose directly from a combat activity of the Armed Forces. The United States is not legally liable for such claims resulting from an act of the Armed Forces of the United States in combat," wrote Maj. John G. Warthen. His letter, dated October 28, 1994, did not say the U.S. military had conducted any investigation of the claim.

Chung Eun-yong wrote back, saying U.S. troops at No Gun Ri were not engaged in combat when they killed the refugees, and the killings constituted a war crime. Six weeks later, Warthen replied, referring him to the first letter and writing, "This is our final and conclusive response to this matter." Said Eun-yong, "My heart collapsed when they told me that it was their last response."

Among the unacknowledged letters, the survivors group said, were those addressed to Vice President Al Gore, in his role as U.S. Senate president; Newt Gingrich, the U.S. House speaker; the U.S. ambassador in Seoul, James T. Laney; and leaders of South Korea's new civilian government. "We thought our own government should take the lead and listen to eyewitness accounts. We thought our government would comfort us that way," Eun-yong said. "But nobody came. It was a severe letdown for us."

IN THE SUMMER OF 1997, THE VILLAGERS HEARD IT WAS POSSIBLE TO seek compensation for damages under the Status of Forces Agreement between the U.S. and South Korean governments, the legal framework for the U.S. military presence in South Korea. Thirty of them traveled together to Chongju, 35 miles from Yongdong, to submit claims at a district prosecutor's office. But an official there refused to give them claim forms, telling them it was pointless. As they stood outside, angry and dejected, one villager telephoned a reporter, an acquaintance of his, at a local television station. He showed up with an empty camera; his editors were uneasy with the story, he told them. But the sight of the camera persuaded the bureaucrat to let the villagers file their claims.

"We asked for compensation because such a gesture would be a sure sign that the United States was truly apologetic," Eun-yong said. "We don't need empty words for an apology. Compensation would tell us they mean what they say." The thirty survivors listed 120 relatives as No Gun Ri victims; they noted only their own families' dead on the claim forms. The list from Im Ke Ri included the poignant entry "Cho (an infant boy born and killed in the tunnel)."

At the time, in 1950, the North Korean journalist Chun Wook had written of 400 dead; Eun-yong's son discovered that report on microfilm at the National Assembly Library. No Gun Ri villager Kim Myong-june, born after the killings, said he remembered older villagers talking about 300 bodies at the scene. The survivors' own list of dead and missing would eventually, after the claims were filed in 1997, surpass 200 names, including almost 50 babies and small children.

For many reasons, fixing a precise death toll for No Gun Ri would prove impossible. People from other villages had mixed into the refugee column; families were wiped out, leaving no one to report their deaths; some babies had not been registered officially; surviving relatives had scattered across the country and were not in touch with the petitioner group or had later died. "Whole families were killed. . . . Those families are still registered to be alive today, even though some would be well over one hundred years old," said Chung Koo-ho. The survivors group—people who were there and saw the aftermath—eventually settled on an estimated death toll of "up to four hundred."

In yet another letter addressed to Bill Clinton, two weeks after filing the compensation claims on August 25, 1997, the villagers wrote of No Gun Ri: "It was an atrocity against innocent Korean refugees, committed by armed U.S. troops. . . . About 400 souls roam around high above the killing field. . . . The victims' families are still suffering today from this nightmare of a tragedy. Please conduct a thorough investigation. . . . We want the truth, justice, and due respect for our basic human rights."

As with the compensation committee in Chongju, the claimants told the U.S. president they suspected troops of the 1st Cavalry Division were responsible for killing the refugees at No Gun Ri.

Six weeks after the compensation claims were submitted, the U.S. military responded. Kelly B. White, a lawyer with the Armed Forces Claims Service in Seoul, wrote to the Chongju District Compensation Committee saying the claims must be denied for several reasons.

"First, there is no evidence to support the claims nor is there any evidence to show that the U.S. 1st Cavalry Division was in the area where the incident allegedly occurred. Additionally, it appears that the alleged incident giving rise to the claims arose directly from combat activities of the armed forces," White wrote. The letter contended that any casualties during that period would have been combat-related, and combat-related incidents were not legally eligible for compensation. Finally, it said, the Status of Forces Agreement required filing of such claims within three years after the incident.

After years of petitions and claims, neither the U.S. military, the U.S. Embassy, the White House, the South Korean government nor anyone else in authority showed any interest in investigating the villagers' accounts of a massacre that midsummer week in 1950. The survivors, for their part, did not have the capacity to conduct their own broader investigation, by researching the vast declassified archive of U.S. military documents in Washington or by trying to find American witnesses.

They did not even have a lawyer, just the elderly, single-minded ex–law student Chung Eun-yong, and they had been ignored or overlooked by the U.S. news media, the newspapers, television networks and news agencies whose reports often prompted Washington officials to take action.

This little-noted campaign by unknown Korean villagers came down to points of law. On December 3, 1997, they got their notification from the Chongju District Compensation Committee. It had ruled against them. It acknowledged that people were killed at No Gun Ri, but said there was no evidence of U.S. involvement—even though dozens of survivors attested to it. The claimants then appealed to a national compensation committee, and on April 28, 1998, that body rejected their claims, noting the statute of limitations' three-year deadline had expired forty-five years earlier.

In Chu Gok Ri, Im Ke Ri and elsewhere among the survivors, a feeling of helplessness set in once more. At age seventy-five, even Chung Eun-yong, for the first time, considered giving up. "Friends were sympathetic," he said, "but they all reminded me that I am nothing but a little man and I can't fight a giant like the U.S. government. They said it was like a praying mantis trying to stop the rolling wheel of an oxcart."

For decades every late July, in the evening quiet of individual homes, villagers stood before ceremonial offerings of food to honor their loved ones killed at No Gun Ri. Confucian tradition dictates such family anniversary memorials. In Chu Gok Ri and Im Ke Ri, the families bowed, the lamps stayed lighted late, all on the same nights.

In 1998, the survivors for the first time gathered at the trestle itself for a memorial ceremony. Chun Choon-ja, up from Pusan, was suddenly frightened once more, like the ten-year-old who lost sight of her grandfather that day in the frenzy of fire from American foxholes. She looked around at the hillsides, now forested where they weren't before. "I still felt as though American soldiers were in the hills, but I couldn't see them because of the woods."

Choon-ja tried to separate out feelings of hate and forgiveness. She hated what they did to her mother, grandfather and others at No Gun Ri, but she tried not to hate the soldiers, she said. "They're old now. I know they came here under orders from their government, far away from home. They had to do what they were ordered to do. It's the government that must be blamed, and the high-ranking people and the kind of war they chose to fight."

THE HERONS STILL FLEW IN, SPRINGTIME DABS OF WHITE, BUT THERE were fewer these days—too many chemicals in the soil, villagers thought, and too few rice paddies. Black grapes, for wine and table, had spread across the valleys of Yongdong. The county had more vineyards, 6,000 acres, than any other in South Korea. Where villagers a half-century earlier bent over rice paddy rows, their offspring now reached up to tend vines.

The countryside around the little valley had been transformed. Park Chung-hee, strongman president of the 1960s and 1970s, had decreed that South Korea's stripped slopes be made green again, and they were reforested. He discouraged thatched roofs, the fire hazard atop every peasant's hut, and blue ceramic or composite tiles now roofed the homes, more substantial houses these days, in Chu Gok Ri and Im Ke Ri. Many rural Koreans still remembered Park as their greatest friend.

Across the valley between Yongdong and Hwanggan marched towering concrete pylons, soon to carry an elevated bullet train from Seoul to southern points. The link would turn the old Japanese main line into a sidetrack, just as expressways had made a backroad of the highway, the old road on which Eun-yong took his bride home to Chu Gok Ri, on which the refugees walked into the guns of the Americans.

Farther south, along the Naktong, the expressways had cut off the town of Samni-dong from the apple orchard, the riverside rise where Art Hunter screamed "Garryowen!" as he got ready to die. Northeast of Waegwan, where another freeway sliced through a maze of valleys, the drivers of speeding Hyundais and Daewoos couldn't know that this was where a barefoot Mel Chandler led a trapped band of GIs through enemy fire to American lines. No plaques marked such spots; more than 700 monuments dotted the South Korean landscape in remembrance of the 1950–1953 war, but they could never tell the story. No marker told where James Hodges died alone, or where Brumagen and Dean were killed while Ralph Bernotas watched, or where countless other ghosts were born to live with old soldiers until the hour of their own deaths.

Even where the monuments were placed, they could bear false witness. Beside the Naktong at Waegwan, a plaque at the rebuilt bridge stated that General Gay of the 1st Cavalry Division ordered the bridge blown up on August 3, 1950, to "deter infiltrating enemy." It didn't note that hundreds of refugees were blown up with it.

At a small concrete railroad trestle 30 miles to the north, nothing would have caused a passerby to stop and ponder what happened there. Only a handful of Koreans and Americans knew. Whenever Chun Choon-ja, one of them, had to take the train to Seoul, she closed her eyes after it pulled out of Hwanggan and didn't open them again until it had crossed the bridge at No Gun Ri.

Up the road from the trestle, a tall, sturdy woman in a sunbonnet, her face tanned and lined, now trimmed the shoots and leaves in her own small vineyard, a patch of land not far from the 4.4 acres of her devoted younger brother, the local grape-grower Yang Hae-chan. Often, she sang to herself as she worked.

"I sometimes think I hear the whispers of the ghosts," Yang Hae-sook said. "Not human voices, but they seem to talk in the wind. It used to terrify me, but not any longer. The hills and tunnel look empty, but in fact they're filled with the spirits of the dead."

Above, on the hill across the tracks, the grave of Chung Koo-ho's mother, the woman who prayed to Buddha as she shielded her children, looked out toward Chu Gok Ri. Each morning her son opened his window in the sleepy village and looked up to see her there. Downhill, among the chattering magpies, another mound rose on the grassy slope, where the schoolteacher Chung Koo-ok, the pride of Chu Gok Ri, lay in her maiden's grave. It bore no marker; Korean custom allows none for the unmarried dead. But everyone knew whose bones rested there.

IN SEOUL, ON A CLEAR DAY, TOURISTS IN THE 1990S COULD SEE ALL the way to North Korea from atop a sixty-three-story skyscraper. A half-century on, the city that was reduced to ash and rubble by the guns and bombs of 1950–1951 had lifted itself up into gleaming towers of glass and steel, had spread out into a complex of ten million people, Asia's second-largest city, crisscrossed by superhighways and grand boulevards jammed with Korean-made automobiles, filled with busy people rushing to the high-rise offices of global conglomerates and the aisles of stylish shopping malls. Two dozen bridges now spanned the broad Han, linking the halves of a metropolis. Below the teeming streets, a world-class subway system carried four million passengers a day, keeping the economic engine turning. And in the heart of it all, the Eighth Army's headquarters, hub of a 37,000-member U.S. military force, sprawled over the riverside Yongsan district, a conspicuous testament to something that had not changed, the confrontation with the north. The first battlefront of the Cold War was the last as well, under a hair-trigger armistice now forty-five years old.

On a Saturday in April 1998, a young journalist rode that subway's Orange Line to work. He was a child of the new South Korea—born thirty-six years earlier and, like many riding with him, a migrant from a farming village who had found a good job in the great city.

He remembered the walls of his village, when he was a boy, painted with red letters calling for the extermination of communists. On his college campus in the 1980s, he saw the clashes of police with anti-American students. He himself served his mandatory two years in the military, as a Korean soldier assigned to a U.S. Army division. He ended up working for a U.S. news organization. He had felt both the overbearing presence of the Americans and the welcome security.

That Saturday was a quiet news day; the political and economic headlines generated by a new president, Kim Dae-jung, had entered a lull. When the young man arrived at his office, he realized it was a good day for a journalist to clean off his desk.

Sorting through stacks of paper, he turned up an old article he once set aside, an intriguing piece from a small Seoul magazine, a story that had gotten little attention. A photograph showed a few graying men standing stiffly outside the U.S. Embassy. A caption said they were petitioning for redress for a "massacre" committed by U.S. troops during the war.

The claim was jarring; it didn't fit the script of history. The books didn't speak of such things. But the reporter remembered his grandparents did, speaking not only of brutality by the communists, but by their own southern soldiers and police, and by American GIs. His grandmother talked of restless souls in the hills and valleys all around, and asked the boy if he saw the flickering lights, the *hon bul*.

He dialed up one of the petitioners. An old man picked up the phone in Taejon. The journalist explained he was with an American news agency and wanted to know more.

There was a long pause at the other end of the line, as the old man cleared his throat. It had been forty-eight years. The father had kept faith with the son. "I always believed someone would listen to my story," Chung Eun-yong finally said.

"Where do you want to begin?"

EPILOGUE AND
NOTES ON SOURCES

The Telling of the Story of No Gun Ri

In April 1998, Sang-Hun Choe, a correspondent in the Associated Press bureau in Seoul, interviewed several of the Korean signatories to the No Gun Ri claim. On April 30, he reported in an AP dispatch that the national compensation committee had rejected their case because the statute of limitations had expired. For Choe and three colleagues, it was the beginning of more than three years' work on what became known as "the story no one wanted to hear."

At AP headquarters in New York, the deputy international editor, Kevin Noblet, thought the Koreans' allegations should be checked at the U.S. end. The first focus was the U.S. military's statement that there was no evidence the 1st Cavalry Division was in the No Gun Ri area at the time of the alleged killings, as claimed by the villagers.

Bob Port, editor of the Special Assignment Team, asked the team's investigative researcher, Randy Herschaft, to look into it. Reviewing the official Army history of the Korean War's first five months, *South to the Naktong, North to the Yalu,* by Roy E. Appleman, Herschaft determined that the claimants were correct: No Gun Ri fell squarely within the area where the 1st Cavalry Division and 25th Infantry Division were operating in late July 1950.

Port then sent Herschaft to the U.S. National Archives in College Park, Maryland, to research the two divisions' operations. The National Archives had no Korean War specialist, and the materials were scattered, but military archivist Richard Boylan was very helpful in familiarizing Herschaft with the records, once secret but now declassified, many since the 1980s.

In Herschaft's long hours of work, largely in Record Group 338 (Records of U.S. Army Commands) and RG 407 (Records of the Adjutant General's Office; Korean War Command Reports), important clues began to emerge. His first key discoveries were of the written order by the 25th Infantry Division's Maj. Gen. William B. Kean to treat civilians as enemy (RG 338: 25th Infantry Division, July 27, 1950) and of the communication from 1st Cavalry Division headquarters to fire on refugees trying to cross U.S. lines (RG 338: Journal, 8th Cavalry Regiment, July 24, 1950).

Martha Mendoza, a Special Assignment Team reporter, subsequently joined Herschaft at the National Archives. They spent days poring through hundreds of boxes of unit histories and war diaries, communications logs, handwritten messages, operations maps and other documents, and began building files of thousands of photocopied pages. Further important discoveries included communications in which Kean's staff interpreted his order to mean civilians would be "considered as unfriendly and shot" (RG 338: 25th Infantry Division, G-1 Journal, July 26, 1950) and that "drastic action" should be taken against them (RG 338: 25th Infantry Division, message from division G-1, July 27, 1950). They found that on July 26, 1950, the day the killings began at No Gun Ri, Eighth Army headquarters issued an order that "no refugees will be permitted to cross battle lines at any time" (RG 338: Eighth Army, radio message from G-1). Herschaft also eventually uncovered the correspondence between the 1st Cavalry Division commander, Maj. Gen. Hobart R. Gay, and Army historian Appleman in which Gay disclosed that hundreds of refugees had been blown up with the Naktong River bridge at Waegwan on August 3, 1950 (RG 319: Records of the Army Staff; U.S. Army Center of Military History; background papers for *South to the Naktong, North to the Yalu*).

The journalists' next job was to narrow the focus, to identify specific smaller units that may have been at No Gun Ri. From various documents—communications journals, war diaries, periodic operations reports of units from the Eighth Army down to the regiments—Herschaft and Mendoza collected hundreds of map coordinates reported for individual units, usually twice a day, as they deployed across the countryside. They then obtained 1950-vintage U.S. Army Map Service topographical maps from the National Archives and the New York Public Library, the maps that were used at the Korean warfront, to track those troop movements.

Mendoza covered the walls of the Special Assignment Team office in New York's Rockefeller Center with many large identical maps ("Yongdong," Army Map Service Series L751, Sheet 6722, scale 1:50,000), one for each day in late July 1950, and painstakingly plotted the movements of U.S. regiments and battalions, of reported refugee groups, of enemy sightings and other events, using stickers whose various colors represented different elements.

At this point, in late May 1998, a fourth member joined the reporting team—Charles J. Hanley, an International Desk special correspondent with long experience in war coverage. From the maps, it was determined that one or more of four battalions, all in the 1st Cavalry Division, were the likeliest to have encountered a refugee group near No Gun Ri around July 26, 1950. Herschaft filed a Freedom of Information Act request with the Army for those units' 1950 rosters. He then traveled to the National Personnel Records Center in St. Louis and returned with dozens of rosters copied from microfilm, some barely legible. The four battalions comprised well over 2,000 men. Armed with names, he and Mendoza began the process of locating veterans, using many resources, including such people-tracking databases as AutoTrack, CDB Infotek and Merlin. A Korean War casualty database and Social Security Administration records helped eliminate the names of those who had died.

As the tracking process continued, Mendoza and Hanley began the calls—"cold" calls to aging veterans to ask whether they witnessed a violent encounter with a large group of refugees in late July 1950. In one lengthy telephone interview after another, many with veterans of the 5th and 8th Cavalry Regiments, the journalists learned much about the mid-1950 warfront, but nothing on No Gun Ri. Then, on the thirty-fourth call, Mendoza found an ex-sergeant who described the shooting of refugees at a trestle in the first days of their deployment. Fifteen interviews later, another man spoke out about the killings at No Gun Ri. The journalists finally were able to zero in— on the 2nd Battalion of the 7th Cavalry Regiment. Although some veterans were simply cryptic or terse or said they didn't remember, more and more were found who were willing to talk about what they saw or participated in at No Gun Ri. Now in their sixties or seventies, they clearly felt a need to unburden themselves.

No surviving 7th Cavalry documents recorded the large-scale civilian killings at No Gun Ri. But the all-important 7th Cavalry "log," the regimental journal for July 1950, was missing without explanation from its assigned place at the National Archives. That log presumably would have recorded, as the 8th Cavalry journal did, standing instructions from above to shoot refugees along the front line, as well as on-the-spot communications within the chain of command about what to do with the refugees at No Gun Ri.

Eventually about twenty veterans of the 7th Cavalry interviewed by the journalists said refugees were killed in the area of their first deployment, and about a dozen of those were strong sources, discussing No Gun Ri in some detail on the record. Some eventually were interviewed on videotape; many identified the trestle from photographs. Some said they believed one hundred or fewer civilians were killed; some said they believed hundreds were killed, as reported by the Korean survivors.

In Seoul, where his work was overseen and edited by AP bureau chief Reid G. Miller, a Korean War veteran, and news editor Paul Shin, Choe assembled a chronology of the shootings based on continuing interviews with survivors and victims' relatives and on Korean historical material providing day-to-day background. He

visited the No Gun Ri site several times, saw the bullets lodged in
the walls and talked to survivors at the scene itself.

On the two sides of the world, the accounts from Koreans and
Americans meshed in their details—of screaming children, ricochets
in the concrete underpasses, bodies piling up in the entrances.

The story was pinned down, but more work needed to be done.
Herschaft traveled to the Harry S. Truman Library in Independence,
Missouri, the U.S. Army Military History Institute in Carlisle, Pennsylvania, and other repositories to examine additional command records, historians' notes and other material. In all, he made about a
dozen trips to the National Archives in Maryland, where the archivist staff proved unfailingly helpful and where many other record
groups were reviewed—of the Army's offices of the Judge Advocate
General (RG 153), the Inspector General (RG 159), the Provost
Marshal General (RG 389), the Chief of Chaplains (RG 247) and
others. Relevant files of photographs in the Still Pictures Branch and
of film in the Motion Pictures Branch were also reviewed.

Herschaft checked 1950 U.S. and European newspapers and relevant bibliographies and periodical indexes in search of references
to the refugee killings. The team examined notebooks and other
personal papers of now-deceased journalists who covered the war.
In Seoul, Choe obtained copies of the North Korean newspaper articles in 1950 that reported the discovery of the civilian slaughter at
No Gun Ri. Throughout, the halves of the international reporting
team worked closely together via teleconferences, electronic mail,
faxes and overnight packages.

Finally, in late July 1998, after an intensive four months, the
story of No Gun Ri was written. But it was not published.

Just weeks before the reporting team completed the draft, the
Cable News Network had retracted a television report alleging that
the U.S. military secretly used nerve gas in the Indochina wars in
1970. The CNN "Operation Tailwind" furor, touched off by complaints from Washington military and political figures, had a chilling effect, leading news executives to view investigative work,
especially relating to the military, ever more cautiously. Skepticism
and nervousness at the AP over the No Gun Ri findings slowed the

story's progress toward the news wire to a crawl, and at times to a stop.

As the delays dragged on, the journalists widened their reporting to refugee killings beyond No Gun Ri. At the U.S. Air Force Historical Research Agency, at Maxwell Air Force Base in Alabama, Hanley found after-mission debriefings from 1950—particularly of the 35th Fighter-Bomber Squadron—in which pilots reported strafing groups of apparent refugees along South Korea's roads. Hanley and Mendoza interviewed old pilots who said they had been troubled at times when directed to such targets. In South Korea, Choe interviewed survivors of refugee strafings.

Herschaft and Hanley wondered whether refugees were killed when U.S. Army engineers blew up the Naktong River bridge at Tuksong-dong on August 3, 1950, the same day on which, General Gay later wrote, hundreds were killed upriver when he ordered the destruction of the Waegwan bridge. The journalists studied documents of the 14th Combat Engineer Battalion and the 21st Infantry Regiment (RG 338) and traced veterans of those units. In a series of interviews in late 1998, they found five American witnesses to the mass refugee killing at the Tuksong-dong bridge, an event long hidden in history. Choe found Korean witnesses as well.

As the months passed, the reporters maintained contact with their No Gun Ri sources. Choe continued to find additional Korean witnesses, including some who were not signatories to the compensation claim and had not been in contact with other No Gun Ri survivors since the war. Their recollections matched those of the claimants. On the U.S. side, meanwhile, the reporters came to understand, more and more, that the civilian killings had psychologically scarred the soldiers who took part or witnessed them. Many were receiving psychiatric treatment at Veterans Affairs hospitals for post-traumatic stress disorder. One veteran told Mendoza from his hospital bed he believed he had been miraculously cured of a serious physical illness because he finally talked about No Gun Ri; he asked her to press harder to get the story out.

By mid-1999, the strength of the story and the obligation to publish were recognized at the AP. The journalism rested on three pillars: the two sets of witnesses, Korean and American, more than forty people an ocean apart whose recollections meshed, down to small details, and the declassified documents that showed that orders to kill refugees had spread across the warfront. The military records, including company morning reports obtained at the St. Louis center, supported the No Gun Ri accounts in other ways as well, by establishing that 7th Cavalry units were present at the time and place of the killings, for example, and by showing that other U.S. troops—5th Cavalry—were, indeed, at Chu Gok Ri and Im Ke Ri the night the Koreans said they were forced by American soldiers to leave those home villages and head toward No Gun Ri. The story also made clear that discrepancies and uncertainties remained, involving, among other things, the number of casualties, the precise sequence of events and the question of who may have ordered the killings.

The story was finally sent on AP's worldwide news wires on September 29, 1999. It made major headlines in newspapers from New York to Paris to Tokyo, and on news broadcasts worldwide. The declassified communications telling troops to shoot refugees were available on the AP's Web site for all to see. The No Gun Ri survivors, who had been unaware that their story was corroborated more than a year earlier, were deeply moved. "I have never been happier before. Now I can rest in peace when I die," said the seventy-five-year-old Park Sun-yong, whose two children were killed at No Gun Ri.

Within hours, the U.S. defense secretary, William Cohen, ordered a U.S. Army investigation of No Gun Ri, to be pursued "wherever it may lead." The South Korean government also began an investigation. The most recent U.S. position on the allegations had been stated six months earlier, on March 22, 1999, in a letter to the U.S. National Council of Churches, which had championed the Koreans' cause at the behest of the Korean National Council of Churches. An Army Department official wrote that Army researchers had reviewed National Archives documents, including the operational records of the 1st Cavalry and 25th Infantry Divisions, and had "found no information to substantiate the claim" of a refugee massacre at No

Gun Ri. The Army presumably did not realize at the time that AP journalists had also reviewed those files and found various orders across the warfront to shoot refugees.

On October 13 and December 28, 1999, the AP team published further reports, detailing other mass killings of South Korean refugees by the U.S. military in 1950–1951. The first focused on the demolition of the Naktong bridges; the second dealt with the strafings of refugee columns by U.S. warplanes. The AP reports and the new democratic freedoms in South Korea combined to open the floodgates of memory. Going public after years of silence, South Korean citizens attested to dozens of large-scale killings of civilians by the U.S. military during the Korean War. By early 2001, at least sixty-one incidents had been reported in complaints filed with the Defense Ministry in Seoul.

Powerful new documentary evidence continued to surface. Bob Port, who left the AP in June 1999, uncovered the series of documents from the spring of 1951 in which an American officer opposes an Eighth Army directive to shoot refugees (RG 338: Staff Section Report of G-3, 2nd Infantry Division, April 1951; S-2 Evaluation, May 1951, 38th Infantry Regiment); Herschaft found the colonel's order to "shoot all refugees" crossing the Naktong River (RG 338: Journal, 1st Battalion, 8th Cavalry Regiment, August 9, 1950); Herschaft, with the help of Korean-American researcher Pang Sun-joo, obtained the captured enemy document whose English translation in August 1950 indirectly informed the U.S. command of No Gun Ri, reporting "barbaric" killings of civilians by U.S. troops near Yongdong. There was no sign in the record that this information led to any investigation (RG 338: 1st Cavalry Division, G-2 Interrogation, Batch BCD 56, Translation 0027, August 17, 1950).

In declassified files of the U.S. Embassy in South Korea, Herschaft found reports and letters showing that U.S. diplomats and officers, up to supreme commander Gen. Douglas MacArthur, were informed by U.S. Army witnesses of mass killings of political prisoners by the South Korean regime (RG 84: Records of the Foreign Service Posts of the Department of State; Korean Embassy Records, Top Secret

Files, August 10–25, 1950). Korean-American researcher Lee Do-young led the AP journalists to similar U.S. documents relating to earlier slaughters, at Taejon in July 1950, and to photographs of the mass summary executions taken by the U.S. military (RG 319: Records of the Army Staff; G-2, Geographical Index to Numerical Series of Intelligence Documents, 1944–1951). This material provided the basis for an AP story published on April 20, 2000.

On June 5, 2000, CBS News was the first to report that the Pentagon's No Gun Ri investigators had turned up the critically important memo from Air Force Col. Turner C. Rogers noting that the Air Force, at the Army's request, was strafing civilian refugee columns in South Korea. Herschaft located the document the next day at the National Archives and the AP also reported on it (RG 342: Fifth Air Force, Office of the Deputy Chief of Staff, Operations and Intelligence, Outgoing Correspondence, "Policy on Strafing Civilian Refugees," July 25, 1950). The USS *Valley Forge* action report noting the Army instructions to Navy pilots to strafe groups of more than eight people was found in a U.S. Navy archive on the World Wide Web ("16–31 Jul 1950" at http://www.history.navy.mil/branches/v-forge.html).

The AP reporting had antagonized some veterans' groups and others, and these critics found a focus in May 2000. An article in *U.S. News & World Report,* written by a 7th Cavalry Association member, speculated that two of AP's many ex-GI sources, Eugene Hesselman and Delos Flint, may not have been present at No Gun Ri because they were wounded around that time and may have been evacuated. But that speculation was not borne out by the company morning reports or by the men's medical records, which the two released to the AP journalists. The magazine also said an incomplete personnel record indicated that another of the more than forty Americans and Koreans cited as witnesses, 7th Cavalry veteran Edward L. Daily, could not have been there. Further AP research determined that Daily, author of two histories of the regiment in Korea and a former 7th Cavalry Association leader, apparently was not at the scene, but had learned about the event secondhand. A spokesman for the ongoing Army investigation noted, however, that "Daily or whoever else is just a small part of a very big picture."

In fact, after years of rejecting the villagers' allegations, the Pentagon and South Korean investigators would ultimately, in their final reports in January 2001, agree with the AP's finding that the 7th Cavalry Regiment, with small arms and heavy weapons fire, killed the refugees at No Gun Ri.

The AP team's reporting received a series of journalism honors: the Pulitzer Prize for investigative reporting; the Polk Award for international reporting; South Korea's Samsung Press Foundation award; the International Consortium of Investigative Journalists Award; the Overseas Press Club's Ross Award for reporting on the human condition; Johns Hopkins University's Novartis Award for international reporting; the Worth Bingham Award for investigative reporting; a Korean Journalists Association special award (for Choe); a National Headliners Award; a Columbia University On-Line Journalism Award; and the Associated Press Managing Editors Association's President's Award.

To broaden and deepen the story, and produce *The Bridge at No Gun Ri*, required many more months of intensive interviewing of the Korean survivors and the ex-soldiers, and extensive research and interviewing in such areas as the political, physical and cultural features of Korea and its people at midcentury, and of Yongdong County in particular; U.S. and Asian geopolitics of the time; the U.S. Army and the 7th Cavalry in particular; the U.S. occupation of Japan; the Korean War itself; and the impact of post-traumatic stress disorder (PTSD) on combat veterans.

Over three years, the authors conducted more than 500 interviews, the majority of them with Korean survivors of No Gun Ri and with former members of the 7th Cavalry Regiment. Choe interviewed more than three dozen survivors, many of them multiple times and at great length. Particularly generous in sharing the stories of their lives with the authors and readers were Chung Eun-yong and his wife, Park Sun-yong, and their son Chung Koo-do; the brothers Chung Koo-hak and Chung Koo-hun; sister and brother

Yang Hae-sook and Yang Hae-chan; Chun Choon-ja; Park Hee-sook; Park Chang-rok and his sister Park Chang-soo; Chung Koo-ho; Kim Hong-ki; the brothers Kim Bok-jong and Kim Bok-hee; and Chung Koo-hong.

Other No Gun Ri survivors and victims' relatives who contributed to the authors' knowledge of the events of 1950 and of the villagers' lives at midcentury included Choi Sang-joon; the late Park Jong-ha; Kim Hak-joong; Chung Koo-shik; Kim Sung-ja; Chung Myong-ja; Chung Shin-woong; the late Cho Nam-il; Chang Hae-ja; Chang Hae-soon; Chung Jin-myong; Suh Jong-gap; Park Hwa-ja; Lee Byong-hoi; Lee Yoo-ja; Sohn Hyun-uk; Suh Jong-ja; Suh Jong-koo; Hwang Sam-ryang; Chun Joo-sup; Kum Cho-ja; Moon Wan-shik; Cho Nam-joo; Park Soon-nam; Chang Sang-ryol; Lee Young-jong; Park Choon-ja; Cho Soo-ja; Chung Jong-ja; Lee Ok-soon; Han Yang-sok; Han Young-ok; Kim Boo-eui; and Chung Soon-ja. Others contributed in other areas: Lee Duk-soo and Kim Jin-sok, among others, recounting the Naktong bridge explosions; Yang Sung-bok, Cho Koon-ja, Lee Hwang-hoon, Chung Kyong-yong, and other residents of No Gun Ri and other Yongdong County villages; and Hong Won-ki and others who described various U.S. strafing attacks on refugees in 1950–1951.

Mendoza and Hanley interviewed almost 100 veterans of the 7th Cavalry, some multiple times and in great depth. Some discussed No Gun Ri; many did not, including men who said they did not observe the killings. But all contributed to a knowledge of the life of 7th Cavalrymen in Tokyo and at the Korea warfront, and to an understanding of the young American soldier of midcentury. Leonard B. "Buddy" Wenzel, Arthur H. Hunter, Ralph Bernotas and Suey Lee Wong were especially open and forthright in helping the authors understand the lifelong impact of a long-ago war. Decar "De" Wenzel, as both the wife of a disabled veteran and the sister of a soldier killed in Korea, bore witness to the long-term havoc of that war, and to the power of love in coping with it. Her sister, the late Juanita Royal, kindly shared brother James Hodges's letters from Korea with the authors, thereby giving readers a special insight into a teen-aged soldier's mind on a distant battlefield.

Of the veterans who recounted what happened at No Gun Ri, some provided more detail than others, and their perspectives often differed, from different foxholes in 1950, from different points of view a half-century later. But all seemed to have a desire to see the truth finally told, and above all they were the ones who ensured that light would be shed on a dark chapter of history. They included James T. Kerns, Herman W. Patterson, George D. Preece, Norman L. Tinkler, Eugene S. Hesselman, Delos K. Flint, Joseph Jackman, the late William T. Collins, Lyle W. Jacobson, Aulton E. Blalock, James Elkins, Robert W. Johnson, Thomas H. Hacha, George W. Early, Lawrence Levine, James Crume, Robert M. Carroll, James McClure, Henry Matthias and the late Melvin Durham.

Other veterans were generous with their time and encouragement in telling the wider story of the 7th Cavalrymen and the 1st Cavalry Division in Korea, particularly Robert C. "Snuffy" Gray; William N. McKown, who with his wife, Lois, helped bring the Tokyo days to life; Alfred B. Clair; the late William C. Kaluf; Charles Leavitt; Donald J. MacFarland; John M. Ramirez; Herbert B. Heyer; Harold D. Steward; Joseph A. McAnany; Clifford Biddle; Donald D. Down; Lyle R. Gibbs; Louis S. Mehl; Jack Haskell; John Finazzo; David Fetter; Elzondo Berryman; Otto R. Bohlender; Royal Bollinger; Crawford Buchanan; Russell McKinley; Francis McManus; Joseph Burton; Tom Boyd; Edwin Klinedinst; Leighton Dodd; John C. Lippincott; Marvin Daniel; the late Lucian Croft; John W. Callaway; Louis B. Trevathan; Jacob Schacter; Robert G. Russell; and the late Gen. Charles D. Palmer. Susan Huff Rush, daughter of Col. Gilmon A. Huff, very helpfully filled in further details about her father after his death on April 29, 1999, nine months after Mendoza and Hanley interviewed him. The Rev. E. T. Cooprider and Patricia Dutton helped the authors gain some understanding of Melbourne C. Chandler, their nephew and stepfather, respectively, thirty years after his death.

Still other veterans, from other units, contributed meaningfully to the authors' knowledge of the events of 1950–1951 in Korea: Carroll F. Kinsman, Joseph Ipock, the late Leon L. Denis, Ronald

W. Crump and Roy L. Meredith of the 14th Combat Engineer Battalion; Donald Lloyd and William Traylor of the 3rd Combat Engineer Battalion; Clyde Keene of the 43rd Engineer Battalion; Rudolph Giannelli, Earl C. Downey, Forrest K. Kleinman, Lacy Barnett, William Wyrick and John J. Doody of the 24th Infantry Division; and Uzal Ent and Sidney Berry of the 25th Infantry Division.

Over three years, the authors consulted many specialists, particularly in the areas of Korean and military history, the law of war and post-combat mental health. Especially helpful were historian Bruce Cumings of the University of Chicago; Yang Young-jo, senior researcher at the Korea Institute for Military History; Kim Dong-dae, unofficial historian of Yongdong County, South Korea; law professors Gary D. Solis of the U.S. Military Academy at West Point and Scott Silliman of Duke University, both former military lawyers; Dr. Robert A. Rosenheck, a psychiatrist, and psychologist Alan Fontana of the Veterans Affairs Northeast Program Evaluation Center, West Haven, Connecticut; and psychologist Glenn Smith of the VA Medical Center in Tampa, Florida.

Besides yards of files of declassified military documents, the authors consulted scores of books and hundreds of newspaper, news wire and magazine articles in pursuing the original story, and then in deepening it to write *The Bridge at No Gun Ri*. Their sources ranged from early twentieth-century Salvation Army yearbook reports on the Korea mission, to a videotape of the 7th Cavalry Association's *Wolakota* reconciliation ceremony in South Dakota in 1994, to South Korean government and U.S. military astronomical and weather data for mid-1950. The July 1950 deck log of the USNS *David C. Shanks*, the troopship that took the 2nd Battalion to Korea, was found at the Military Sealift Command in Washington and proved invaluable.

The full declassified source documents for *The Bridge at No Gun Ri* can be viewed at www.henryholt.com.

A selection of the more important published sources, by subject, follows:

The Korean War

Three official U.S. histories cover the first year of the war: Appleman's *South to the Naktong, North to the Yalu* (1960); Billy C. Mossman's *Ebb and Flow: November 1950–July 1951* (1990); and James F. Schnabel's *Policy and Direction: The First Year* (1972). All Center of Military History, U.S. Army.

Two official Korean-language sources: *A History of the Korean War*, Korean Military Academy, 1987; *The History of the United Nations Forces in the Korean War*, compiled by the South Korean Defense Ministry.

Bruce Cumings's two-volume *The Origins of the Korean War*, Princeton University Press, 1981 and 1990.

Clay Blair's *The Forgotten War*, Times Books, 1987.

Max Hastings's *The Korean War*, Simon and Schuster, 1987.

Harold Joyce Noble's *Embassy at War*, edited by Frank Baldwin, University of Washington Press, 1975.

Uzal W. Ent's *Fighting on the Brink*, Turner Publishing, Paducah, Ky., 1996, a densely detailed account of the Pusan Perimeter campaign.

Encyclopedia of the Korean War, ABC-CLIO, 2000.

The Korean War: An Encyclopedia, Garland Publishing, 1995.

John G. Westover's *Combat Support in Korea*, Combat Forces Press, 1955.

James A. Huston's *Guns and Butter, Powder and Rice: U.S. Army Logistics in the Korean War*, Susquehanna University Press, Selingsgrove, Pa., 1989.

Two memoirs offered valuable insights into the combat soldier's life: Boris R. Spiroff's *Korea: Frozen Hell on Earth*, Vantage Press, 1995, written by a former 7th Cavalry sergeant; and Addison Terry's *The Battle for Pusan*, Presidio Press, 2000.

Many articles in military and other journals provided useful information. One of particular importance was Martin Blumenson's "The Rangers at Hwachon Dam: An Operation in Frustration," *Army* magazine, December 1967.

Korea

Do You Know Our Agony? (Dari publishing, 1994), the book written by Chung Eun-yong to expose the No Gun Ri killings, was useful not only in providing an account of events there but also in illuminating the Chung family and village life before and after the war.

Some other Korean-language sources:

Defense Ministry Investigation Report on the No Gun Ri Incident, Seoul, 2001.

Lee Ki-baik's *A New History of Korea*, Ilchokak, Seoul, 1984.

Kang Man-gil's *A History of Modern Korea*, Changjak Kwa Pipyong, Seoul, 1984.

Chung Hee-sang's *I Cannot Die Without Telling This Story*, Dolbaege, 1990, an account of civilian massacres by South Korean police and soldiers during the war.

A History of Yongdong County, Yongdong County Office, 1997.

Some English-language sources:

Cornelius Osgood's *The Koreans and Their Culture*, The Ronald Press, New York, 1951.

V. T. Zaichikov's *Geography of Korea*, Institute of Pacific Relations, 1952.

Chae Kyung-oh's *Handbook of Korea*, Pageant Press, New York, 1958.

Shannon McCune's *Korea's Heritage: A Regional and Social Geography*, Charles E. Tuttle Co., Rutland, Vt., 1956.

Koreana, Korean Cultural Heritage, Volume II, Thought and Religion, and *Volume IV, Traditional Lifestyles*, Korea Foundation, Seoul, 1997.

Occupation of Japan and the Cold War

The authors reviewed issues of the Tokyo-based newspapers *Pacific Stars and Stripes* and the *Nippon Times* from the late 1940s and

1950 for information about the occupation and the early months of the Korean War.

Other sources included:

John W. Dower's *Embracing Defeat,* W. W. Norton/The New Press, New York, 1999.

Walt Sheldon's *The Honorable Conquerors: The Occupation of Japan, 1945–1952,* Macmillan, New York, 1965.

Michael Schaller's *The American Occupation of Japan: The Origins of the Cold War in Asia,* Oxford University Press, 1985.

Occupation Diary, First Cavalry Division, U.S. 1st Cavalry Division Public Information Office, Tokyo, 1950.

Lisle A. Rose's *The Cold War Comes to Main Street: America in 1950,* University Press of Kansas, 1999.

James R. Kerin Jr.'s "The Korean War and American Memory," Ph.D. dissertation, University of Pennsylvania, 1994.

Post-Traumatic Stress Disorder

The authors benefited from the useful expository material of the Department of Veterans Affairs posted on a VA Web site (http://www.long-beach.va.gov/ptsd/stress.html), and read dozens of papers on the subject in such professional journals as the *American Journal of Psychiatry, U.S. Armed Forces Medical Journal, Journal of Consulting and Clinical Psychology, Journal of Clinical Psychiatry* and *Journal of Traumatic Stress.*

Other useful published works included:

Dave Grossman's *On Killing: The Psychological Cost of Learning to Kill in War and Society,* Little, Brown and Company, Boston, 1995.

Trauma and the Vietnam War Generation; Report of Findings from the National Vietnam Veterans Readjustment Study, Brunner/Mazel Publishers, New York, 1990.

Robert Jay Lifton's *Home from the War,* Simon and Schuster, 1973.

Albert E. Cowdrey's *The Medics' War,* Center of Military History, U.S. Army, 1987, an official history of the Medical Service Corps in the Korean War.

On January 11, 2001, the U.S. Defense Department and the South Korean Defense Ministry issued reports on their parallel investigations of the events at No Gun Ri in July 1950. After years of rejection of the villagers' allegations, the inquiry led by the U.S. Army inspector general affirmed that the U.S. military killed and wounded an "unknown number" of South Korean refugees at No Gun Ri with small-arms, artillery and mortar fire and aerial strafing. President Bill Clinton issued a statement expressing deep regret and said a memorial would be built and a scholarship fund established to honor all Korean civilians killed in the 1950–1953 war. The U.S. government did not make a formal apology or offer compensation to the No Gun Ri survivors, as asked for in their petition.

The reports' release was preceded by weeks of friction between the American and South Korean investigators.

The South Koreans' report said their investigators believed U.S. pilots had been instructed to attack South Korean refugees to guard against North Korean infiltrators, and it was possible that U.S. ground troops received orders to fire on the No Gun Ri refugees.

The Pentagon report, on the other hand, maintained without citing definitive evidence that U.S. pilots were not told to attack the No Gun Ri civilians and that no Army officers issued orders to shoot them, implying that enlisted men took it upon themselves to fire. It called the killings at No Gun Ri, carried out over three days, "an unfortunate tragedy inherent to war and not a deliberate killing." It found no wrongdoing and assigned no blame.

In taking that position, however, the Army's 300-page report omitted vital information and misrepresented some important documents. Major examples:

- Despite the Korean investigators' request, the American investigators did not share with their Korean counterparts the mission reports of the U.S. Air Force's 35th Fighter-Bomber Squadron; nor did they discuss the documents' contents in the U.S. report. The 35th Squadron documents showed that apparent civilian groups were targeted during this period; noted pilots' concerns that they were killing refugees; and reported three air attacks in the No Gun Ri area on July 26–27, 1950.
- The Pentagon did not include in its report any reference to what the Korean-language report said were interviews with five ex-pilots who told U.S. investigators they had been ordered to attack apparent refugee groups in mid-1950 in South Korea.
- It omitted the key passage from the "Rogers memo" of July 25, 1950, in which the Fifth Air Force's operations chief wrote that "to date, we have complied" with an Army request to strafe refugees approaching U.S. lines. These essential words, a colonel's statement that deliberate strafings were taking place, were not included in the Pentagon's presentation of the memo.
- It did not disclose that the all-important 7th Cavalry Regiment communications log for July 1950 was missing from the National Archives. That is the single document most likely to have recorded orders for ground troops to shoot the No Gun Ri refugees.
- It did not report, as the Korean investigators did, that seventeen of the former 7th Cavalrymen interviewed by the Pentagon said they believed there were orders at No Gun Ri to shoot the refugees.
- It did not report the existence of at least fourteen U.S. Army documents showing that high-ranking officers ordered or authorized the shooting of refugees during the Korean War's first months. It acknowledged the existence of only two such directives, previously made public by the Associated Press: the one in the 1st Cavalry Division to "fire everyone," including refugees, trying to cross U.S. lines, and General Kean's order in the 25th Infantry Division to treat civilians as enemy. In the case of the 1st Cavalry

Division communication, it asserted that this was an officer's "misinterpretation" of policy. But subsequent orders in that division, undisclosed in the Pentagon report, said just as plainly that refugees should be shot. As for Kean's order, the report said the general meant civilians should be "arrested." But one communication the Pentagon did not report was from a Kean aide, a colonel, who instructed troops that the order meant civilians should be "shot."

- While discussing at length the perceived threat of North Korean infiltration among South Korean refugees, the Pentagon did not report the fact that no hard evidence emerged of infiltration among the group at No Gun Ri.

There were other examples, and former U.S. Representative Paul N. "Pete" McCloskey Jr. of California, one of eight members of an advisory panel that oversaw the U.S. inquiry, concluded afterward that the Pentagon report was a "clear failure to report the truth." He was the only adviser to write and distribute a detailed analysis, although another, retired Marine Lt. Gen. Bernard E. Trainor, wrote afterward in the *Washington Post* that "the blame (at No Gun Ri) ultimately fell on some level of leadership."

On January 12, 2001, the day after the Pentagon report's release, President Clinton commented further when asked whether his statement of regret amounted to an apology: "I don't think there is any difference in the two words. They both mean that we are profoundly sorry for what happened, and that things happened which were wrong. I think the word which was agreed on . . . was thought to be appropriate in a—if you will—a legal and a political sense, because the evidence was not clear that there was responsibility for wrongdoing high enough in the chain of command in the Army to say that, in effect, the government was responsible."

In South Korea, Chung Koo-do, as spokesman for the No Gun Ri petitioners, said: "Any final report that does not deal with the responsibility of commanders has a serious defect. It can't be construed as anything other than a Pentagon attempt to whitewash the massacre." Chung Eun-yong, his father, concluded, "America has no justice or conscience."

An acknowledgment of responsibility and granting of compensation for No Gun Ri would have set a precedent for dozens of other reported cases of large-scale, indiscriminate killings of South Korean civilians by the U.S. military in 1950–1951, all cases reported after the original AP articles on No Gun Ri were published in 1999. An examination of those cases would shed further light on a long-hidden underside of an American war.

The Pentagon report, in its 300 pages, took note of these many other deaths in a footnote on page 18, in which it said the Army interrogators learned of other civilian killings in the course of their interviews. Those other killings, Pentagon officials indicated, would not be investigated.

(별첨 13) : 영문

Eunyong Chung
Representative of Petitioners
of Nokun Ri Incident
797-7 Kasuwon-dong, So-gu
Taejon, Republic of Korea, 302-241

His Excellency Bill Clinton   September 10th, 1997
President
The United States of America

Dear Mr. President ;

We, the remaining families of the Korean War victims who were killed or wounded by U.S. soldiers from July 26th to 29th, 1950, are petitioning for your recognition of the incident, a formal apology and compensation.

We had previously sent similar letters to you via the U.S. Embassy in Korea on July 5th and October 5th of the year 1994. We are deeply regretful of not having received your response yet.

The incident took place during the Korean War in NoKun Ri, Hwanggan Myon, Yongdong Gun, North Chungchong Province. It was an atrocity against innocent Korean refugees, committed by armed U.S. troops. Even though it has been 47years since the slaughter of July 26th through July 29th, 1950, the incident still lives in our hearts and our minds daily. We are still suffering from the vivid memory of this unforgetable day. Some survivors live with permanently disfigured bodies (without one eye or nose and so on). Others are in sorrow because they live without thier families. About 400 souls roam around high above the killingfield

We sincerely hope that you will find it in your heart to sympathize with us and share the pains of the bereaved families. The victim's families are still suffering today from this nightmare of a tragedy. Please conduct a thorough investigation on the survivors and the actual site, and find out which of the 1st Cavalry Division committed such a grave mistake. We want the truth, justice and due respect for our basic human rights.

We thank you for your kind attention again. May God bless you and your country.

Respectfully yours,

鄭 殷溶

Eunyong Chung

Representative of Petitioners
of Nokun Ri Incident

A SIGNATURE PAGE OF THE PETITION

The List of Name of Petitioners

Name	Address	Signature	Remark
정은용 Eunyong Chung	대전시 서구 가수원동 797-7 797-7 Kasuwondong, Sogu, Taejon city, R.O.K		*
전태철 Taechul Chun	대전시 서구 갈마동 큰마을Apt. 116동 1503호 116-1503 Kunmaul Apt, Galmadong, Sogu, Taejon city		*
정순자 Sunja Chung	경기도 의정부시 용현동 용현주공아파트 107동 107호 107-107 Yonghyun Jugong Apt, Yonghyundong, Uijongbu City, Kyonggido Province		*
박정하 Jungha Park	서울특별시 송파구 삼전동 120-1 120-1 Samjundong, Songpagu, Seoul		*
정진웅 Jinwoong Chung	경기도 용인군 외사면 옥산리 835 835 Oksan Ri, Oisa myun, Yongin Gun, Kyonggido Province		*
김학중 Hakjung Kim	충청북도 청주시 수곡동 52-33 52-33 Sukogdong, Chongju City, North Chungchong Province		*
양해식 Haeshik Yang	충청북도 영동군 영동읍 회동리 90 90 Hoidong Ri, Yongdong Eup, Yongdongkun, North Chungchong Province		**
박선용 Sunyong Park	대전시 서구 가수원동 797-7 797-7 Kasuwondong, Sogu, Taejon		**
김성자 Sungja Kim	서울시 성북구 정능3동 665-12 665-12 Jungneung 3dong, Sungbukgu, Seoul		*
서범식 Bumsok Suh	서울시 서초구 서초동 1350-5 금성빌라 303호 303 Kumsung villa, 1350-5 Sochodong, Sochogu, Seoul		*

Remark   * bereaved families
              ** wounded

As of early 2001, survivors had reported the names of 181 people said to have been killed, 20 reported missing and 50 wounded in the U.S. military attack on refugees at No Gun Ri in July 1950. Survivors estimated up to 400 were killed, but they and South Korean government investigators said fixing a precise number was impossible, since whole families were wiped out, records were destroyed in the war and many refugees likely came from distant villages.

Most names on the list, maintained by the Yongdong County Office, were reported by families from the villages of Im Ke Ri and Chu Gok Ri. Of the dead, 83 percent were women and children or men over age forty. About one-quarter of the dead were babies or other children under age ten.

In the victims' list below, a few females bear only family names. According to customs at the time, families often registered housewives by surnames only in lineage books, married women's names were seldom used in conversation and the wartime destruction of records made it difficult for surviving children to trace mothers' full names.

(Key: F = female. M = male. The age and hometown are given. N/A = not available. "Yongdong" designates people from other Yongdong County villages, many of whom sought shelter with relatives at Chu Gok

Ri or Im Ke Ri. "Elsewhere" designates those from outside Yongdong County.)

Reported Killed

Park Soon-im (F, 73, Yongdong)
Hwang Jae-young (M, 23, Yongdong)
Kim Chang-keun (M, 30, Yongdong)
Lee Kyong-yoel (F, 39, Yongdong)
Kim Duk-joo (M, 42, Yongdong)
Kim Dong-eui (M, 39, Yongdong)
Park Choon-duk (M, 39, Yongdong)
Sohn Jong-eui (F, 59, Im Ke Ri)
Park Chang-won (M, 4, Im Ke Ri)
Lee Jong-son (M, 5, Im Ke Ri)
Lee Jong-sup (M, 2, Im Ke Ri)
Park Boot-dul (F, 1, Yongdong)
Kim Duk-shi (M, 8, Yongdong)
Kim Bong-joon (M, 29, Yongdong)
Kim Byong-hyun (M, 28, Yongdong)
Yang Eun-nyon (F, 48, Yongdong)
Kim Sool-yi (M, 55, Yongdong)
Song Jae-hwa (M, 16, elsewhere)
Hwang Doo-chok (F, 44, Im Ke Ri)
Lim Kan-nan (F, 43, Yongdong)
Chang Man-im (F, 54, Im Ke Ri)
Sohn Yong-woon (M, 61, Im Ke Ri)
Chang Jae-sung (M, 36, Yongdong)
Han Dae-gil (M, 44, Chu Gok Ri)
Han Dae-son (M, 36, Chu Gok Ri)
Han Wol-soon (F, 14, Chu Gok Ri)
Han Myong-soo (M, 3, Chu Gok Ri)
Sohn Myong-sook (F, 26, Chu Gok Ri)
Chung Soon-ja (F, 8, Yongdong)
Sohn Ssang-dae (F, 39, Chu Gok Ri)
Lee Sung-nam (F, 57, Chu Gok Ri)
Kim Ke-soon (F, 18, Chu Gok Ri)
Park June-ha (M, 55, Im Ke Ri)

Park Hee-soon (F, 20, Im Ke Ri)
Sohn Soon-nam (F, 48, Im Ke Ri)
Lee Young-ja (F, 2, Im Ke Ri)
Min Young-ok (F, 30, elsewhere)
Chung Soon-rye (F, 3, elsewhere)
Chung Koo-sung (M, 1, elsewhere)
Kim Dae-ak (F, 46, Chu Gok Ri)
Chang Shi-hun (M, 21, Chu Gok Ri)
Hong Sung-mee (F, 8 months, Chu Gok Ri)
Chang Myong-ja (F, 5, Chu Gok Ri)
Chun Young-ja (F, 15, Yongdong)
Chun Young-ja (same name, F, 16, Im Ke Ri)
Kim Yoon-boon (F, 43, Im Ke Ri)
Koo Chul-dong (M, 56, Chu Gok Ri)
Koo Hoi-woo (M, 21, Chu Gok Ri)
Chung Chang-keun (M, 65, elsewhere)
Kim Kan-ran (F, 58, elsewhere)
Kim In-sun (F, 17, elsewhere)
Chung Myong-rae (F, 16, elsewhere)
Kal Yong-yi (M, 53, Yongdong)
Kal Keun-ok (M, 85, Yongdong)
Lee Ja-sun (F, 85, Im Ke Ri)
Yang Hae-young (M, 16, Im Ke Ri)
Yang Hae-yong (M, 6, Im Ke Ri)
Yang Ke-soon (F, 42, Im Ke Ri)
Min Eun-soon (F, 21, Im Ke Ri)
Chung Hyun-mok (M, 2, Im Ke Ri)
Park Ne-eung (M, 41, Yongdong)
Yang Mal-soon (F, 38, Yongdong)
Park Sang-ja (F, 13, Yondgong)
Park Hwa-soon (F, 4, Yongdong)
Song Jae-ok (F, 19, Im Ke Ri)

Lee (F, 59, Im Ke Ri, mother of survivor Kim Hak-joong)

Kim Im-soon (F, 28, Im Ke Ri)

Park Chil-bong (M, 35, Im Ke Ri)

Park Sun-nye (F, 2, Im Ke Ri)

Kim Hal-reh (F, 60, Im Ke Ri)

Cho Hong-koo (M, 30, Im Ke Ri)

Lee Myo-sun (F, 50, Im Ke Ri)

Ban Kyong-ho (M, 27, Yongdong)

Chang Bong-rye (F, 50, Yongdong)

Lee Bok-yong (M, 51, Im Ke Ri)

Kim Kap-yon (F, 45, Im Ke Ri)

Lee Won-shik (M, 17, Im Ke Ri)

Lee Chang-shik (M, 13, Im Ke Ri)

Lee Bong-ja (F, 7, Im Ke Ri)

Won Ho-yol (F, 11, Im Ke Ri)

Nam Hee-yong (F, 38, Yongdong)

Chung Young-hee (F, 17, Yongdong)

Chung Ok-hee (F, 13, Yongdong)

Chung Jong-ja (F, 7, Yongdong)

Chung Jin-koo (M, 3, Yongdong)

Moon Kwang-se (M, 39, Yongdong)

Park Young-soon (F, 47, Chu Gok Ri)

Hwang Pal-keun (M, 37, Yongdong)

Hwang Yon-hwa (F, 15, Yongdong)

Hwang Kyong-ja (F, 6, Yongdong)

Hwang Chong-soo (M, 4, Yongdong)

Hwang (M, 2, Yongdong, Chong-soo's brother)

Kim Jam-sun (F, 41, Im Ke Ri)

Kim Woo-jae (M, 17, Im Ke Ri)

Kim Jong-woong (M, 13, Im Ke Ri)

Kim Ko-mee (F, 10, Im Ke Ri)

Sohn Im-soon (F, 11, Im Ke Ri)

Lee Yi-moon (M, 57, Yongdong)

Lim Soon-ja (F, 3, Im Ke Ri)

Cho Jong-koo (M, 49, Im Ke Ri)

Cho Kil-jin (M, 9, Im Ke Ri)

Cho Nam-gak (M, 2, Im Ke Ri)

Cho Nam-yol (M, 11, Im Ke Ri)

Cho Chong-rye (F, 14, Im Ke Ri)

Chung Sun-boon (F, 47, Im Ke Ri)

Chun Kyong-moon (M, 63, Chu Gok Ri)

Chun Joon-pyo (M, 23, Chu Gok Ri)

Lee Young-ja (F, 21, Chu Gok Ri)

Kim Ae-shim (F, 27, Chu Gok Ri)

Chun Tae-sung (M, 5 months, Chu Gok Ri)

Chung Pan-suk (M, 50, Yongdong)

Park (F, 41, Yongdong, wife of Chung Pan-suk)

Chung Jin-ok (M, 14, Yongdong)

Chung Soon-duk (F, 11, Yongdong)

Chung Soon-oh (M, 7, Yongdong)

Park Hee-won (M, 53, Yongdong)

Lee Bok-soon (F, 36, Im Ke Ri)

Bae Soon-bok (M, 3, Chu Gok Ri)

Ahn Moon-sam (M, 66, Im Ke Ri)

Kang Soon-hee (F, 61, Im Ke Ri)

Park Oh-soon (F, 21, Im Ke Ri)

Ahn Bok-dol (M, 17, Im Ke Ri)

Suh Moon-sam (M, 76, Chu Gok Ri)

Kim Il-soon (F, 61, Chu Gok Ri)

Suh Kan-ran (F, 1, Chu Gok Ri)

Kim Il-yong (F, 14, Chu Gok Ri)

Suh Jong-hoon (M, 2, Chu Gok Ri)

Suh Byong-jik (M, 44, Chu Gok Ri)

Park Young-hyun (M, 1, Chu Gok Ri)

Chung Jo-woong (M, 32, Im Ke Ri)

Chung Chong-tae (M, 7, Im Ke Ri)

Sohn Hyun-koo (M, 43, Im Ke Ri)

Lee Soon-suk (F, 45, Im Ke Ri)

Hwang Eun-yon (F, 43, Chu Gok Ri)

Chung Young-sook (F, 1, Chu Gok Ri)

Lee Soon-kum (F, 57, Chu Gok Ri)

Chung Koo-ok (F, 20, Chu Gok Ri)

Chung Koo-yon (F, 27, Yongdong)

Kim Kook-hun (M, 3, Yongdong)
Ahn Il-joon (M, 52, Yongdong)
Chung Jin-tae (M, 1, Yongdong)
Park Byong-shik (M, N/A, Yongdong)
Oh (F, N/A, Yongdong, Park Byong-shik's wife)
Park Chang-ki (M, N/A, Yongdong)
Lee Ye-joo (F, 27, Yongdong)
Hong Suk-tae (M, 16, elsewhere)
Sohn Hyun-koo (M, 13, Im Ke Ri)
Lee Soon-suk (F, 45, Im Ke Ri)
Sohn Dae-shik (M, 1, Im Ke Ri)
Chung Koo-hee (F, 2, Chu Gok Ri)
Chung Koo-pil (M, 4, Chu Gok Ri)
Han Yong-kwon (M, 63, Chu Gok Ri)
Han Jong-ja (F, 9, Chu Gok Ri)
Han Kyong-yi (F, 28, Chu Gok Ri)
Kim Bu-duk (F, 63, Chu Gok Ri)
Kim Chong-suk (M, 34, Yongdong)
Kim Chong-yol (M, 30, Yongdong)
Suh Choon-suk (M, 38, Yongdong)
Park Won-jong (M, 33, Yongdong)
Han Kum-suk (M, 1, Chu Gok Ri)
Kim Chang-yong (M, 23, elsewhere)
Chung Woo-young (M, 28, Yongdong)
Suh Sang-kook (M, 36, elsewhere)
Suh Byong-gon (M, 9, elsewhere)
Suh Byong-kyun (M, 1, elsewhere)
Byon Boon-dan (F, 77, Yongdong)
Bae Jong-woon (M, 23, Yongdong)
Kang Sung-keun (M, 55, Yongdong)
Park Bong-woo (M, 29, Yongdong)
Kim Sam-jo (M, 22, Yongdong)
Kang Chang-gil (M, 26, Yongdong)
Kim Han-dong (M, 17, elsewhere)
Kim Dal-je (M, 54, Im Ke Ri)
Han Min-suk (M, 6 months, Chu Gok Ri)

Kim (F, 35, Chu Gok Ri, Han Min-suk's mother)
Park Chang-ha (M, 23, Im Ke Ri)
Han Soon-suk (F, 20, Im Ke Ri)
A baby (Han Soon-suk's son, born and killed in the tunnel, posthumously named Park No-myong)
Lee Ja-sun (F, 52, Im Ke Ri)
Cho Dae-yon (M, 3, Im Ke Ri)
A baby (born and killed in the tunnel; Dae-yon's brother, posthumously named Cho Seung-yon)

Reported Missing

Kim Duk-han (M, 61, Yongdong)
Kim Tae-young (M, 29, Chu Gok Ri)
Park Rae-hun (M, 25, Yongdong)
Chang Kyong-man (M, 26, Yongdong)
Oh Ki-young (M, 34, Yongdong)
Kim Soo-hyun (M, 25, Yongdong)
Cho Wol-ok (F, 27, Yongdong)
Kim Ki-bok (M, 26, Yongdong)
No Jae-dong (M, 24, Yongdong)
Sohn Kyu-won (M, 31, Yongdong)
Lee Byong-wook (M, 58, Yongdong)
Kwon Hee-yong (M, 25, Yongdong)
Kwon Tae-yong (M, 27, Yongdong)
Kwak Young-chul (M, 23, Yongdong)
Kim Ki-myong (M, 10, Yongdong)
Kim Byong-hyun (M, 26, Yongdong)
Park Duk-shi (F, 20, Yongdong)
Lee Choon-nyon (F, 6, Yongdong)
Nam Sung-woo (M, 25, Yongdong)
Kim Young-sun (M, 15, Yongdong)

Reported Wounded

(Three named Kim Sung-ja on the list are all different females.)

Kim Chul-hoon (M, 6, elsewhere)

Lee Suk-ki (M, 47, Im Ke Ri)

Lee Ok-soon (F, 8, Im Ke Ri)

Park Choon-ja (F, 10, Yongdong)

Lee Byong-hoi (M, 16, Im Ke Ri)

Chun Sun-bong (F, 33, Chu Gok Ri)

Kim Kyong-sok (M, 52, Chu Gok Ri)

Kim Sung-ja (F, 12, Chu Gok Ri)

Kim Kum-soon (F, 21, Chu Gok Ri)

Chang Shi-gon (M, 11, Chu Gok Ri)

Kim Ahn-hyang (F, 59, Im Ke Ri)

Park Hee-jin (M, 13, Im Ke Ri)

Cho Dong-soon (M, 59, Im Ke Ri)

Yang Hae-sook (F, 13, Im Ke Ri)

Kum Cho-ja (F, 11, Yongdong)

Kim Kum-rye (F, 34, Im Ke Ri)

Won Taek-kyu (M, 35, Im Ke Ri)

Chung Shin-woong (M, 8, Yongdong)

Lee Soon-yi (F, 36, Im Ke Ri)

Kim Myo-nam (F, 38, Im Ke Ri)

Chung Jin-myong (M, 20, Im Ke Ri)

Lee Choon-keun (M, 44, Im Ke Ri)

Lee Soo-hwan (M, 12, Im Ke Ri)

Chun Chang-sup (M, 22, Im Ke Ri)

Park Jong-im (F, 14, Im Ke Ri)

Chun Ok-boon (F, 13, Chu Gok Ri)

Suh Jong-gap (M, 10, Chu Gok Ri)

Chung Koo-hak (M, 8, Chu Gok Ri)

Chung Myong-hwa (F, 1, Chu Gok Ri)

Kim Sung-ja (F, 1, Chu Gok Ri)

Lee Taek-soon (F, 18, Yongdong)

Yang Hae-chan (M, 10, Im Ke Ri)

Chung Koo-ho (M, 13, Chu Gok Ri)

Kim Hong-ki (M, 15, Chu Gok Ri)

Park Sun-yong (F, 24, Chu Gok Ri)

Cho Soo-ja (F, 6, Im Ke Ri)

Shin Yong-ki (M, 27, elsewhere)

Kim Sung-ja (F, 8, Yongdong)

Chung Kap-duk (F, 38, Yongdong)

Park Hee-yong (M, 35, Yongdong)

Suh Byong-nim (F, 4, elsewhere)

Suh Jong-ja (F, 19, Chu Gok Ri)

Chang Hae-ja (F, 19, Chu Gok Ri)

Chang Hae-soon (F, 16, Chu Gok Ri)

Cho Kyong-koo (M, 51, Im Ke Ri)

Chung Woi-sool (F, 24, Im Ke Ri)

Chun Joo-sup (M, 18, Im Ke Ri)

Chun Sung-ja (F, 8, Im Ke Ri)

Suh Jong-hak (F, 13, Chu Gok Ri)

Park Hee-moon (F, 54, Chu Gok Ri)

ACKNOWLEDGMENTS

Dae ki mahn sung, they say in Korea. A large vase takes a long time. In the case of the story of No Gun Ri, it also took many hands.

Our lasting gratitude goes to Bob Port, Kevin Noblet, Reid Miller and Tom Wagner of the Associated Press, editors who inspired and encouraged the pursuit of the truth of No Gun Ri, and then worked to get that truth out. Madge Stager, Ahn Young-joon, Steve Fluty, Bill Gorman, Seung-jai Moon, Richard Pyle, Tonia Cowan, Bob Bianchini, Jason Fields and many others, all in their special ways, contributed significantly to the reporting and the presentation of the journalism.

Above all, however, we are grateful to Randy Herschaft of the AP, the investigative researcher without whose intelligence, intensity and integrity the story of No Gun Ri would never have been told.

From the outset our spouses—Pamela Hanlon, Eun-Young Suh and Raymond G. Mendoza—were our strength through difficult days. In the end, our agent, Alex Smithline of Scovil Chichak Galen, and our editor, Liz Stein of Henry Holt and Company, were our strength in ensuring the story of *The Bridge at No Gun Ri* would be told in depth and would be told well.

Our deepest bows, ultimately, are reserved for the U.S. Army veterans, men of conscience, who finally spoke about No Gun Ri and helped us, and through us many others, understand the young soldiers of a "forgotten war," and for the people of Chu Gok and Im Ke villages, the mothers and fathers, sisters and brothers, children and grandchildren, survivors of No Gun Ri, who refused to let the memory and the quest for truth die.

Portions of the royalties from *The Bridge at No Gun Ri* will be donated to benefit elderly and other needy of Chu Gok Ri and Im Ke Ri, South Korea, and the post-traumatic stress disorder (PTSD) program at the Veterans Affairs medical center at Fort Meade, South Dakota.

ABOUT THE AUTHORS

CHARLES J. HANLEY, SANG-HUN CHOE and MARTHA MENDOZA were awarded the Pulitzer Prize for Investigative Reporting in 2000. Hanley is a special correspondent with the Associated Press International Desk in New York who has covered a half dozen wars over thirty years. He is a U.S. Army veteran of Vietnam. Choe is an AP reporter in Seoul, South Korea. Also a military veteran, Choe received a special award for his No Gun Ri work from the Korean Journalists Association. Mendoza, the recipient of a John S. Knight Fellowship at Stanford University in 2000–2001, is an AP national reporter based in San Jose, California, who has won numerous awards for her investigative work. RANDY HERSCHAFT, an Associated Press investigative researcher, is an expert in public records and electronic research.